T0305517

The Rise of the Hybrid Domain

The Rise of the Hybrid Domain

Collaborative Governance for Social Innovation

Yuko Aoyama

Professor, Graduate School of Geography, Clark University, USA

with

Balaji Parthasarathy

Professor, International Institute of Information Technology, Bangalore, India

 Edward Elgar
PUBLISHING

Cheltenham, UK • Northampton, MA, USA

Published by
Edward Elgar Publishing Limited
The Lypiatts
15 Lansdown Road
Cheltenham
Glos GL50 2JA
UK

Edward Elgar Publishing, Inc.
William Pratt House
9 Dewey Court
Northampton
Massachusetts 01060
USA

A catalogue record for this book
is available from the British Library

Library of Congress Control Number: 2016949920

This book is available electronically in the
Social and Political Science subject collection
DOI 10.4337/9781785360435

ISBN 978 1 78536 042 8 (cased)
ISBN 978 1 78536 043 5 (eBook)

Printed and bound by CPI Group (UK) Ltd, Croydon, CR0 4YY
Typeset by Columns Design XML Ltd, Reading

Contents

List of tables   ix
Acknowledgments   x
List of abbreviations   xii

1   Introduction   1
    1.1   The hybrid domain   1
    1.2   Social innovation in India   5
    1.3   Methodology   9
          1.3.1   Questionnaire survey of R&D activities of
                  multinational enterprises   9
          1.3.2   Semi-structured interviews with social innovation
                  stakeholders   10
    1.4   Book organization   11
    1.5   Caveats   13

2   Rescaling collective action for governance in the twenty-first
    century   15
    2.1   Governing global public goods   15
          2.1.1   State–market dichotomy   16
          2.1.2   Problems with public goods   18
          2.1.3   From local to global commons: global merit goods   20
    2.2   Polycentric and network forms of governance   22
          2.2.1   Polycentric governance   22
          2.2.2   Network forms of governance   24
          2.2.3   Heterarchies   24
          2.2.4   Institutional "bricolage"   26
    2.3   Conclusion   27

3   The hybrid domain: bridging the state–market divide   28
    3.1   The rise of the hybrid domain   29
    3.2   Domain and scalar flexibility   31
    3.3   Actors in the hybrid domain   33
          3.3.1   Corporations: from shareholder to stakeholder
                  governance   34

3.3.2   Corporate social responsibility (CSR) initiatives   37
3.3.3   NGOs in transition   38
3.3.4   Social enterprises   40
3.3.5   Transnational social entrepreneurs (TSEs)   43
3.3.6   From traditional to venture philanthropy   44
3.3.7   The rise of impact investment   49
3.4   Conclusion   51

4   Social innovation in global contexts   53
4.1   Social innovation   53
4.1.1   Defining social innovation   53
4.1.2   Context in social innovation   56
4.1.3   Proximity in social innovation   57
4.1.4   Technology in social innovation   59
4.1.5   Sustainability in social innovation   60
4.2   Collaborative governance for social innovation   61
4.2.1   Corporations   61
4.2.2   Users and consumers   64
4.2.3   Incentivizing social innovation   65
4.2.4   The state in social innovation   67
4.3   Conclusion   68

5   Social innovation in India   69
5.1   Failure of the state to provide public goods   70
5.1.1   The Nehruvian ideal of scientific and technological
        self-sufficiency   71
5.1.2   The Gandhian ideal of decentralized self-reliance   76
5.1.3   Inclusive development   80
5.2   Failure of the market to provide public goods: the myth
      of the BOP   82
5.2.1   The myth of profitability   84
5.2.2   Opportunities and challenges   87
5.2.3   From BOP to "emerging market" consumers   90
5.3   Conclusion   91

6   Designing solutions for "wicked problems"   93
6.1   Designing solutions   93
6.1.1   De-featuring and frugal innovation   94
6.1.2   Bottom-up design   95
6.1.3   Design for constraints   96
6.1.4   Cross-sectoral solutions   99
6.2   India as a laboratory for social innovation   101

	6.2.1 Learning for social impacts: contexts and proximity	101
	6.2.2 South–South knowledge transfer and reverse innovation	106
6.3	Conclusion	111
7	**Case studies from India**	**112**
7.1	Innovating on healthcare delivery and medical diagnostics	112
	7.1.1 Rural healthcare franchising with local social networks	113
	7.1.2 From thermoplastics to silk fabric chips for immunoassays	115
	7.1.3 Dry reagents for resource-constrained supply chains	116
7.2	Resolving information asymmetries for small-scale farmers	117
	7.2.1 Video-based content creation and distribution	118
	7.2.2 Text messaging service for crop prices	119
	7.2.3 Building farmers' capacities to reach markets	121
7.3	Promoting inclusive development for rural populations	122
	7.3.1 Voice-enabled mobile phone platform for tribal communities	122
	7.3.2 ICT employment creation and training in rural areas	124
	7.3.3 "Bank-less" banking for rural migrants	125
7.4	Sustaining livelihoods in the informal sector	127
	7.4.1 Training and skill certification for construction workers	127
	7.4.2 An employment portal for informal work	129
	7.4.3 Enhancing the cash flows and creditworthiness of rural informal retailers	131
7.5	Introducing renewable energy	132
	7.5.1 Solar systems as a catalyst for social change	133
	7.5.2 Micro-franchises for renewable energy	135
7.6	What the cases tell us	136
8	**Domain flexibility**	**138**
8.1	From CSR to shared value creation	138
	8.1.1 The limits of goodwill	138
	8.1.2 Shared value creation: opportunities and challenges	140

8.1.3   The socially sustainable business model (SSBM)   142
8.2   Learning through collaborating   144
    8.2.1   Varieties of collaborative arrangements   145
    8.2.2   Collaborating with the state   154
    8.2.3   Challenges in collaboration   156
8.3   The rise of hybrid organizations   163
    8.3.1   Transitions from NGOs to social enterprises   164
    8.3.2   NGOs established by social enterprises   167
    8.3.3   The Robin Hood model   169
    8.3.4   Corporations established by NGOs   170
    8.3.5   Joint NGO–corporate set-up and collaborative
        polygon   171
8.4   Conclusion   172

9   Scalar flexibility   174
9.1   Globalizing social enterprises   174
9.2   The role of universities in the Global North   176
9.3   Looking for impacts, practice-oriented research   179
9.4   Accessing transnational financing   182
9.5   Conclusion   185

10   Conclusions   187

Appendix   192
References   195
Index   223

Tables

3.1	Private foundations in the United States	46
5.1	Macro-economic indicators: BRICS countries	69
5.2	Education, health, and infrastructure indicators, BRICS countries	71
5.3	Average annual GDP growth rate in India	73
5.4	Infrastructure spending as a share of GDP, India	74
5.5	Registered NGOs in India	78
5.6	Sources of funding for NGOs in India	79
5.7	Results from the survey questionnaire: R&D for BOP markets	83
6.1	Results from the survey questionnaire: sources of knowledge for the BOP market	102
7.1	Healthcare system indicators, BRICS countries	113
7.2	Urban non-agricultural informal employment, India (percentage distribution by sector, 2011–2012)	128
8.1	Illustrative examples of collaboration in the hybrid domain	145
8.2	Results of the questionnaire survey: MNE–NGO collaboration	150
A.1	List of interviewees	192

Acknowledgments

We are grateful to many organizations and individuals who supported us throughout the research and writing phases of this project. The book is an outcome of a collaborative research conducted with funding from the National Science Foundation (BCS-1127329), with field research conducted in India and elsewhere between 2011 and 2015. A Rockefeller Foundation Academic Writing Residency in Bellagio in 2015 gave us invaluable encounters with a wide-ranging set of colleagues from various interdisciplinary backgrounds. We are grateful to Judith Rodin, Claudia Juech, Pilar Palacia and Elena Ongania, in their respective capacities for supporting our work, giving us new exposure, and an enormously rewarding intellectual experience. We much appreciate valuable inputs from fellow residents who attended our seminar: Michael Blake, Alex Freund, Suzanne Lacy, Christine Lucia, Afaf and Mahmoud Meleis, Kate O'Regan, Barbara Rubin, Pierre Sauvage, and Anya Stiglitz; and our special thanks goes to Joseph Stiglitz, Julia Marton-Lefèvre, Djavad Salehi-Isfahani, and Evan Thomas who spent extra time sharing their thoughts on our project. Balaji Parthasarathy would also like to thank Amitabh Matoo and the Australia India Institute at the University of Melbourne for offering him an Emerging Leader Fellowship in 2013. The Fellowship allowed him to sharpen the conceptualization of the project in its early stages.

We are also grateful to many colleagues for moral, intellectual, and substantive support. In particular, we thank Bjørn Asheim, Cristina Chaminade, S. Sadagopan, AnnaLee Saxenian, Allen Scott, Jonathan Storper, and Henry Yeung, for their support and helping us through the process. Special and enormous thanks goes to Michael Storper, Karen Chapple, Rory Horner, Vinod Vyasulu, Haripriya Rangan, and Norma Rantisi for reading drafts of the manuscript and offering incisive criticism as well as encouragement. We also acknowledge doctoral students at Clark, and post-docs and research assistants at IIITB who worked on the project: Rory Horner, Seth Schindler, Younglong Kim, Yifan Cai, Niveditha Menon, Mandar Kulkarni, Kavitha Narayanan, and Rishi Singh.

Our thanks go to all the interview and survey participants who volunteered their time and shared insights for this research. They spanned across for-profit and non-profit arenas, and it is their insights, dedication, and hard work that allowed us to get a glimpse of the realities on the ground. Without their generous contributions and their sharing of time, thoughts, and inputs, this project would not have been possible, for which we are deeply indebted. And last but not least, we are indebted to our family and friends, near and far, whose support and understanding makes our work not only possible, but also enjoyable.

Yuko Aoyama led the conceptualizing and writing of this book. Field work was undertaken jointly. Balaji co-authored Sections 2.2, 5.1 and Chapter 7, besides providing inputs to the rest of the book. We remain jointly responsible for any errors that remain.

Yuko Aoyama,
with Balaji Parthasarathy
Bangalore, Bellagio, Worcester

Abbreviations

ATM	Automated teller machine
BOP	Base-of-the-pyramid
BPO	Business process outsourcing
BRAC	NGO in Bangladesh, formerly Bangladesh Rehabilitation Assistance Committee
BRICS	Brazil, Russia, India, China, South Africa
CEO	Chief Executive Officer
CIC	Community Interest Company (UK)
CSO	Central Statistical Office (India)
CSP	Customer Service Point
CSR	Corporate social responsibility
DAC	Development Assistance Committee
EPA	Environmental Protection Agency (USA)
FDI	Foreign direct investment
FMCGs	Fast-moving consumer goods
GBP	British Pound Sterling
GDP	Gross domestic product
GPPP	Global public–private partnership
HBS	Harvard Business School
HNWI	High-net-worth individual
HQ	Headquarters
ICT	Information and communication technology
IMF	International Monetary Fund
INR	Indian Rupee
IP	Intellectual Property
ISI	Import substitution-led industrialization
L3C	Low-profit limited liability company (USA)

MGNREGA	Mahatma Gandhi National Rural Employment Guarantee Act (India)
MIT	Massachusetts Institute of Technology
MNE	Multinational enterprise
MOP	Middle-of-the-pyramid
MOU	Memorandum of understanding
MSMEs	Micro, small and medium enterprises
NASSCOM	National Association of Software and Services Companies (India)
NCX	National Commodity Exchange (India)
NGO	Non-governmental organization
NRHM	National Rural Health Mission (India)
NRI	Non-resident Indian
ODA	Official development assistance
OECD	Organisation for Economic Co-operation and Development
PMGSY	*Pradhan Mantri Gram Sadak Yojana* or the Prime Minister's Rural Roads Program (India)
POS	Point-of-sale
PPP	Public–private partnership
PV	Photovoltaic
R&D	Research and development
RFP	Request for proposal
RTBI	Rural Technology and Business Incubator
S&T	Science and technology
SE	Social enterprise/entrepreneur
SHG	Self-help group
SMEs	Small- and medium-sized enterprises
SMS	Short message service
SSA	*Sarva Shiksha Abhiyan* or the Education for All Movement (India)
SSBM	Socially sustainable business model
STs	Scheduled Tribes
TSE	Transnational social enterprise/entrepreneur
UNCTAD	United Nations Conference on Trade and Development

USD   US Dollar
VAT   Value-added tax

1. Introduction

Policymakers, academics, and the public are acutely aware of the urgent need to redesign the governance of global capitalism in response to recent financial, environmental, and social crises. The objective of this book is to explore new possibilities for the innovation, production, and delivery of solutions for some of the most pressing social challenges of the twenty-first century. Among the challenges facing the world at present, with long-term consequences, are inequality, including unequal access to education, health, and energy. With growing recognition that policy responses that posit states against markets produce dismal results, various actors are addressing social challenges requiring collective mobilization and action, and correspondingly, scholars are reconceptualizing governance as an outcome of these actions. Persistent inequality amidst low levels of socio-economic development calls for new institutional arrangements. How this challenge is being addressed with the rise of the hybrid domain lies at the heart of this book. Our goal is to engage with the question of collective capacity-building for a broad and multi-disciplinary audience, from those in innovation, science and technology policy, entrepreneurship, governance, and development.

1.1 THE HYBRID DOMAIN

The book will conceptualize the hybrid domain, which refers to an ever-growing "middle" that lies between states and markets. As Stiglitz (2008) notes, "the closer integration of the countries of the world – globalization – has given rise to a greater need for collective action." Based on observations of social innovation in India, we develop a conceptual framework that acknowledges the shifting boundaries and blending interests between the public and the private domains. Collaboration has been acknowledged as a key organizational attribute in various forms of governance, including polycentric governance, network governance, and heterarchies. Yet, the emphasis has remained on the role of the state in governance, with little acknowledgment of the subtle changes in capitalist societies that defy previously accepted categorization. For

1

instance, acknowledging the the role of civil society organizations and social enterprises, if at all, is very nascent.

We conceptualize the hybrid domain as a newly emerging domain that overlaps public and private interests. We analyze the stakeholders in this hybrid domain – to demonstrate the swelling of the middle – and, by doing so, critique what has become the basic analytical framework in understanding economic governance – state versus markets. The rise of the hybrid domain signifies the shift from shareholder-driven to stakeholder-driven capitalism on the one hand, and the growing role of civil society organizations as key stakeholders working in conjunction with the state and corporations in pursuing social missions on the other. However, there is an important distinction between social needs and market opportunities, even if they may converge or overlap in many instances. Such convergence of needs and opportunities has been observed from multiple perspectives, ranging from "shared value" (Porter & Kramer, 2006) in business management to inclusive development (Dreze & Sen, 1999) in the development literature. Finance increasingly intersects with social missions as well, as the concept of "philanthro-capitalism" indicates (Bishop & Green, 2008).

While the hybrid domain involves both social and economic missions, new organizational entities ensure the integrity of dual missions by emphasizing stakeholders, not shareholders. Moreover, various aspects of the hybrid domain have been reported and analyzed as separate processes; the marketization of the state on the one hand, and the socialization of markets on the other. We believe it is useful to understand the two processes in a single conceptual framework, and examine the interactions among for-profit, non-profit, and various hybrid entities that produce social innovation. Most broadly defined, social innovation refers to innovation with strong social impacts, one that is designed to fulfill unmet social needs of underserved populations.

The reasons for the rise of the hybrid domain are many and complex. Most broadly, both statism and capitalism of the twentieth-century variety are no longer viable. The collapse of the Soviet Union in the late 1980s was the final nail in the coffin to the centrally planned economy model. The weaknesses of the market as a mode of governance have been regularly exposed by economic crises – the most recent of which was the 2008 financial crisis that began in the United States, followed by the European crisis from 2010 and the Greek crisis of 2015. More specifically, the retreat or failure of the state and growing inequality has brought the role of the state under scrutiny on the one hand, while corporate scandals have led to increasing suspicion of the private sector on the other hand. These tendencies have all contributed to the shift in societal legitimacy and the division of labor in balancing economic and social objectives. As a result, an increasingly important role for non-governmental, non-profit organizations as representatives of civil society, combined with technological innovation, particularly in information and communication technologies (ICTs), is having a profound effect on the lives of people around the world.

Social innovation lies at the intersection of changing state–market relations, institutional design, and technological innovation. The use of the term "social innovation" grew more than 67 times in the past 15 years, from 24 in year 2000 to 1,614 in 2014 in the legal and journalistic database compiled by LexisNexus. Despite its appeal and potential, a precise definition of social innovation remains elusive, and its current usage varies widely in the literature. Although social innovation has long been attempted under various guises, and technological advances have promised to tackle poverty, illiteracy and poor physical infrastructure, the impacts on the poor have thus far been limited. For example, the "appropriate" technologies movement of decades past suffered from limited transferability and weak institutional support including insufficient funding, along with a perception that the technologies deployed were inferior (Zelenika & Pearce, 2011). By contrast, grassroots innovation, such as *jugaad* (Hindi for local improvisation) in India's informal sector, has recently come to be celebrated as a reflection of ingenuity in meeting needs in conditions of scarcity (Radjou et al., 2012). But its diffusion, for commercial ends or otherwise, still faces significant challenges, including the high transaction costs for scouting and documentation, the need for value-addition and finance, and ambiguous intellectual property rights (World Bank, 2007).[1]

With recent attention turning to systems and policies oriented toward more socially inclusive and pro-poor designs (Altenburg & Lundvall, 2009; Foster & Heeks, 2013; Sonne, 2012), the timing is ripe to develop a synthetic approach that involves the state, markets and civil society. This is especially so with growing public interest in ethical investments and the priorities of corporations in the Global North shifting from the single- to the triple-bottom-line of social, environmental, and economic objectives, following Elkington (1997). Corporate social responsibility (CSR), and the rise of benefit and certified B corporations in the United

---

[1]   Other examples of grassroots innovations involving improvised solutions in one form or another include *shanzhai* in China, and *jeito* in Brazil, although contexts shape the meanings of these terms. As a result, *jeito,* which circumvents state regulations, is associated with corruption, and *shanzhai,* which circumvents intellectual property (IP) regulations, often translates as counterfeit products.

States, also suggests the reconceptualization and the reconfiguration of economic and social objectives. Non-governmental organizations (NGOs)[2] too have become more professional, at times commercialized, increasingly globally networked, and technologically proficient (Roberts et al., 2005; Weisbrod, 2000). In addition, there is heightened interest in social entrepreneurship in North America and Europe, with social entrepreneurs becoming transnational to address social missions. The phenomenon of social entrepreneurs crossing borders to operate beyond their domestic markets has not been analyzed in the academic literature.

While social innovation is also observed in the Global South, empirical evidence has not been collected systematically to understand how the process of macro-level and micro-level shifts in institutions and innovation intersect with shifts in global governance. Our goal is to reconceptualize multi-stakeholder collaborative governance through the concept of the hybrid domain that better combines economic and social goals more effectively in the context of the Global South.

By conceptualizing governance in emerging markets beyond the traditional division of labor between for- and non-profit entities, and state versus non-state actors, we aim to better understand the significance of social innovation emerging in the Global South. Particularly in the context of "state failure," where states fail to deliver services that fulfill the basic needs of the population, collaborative governance can serve as a useful alternative to blend economic and social objectives by overriding organizational boundaries which were previously considered ideologically incompatible and, therefore, unbridgable. We seek to articulate how corporations, states, and civil society organizations develop common agendas, despite the differences in their primary objectives. The process of coordination in developing a common agenda, in innovating and designing solutions, and in generating relevant institutions constitutes the rise of the hybrid domain.

---

[2] According to the UN (2003), NGOs are non-profit, self-organizing institutions in which membership is voluntary. The non-profit status has been created "for the purpose of producing goods and services whose status does not permit them to be a source of income, profit, or other financial gain for the units that establish, control or finance them" (p. 12). For the World Bank, NGOs encompass a broader range of private organizations, "that pursue activities to relieve suffering, promote the interests of the poor, protect the environment, provide basic social services or undertake community development" (Malena, 1995, p. 7).

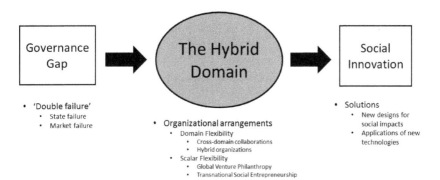

Figure 1.1   The rise of the hybrid domain

1.2 SOCIAL INNOVATION IN INDIA

As Sheppard and Leitner (2010) observe, the contemporary socio-spatial imaginary of development "repeatedly reconstitutes the first world as the source of development expertise" (p. 192). Using empirical evidence on social innovation in India, this book conceptualizes hybrid governance as a new form that combines economic and social missions and blends the public and the private domains. India serves as a useful case to understand how local innovations to solve local problems can be devised with global technologies for scalable solutions. The inclusion of low-income populations in the Global South as contributors of knowledge for social innovation promises impacts that earlier attempts could not deliver. At the macro level, social innovation offers potential for systemic changes and inclusive development through new organizational configurations. At the micro level, we examine how various styles of collaboration are catalyzing social innovation.

Today, India is recognized for its production and delivery of ICT/BPO (business process outsourcing) services (Wessner & Shivakumar, 2007). This has been attributed to state initiated liberalization policies since the mid-1980s (Evans, 1995; Heeks, 1996; Heitzman, 2004; Kohli, 2006; Parthasarathy, 2000), the shortage of engineers in the developed world (Parthasarathy, 2004), the onset of the Internet (Arora et al., 2001), and the role of Non-resident Indians in Silicon Valley (Parthasarathy, 2004; Saxenian, 1999, 2006).

India's strength is still understood to rely largely on cost arbitrage. In fact, the country has long been viewed to be an inappropriate location for

R&D. As recently as 2001, India was ranked among the bottom third of countries in the world in UNCTAD's (2005) innovation capability index. Only in the past decade has India emerged as a location of knowledge production (Aoyama & Parthasarathy, 2012; Chaminade & Vang, 2008; Parthasarathy & Aoyama, 2006). Correspondingly, India has recently moved up the ranks in a more recent Global Innovation Index, ranking 81st among 142 countries (Dutta et al., 2015).

Our focus on India is motivated by the country's recent shift from being merely an offshore delivery center for ICT services to a favored location for global corporate research and development (R&D) activities. There are over 1,700 private sector R&D facilities in India (Department of Scientific & Industrial Research, 2014), and they are highly concentrated in major cities, as shown in Figure 1.2. Many multinational enterprises (MNEs) have R&D facilities in the country for reasons beyond cost arbitrage. It is estimated that over 1,000 MNEs conduct R&D in India, including 30 percent of the top 1,000 global R&D organizations.[3] Patent applications in India almost doubled in the eight-year period from 24,505 in 2006 to 42,951 in 2014,[4] and applications for US patents grew six-fold, from 506 to 3,044 during the same period.[5]

Against the backdrop of this development, we contend that various social innovation stakeholders are increasingly viewing India as an ideal learning laboratory. India makes an attractive laboratory for social innovation for many reasons. First, even among Asian countries, which are home to the largest number of poor people in the world, the situation in India continues to be dire. Despite the rapid economic growth in the past 15 years, a large percentage of the population still lives in poverty (see Chapter 5).[6] India's predominant post-independence development models, whether the Nehruvian strategy for industrial self-sufficiency or the Gandhian ideal for self-reliance, failed to produce adequate infrastructure. Competing ideological frameworks, the reality of a lumbering (and often corrupt) state bureaucracy amidst institutionalized socio-economic inequalities, and urban–rural gaps, have given rise to active grassroots innovation and the engagement of various hybrid domain

---

[3]   According to data provided by India Brand Equity Foundation.

[4]   Data provided by the Government of India, Controller General of Patents Designs and Trademarks.

[5]   Number of patents applied from India Granted by US State and Foreign Country of Origin http://www.uspto.gov/web/offices/ac/ido/oeip/taf/cst_all.htm (accessed October 11, 2015).

[6]   According to the UNDP (2014) India's Human Development Index ranked 135 among 187 countries.

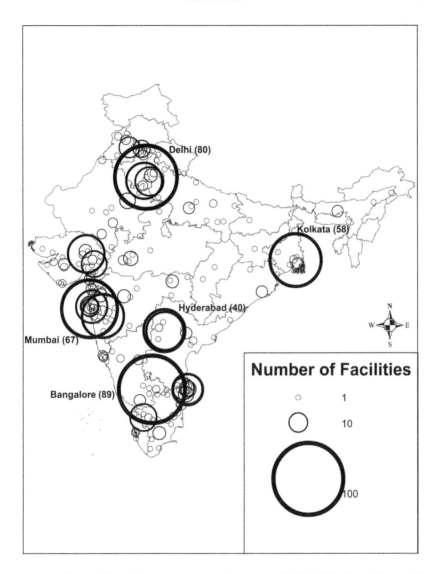

Notes: The smallest circle represents one private sector R&D facility located in a taluk (village). The size of the circles corresponds to the number of R&D facilities in each taluk where such facilities are present

Source: Developed by authors with support of REU Supplement to National Science Foundation Grant (BCS-1127329). Based on the data provided by the Government of India, NSTMIS (National Science and Technology Management Information System) Division, 2015

Figure 1.2   *R&D Facilities (Private Sector) in India, 2015*

stakeholders and transnational interests. India thus offers a unique and prominent vantage point from which to observe the hybrid domain.

Second, India's inadequate infrastructure and its diverse socio-cultural environment serves as a laboratory for the challenges commonly faced in many multi-lingual and multi-ethnic countries of the Global South. Third, the Indian government's recent emphasis on *inclusive development* has generated interest in exploring a new avenue of empowerment for the poor by articulating their role beyond traditionally conceived livelihood sustenance. Fourth, the Indian economy is known as among the most entrepreneurial in the Global South, with a high rate of business start-ups. For instance, according to the Indian industry association Nasscom (2015), India's start-ups number over 3,100, with only the United States, United Kingdom and Israel boasting of more.

India is emerging as a location that specializes in conducting design engineering based on perceived needs of populations in the Global South. Those MNEs which hoped to generate profit by tapping into the base of the pyramid (BOP) market (Kolk & van Tulder, 2006; Prahalad, 2002, 2009; Prahalad & Hammond, 2002; Whitney & Kelkar, 2004), however, now acknowledge that a wide gap exists between their hope and the reality of poor consumers. Instead, the fastest road to MNEs' future bottom lines may well be through their contributions to development initiatives, in the form of CSR initiatives, collaboration with the state for social innovation, and the transfer of knowledge and enabling technologies among various stakeholders, including grassroots NGOs.

The emerging collaboration between MNEs and NGOs signals a new organizational approach in the context of the Global South to overcome entrenched information and power asymmetries. Befitting the world's largest democracy, civil society organizations thrive in India, with the official figure at nearly 3.2 million (Central Statistical Office [CSO], 2012). Furthermore, transnational social entrepreneurs (TSEs), mainly transplants from the Global North, including those not of Indian origin, play an increasingly pivotal role in coordinating globally sourced technology, business know-how, and financing, to develop solutions to critical local problems.

The emergence of India as a location of social innovation demands a reorientation in our theoretical and empirical understanding of the geography of innovation. Innovation has long been assumed to be predominantly skill-driven, rather than market-driven. But, as recent research on "frugal innovation" (Ramdorai & Herstatt, 2015; Zeschky et al., 2011) has shown, there is greater recognition that contextual intelligence held by users and consumers in India plays a central role in successful social innovation. Also, knowledge gained in India can generate new demand in other parts of the Global South with similar infrastructural or institutional conditions, or in some cases, making its way to markets in the Global North. As Govindarajan and Trimble (2012) note, it can take the form of "reverse innovation," evident in, for example, General Electric's ultra-portable electrocardiograph equipment which was designed for emerging markets such as India.

1.3 METHODOLOGY

This book is based on our joint research, which was funded by the US National Science Foundation (BCS-1127329).[7] To develop in-depth case studies of corporate and civil society involvement in social innovation, we relied on a questionnaire survey and in-person, semi-structured interviews. The questionnaire survey was designed to generate comparable indicators for the broadest possible number of firms, and was distributed to MNEs conducting R&D in India. Semi-structured interviews were conducted with various social innovation stakeholders including MNEs, NGOs, and social enterprises in major Indian cities to access information unavailable from published sources. This generated new insights and qualitative evidence that informs the nature and extent of social innovation taking place in the country.

1.3.1 Questionnaire Survey of R&D Activities of Multinational Enterprises

In the absence of a comprehensive and publicly accessible database, we began by compiling a list of R&D facilities in India from government sources. We then manually selected all firms that were deemed R&D intensive and excluded those that were no more than glorified data processing or production facilities, as the database included a few "offshore development centers" which typically conduct neither research nor product development. To ensure the inclusion of MNEs that conduct innovation without stand-alone R&D facilities, an extensive media analysis of recent articles in Indian business and technology magazines was conducted to add to this database. The database constructed as a result

---

[7] National Science Foundation Grant (BCS-1127329), *The Global Shift in R&D Alliances: Multinational Enterprises (MNEs) and the Quest for the "Base of the Pyramid" (BOP) markets*. Geography and Spatial Science Program, 2011–16.

was our primary sampling frame of 620 MNEs with R&D facilities in 2012.[8] Email requests to participate in the questionnaire survey were sent to firms identified in the sampling frame, and we received 158 valid responses.[9] We used cross-tabulation to examine the interdependence between pairs of key questions in the survey.[10]

1.3.2 Semi-structured Interviews with Social Innovation Stakeholders

We conducted semi-structured interviews with social innovation stakeholders in six major cities (Bangalore, Chennai, Hyderabad, Mumbai, Pune, and the National Capital Region around Delhi). The list of interviewees, with their affiliations and identity suppressed, is included in the Appendix as Table A.1. We identified social innovation stakeholders through media and website analysis, and among the attendees of two conferences in Bangalore.[11] We also employed snowballing techniques during the interviews to identify additional stakeholders. The social innovation stakeholders interviewed included MNEs, NGOs, social entrepreneurs, and global foundations. In total, 115 interviews were conducted between May 2012 and December 2014, roughly half of which were executives of foreign MNEs with R&D facilities in India, while the rest were NGO collaborators in R&D alliances and social enterprises. We also conducted in-person and telephone/skype interviews outside India (the United States, Japan, Singapore, Hong Kong, and the Netherlands), to access Indian experts in those locations or to get a perspective from the corporate headquarters. The majority of MNEs interviewed established R&D facilities in India after 2005.

Social enterprises were a diverse group and situated across a broad spectrum, with some transitioning from non-profit to for-profit status,

---

[8] Zinnov, a consulting firm in India claims that there were over 900 MNEs with R&D facilities operating in India in 2015, and over 3,100 start-ups in technology fields.

[9] Our primary targets were R&D lab directors or section heads. When formal R&D sections did not exist, the survey was sent to the Directors of Marketing.

[10] Cross-tabulation analysis shows a relationship between two variables using a bi-variate contingency table. The existence and strength of the interdependence can be determined by the chi-square.

[11] The two conferences were the 13th International Conference on Mobile Data Management, July 23–26, 2012, and the Association of Computing Machinery's 3rd Annual Symposium on Computing for Development, January 11–12, 2013.

while others were closer to commercial enterprises active in social sectors. In general, self-identified social enterprises adopt corporate governance that prioritizes stakeholder rather than shareholder perspectives. Most social enterprises we interviewed were established after 2005, with a cluster of firms established around 2009–10. The NGOs we interviewed included grassroots, national and global NGOs, and most had been active for at least a decade in India. The majority of interview participants were Indian nationals.

1.4 BOOK ORGANIZATION

Chapter 2 explores existing frameworks of collective action problems, including Ostrom's common property resources framework and her polycentric governance. It also explores network forms of governance, Jessop's notion of heterarchy, and institutional bricolage. The goal of the chapter is to broaden the scope of the debate over social innovation, and to situate it as both an outcome of governance in transition and an essential vehicle to produce global public goods.

Chapter 3 elaborates the key conceptual framework of this book, the hybrid domain. Particular emphasis is placed on how it fulfills economic and social missions, and how it conceptualizes competing missions, or seeks synergies between missions. The chapter also discusses the stakeholders of social innovation, where their perspectives converge and diverge, the nature of their involvement, and how they have transformed in recent decades.

In Chapter 4, we develop a geographically nuanced definition of social innovation that is conceptually useful in the contemporary global context. We discuss controversies and competing paradigms, with firms viewing knowledge resources as market intelligence on the one hand, and non-profit organizations conceptualizing social innovation as community assets for empowerment on the other. The chapter includes an overview of the debates on social innovation in the Global North and discusses how state devolution, privatization, and austerity measures provide the context. We then discuss how social innovation in the Global South differs in its features, orientation, and emphases due to its distinctive context, such as state failures and grassroots self-help movements. We examine the role of learning-through-collaborating in inducing and incentivizing social innovation, and propose a shift in conceptualizing the knowledge of market demand to a knowledge of community needs.

In Chapters 5–9, we extrapolate trends, generalizable challenges, and lessons learned from empirical evidence in India to other areas of the world. In Chapter 5, we present a brief overview of the historical-institutional underpinnings of India's capability for social innovation. This capability is an outcome of the evolution of state policy and the private sector, and a combination of state and market failures. The first section focuses on how the influence of different ideologies has led to the present condition and policy orientation toward "inclusive development," while the second section focuses on the extent to which the BOP market advocacy by Prahalad is influential and/or perceived and viable by stakeholders. Our findings suggest that the limits of the concept of the BOP market are well understood and shared across various social innovation stakeholders in India today, and a far more pragmatic approach in learning the needs that arise out of emerging market conditions is adopted.

In Chapter 6, we discuss both the engineering and institutional dimensions of design in the private sector, deployed to narrow the gap between technology and needs. We begin with misconceptions about India's contemporary innovation. We discuss how R&D activities in India are no longer confined to cost arbitrage and how de-featuring, or "frugal" innovation, and "secondary marketing" are increasingly viewed as an ineffective strategy for market share expansion. Instead, the focus has shifted toward bottom-up design, design for constraints, and cross-vertical/industrial solutions. India is emerging as a laboratory where needs for emerging market living conditions are learned and solutions are devised. Learning contextual knowledge is done through local presence, experiencing, amplifying, and by seeking synergies across sectors. Finally, as India becomes a seedbed for social innovation, new designs, business models and organizational innovation are also increasingly transferred to other areas, not only to areas where similar emerging economy conditions apply, but also to affluent economies in the Global North.

Chapter 7 presents 14 case studies, which illustrate how cross-domain collaborations and new technologies, in different measures, are combined for social innovation. Examples include affordable medical diagnostic tools; an employment-matching service between urban middle-class clients and domestic help combining a web platform and mobile phone access; and a mobile telemedicine system micro-franchising, complete with a mobile pharmacy. These examples represent not only Indian conceived innovations, but are also intended for exports to other areas of the Global South.

In Chapter 8, we focus on domain flexibility of the hybrid domain, and examine various forms of organizational transitions and the blurred boundaries between stakeholders of social innovation. We compare and contrast the effectiveness of charity and social innovation collaborations, both of which involve NGOs as collaborators but with distinctive functions. We examine the rationale behind establishing social enterprises, and why some NGOs are converting to social enterprises. We explore the opportunities and challenges in, and the variety of forms of learning through, collaborating. We also examine the rise of hybrid organizations: those that combine, in one way or another, for- and non-profit sub-entities in their organization. We conclude this chapter by demonstrating the variety of collaborative governance that surrounds social innovation, identifying common features and examining differences.

In Chapter 9, we explore the rise of TSEs as empirical evidence of scalar flexibility of the hybrid domain. In particular, we examine TSE relcoating to India from the Global North (USA, Australia, UK, the Netherlands), to fulfill social and economic objectives. Our research suggests that they are inspired by the needs of the poor in the Global South, are networked among themselves as well as with global sources of finance, and are often supported by communities and mentors in elite academic institutions.

Chapter 10 draws our theoretical claims and empirical evidence together to substantiate the rise of the hybrid domain. We explore how collaborative governance for social innovation in the preceding chapter can be rescaled to address issues in the global commons.

1.5 CAVEATS

A book as interdisciplinary as this demands a few explanations for readers and caveats for our arguments. This book focuses on the changing nature of governance with both state and market involvement, through understanding newly emerging stakeholder involvement in social innovation in the twenty-first century. We left out other dimensions of state–market relations, such as the political dimensions of corporate citizenship and corporate influences in politics (for example, campaign finance reform in the United States). By highlighting the emergence of the hybrid domain, our goal is to remind scholars and practitioners of the conceptual deficiencies of single-stakeholder advocacy that relies on conventional actors such as the state, the market, or grassroots solutions. We also aim to contribute to debates over theorizing governance. Given the complexities, the heterogeneity and the risks of failure of collaborations, scholars have often shied away from conceptualizing the "middle-ground." Yet, through this book we argue that the empirical evidence more than suggests that it is time to acknowledge, understand, and conceptualize head-on what lies at the intersection of governance and innovation.

Strongly dichotomous views are often easier to argue than fusing multiple views. Blended logics and mixed strategies are more difficult to convey convincingly, particularly when newly emerging phenomena could easily be disregarded as temporary, marginal, or isolated examples that do not follow as incipient trends. By way of example, when one of us (Parthasarathy, 2000) proposed to write about the rise of Bangalore as a new ICT agglomeration as a dissertation at the University of California, Berkeley in 1994, a committee member commented that the phenomenon may well turn out to be short-lived.

As Sassen (2006) notes, "tipping points", or galvanizing moments of foundational shifts in governance, are often gradual and difficult to detect. Although time will be the ultimate judge, we believe that our perspective offers an avenue to consider the possibility of an impending tipping point, in which the process of reformulation is taking place in various formal and informal institutions to cope with the societal challenges of the twenty-first century that are increasingly global in nature.

2. Rescaling collective action for governance in the twenty-first century

We contend that growing functional and systemic interdependencies across various social, spatial, and temporal horizons, have led to the geographical rescaling of public interest. On the one hand, as Rifkin (2010) notes, a new global consciousness is emerging, facilitated by ICTs, as mass and social media disseminate messages and images about the perils and promises of distant societies. On the other hand, geographical and cultural distance can still lead to empathy gaps. As recent debates over economic and refugee crises demonstrate, national borders continue to define access to rights and resources. What is clear is that, as globalization leads to rescaling and shifting boundaries, there are implications for how each society defines public and private interests. Yet, conceptual tools to understand and respond to shifting public interests are limited. There is an urgent need to reconceptualize the intersection of governance and rescaled public interests.

In this chapter, we examine the concepts of governance, public goods and common property resources, and discuss how public goods are being rescaled from the sub-national to the global level. We then discuss existing frameworks of collective action governance, including polycentric and network forms of governance, and analyze their significance and limits for global collective action challenges.

2.1 GOVERNING GLOBAL PUBLIC GOODS

The usage of the term "governance" in the academic literature has grown phenomenally since the beginning of the twenty-first century (Dixit, 2009). Historically, governance was synonymous with government (Stoker, 1998). In 1989, the World Bank, as a leading constituent of the Washington Consensus, used governance to mean "the exercise of political power to manage a nation's affairs," when describing the need for institutional reform and an effective public sector in sub-Saharan

Africa (World Bank, 1989, p. 60). The Bank also used the term "good governance" to refer to a "public service that is efficient, a judicial system that is reliable, and an administration that is accountable to its public" (World Bank, 1989, p. xii). Subsequently, the definition was elaborated as follows:

> Governance is epitomized by predictable, open, and enlightened policymaking (that is, transparent processes); a bureaucracy imbued with a professional ethos; an executive arm of government accountable for its actions; and a strong civil society participating in public affairs; and all behaving under the rule of law. (World Bank, 1994, p. vii)

Although "there is no agreed definition of governance that would provide a convenient device for organizing the literature" (Keefer, 2009, p. 439), the term is increasingly invoked by international development agencies, corporations and civil society organizations. Similarly, "good" governance is normatively charged and controversial, but has come to imply "managing public affairs in a transparent, accountable, participatory and equitable manner" (Santiso, 2001, p. 5).

Nevertheless, the use of the terms "governance" and "good governance" today signify a shift beyond the state–market dichotomy and the reliance on partnerships to address social challenges (Mohan, 2014). As the public domain is being redefined by an increasing recognition of intergenerational responsibilities on the one hand, and the "moral hazard of efficiency failures" (Drache, 2001) on the other, neither territorially confined natural monopolies (i.e. the state) nor the market can effectively serve as the provider of global public goods. Therefore it becomes necessary to develop alternative conceptions of the role of the public and private domains.

2.1.1 State–Market Dichotomy

Traditionally, the state has been the principal actor in the public domain, acting in the public interest. The logic of the state is dichotomously contrasted with that of the market, which is subject to various state "interventions" on an allegedly "pure" form that is stripped of any socio-political and cultural relations. Yet, the "two-sector bargaining" model that pits the states against markets is increasingly obsolete (Sending & Neumann, 2006; Teegen et al., 2004) for at least two reasons.

First, the distinction between the public and private is not only contextual, but also temporal (Hirschman, 1982; Weintraub & Kumar, 1997). As Sassen (2006) argues, "the distinction between a private and a public sphere in the modern state is one historically constructed under specific conditions and alignments" (p. 188). Second, while the legitimacy of the capitalist state depends on safeguarding the public interest, it also derives from the smooth functioning of markets and the prosperity of the private sector (Friedmann, 1987). Markets, in turn, cannot function smoothly without effective state regulation (Evans, 1995; Schoenberger, 2015). Thus, markets and states complement one another and making a choice between the two is a choice between "imperfect alternatives" (Wolf, 1993, p. 64).

Instead of characterizing state–market relations in oppositional terms, Evans (1996) emphasizes synergy between sectors based on complementarity and embeddedness. Stoker (1998) seeks "the blurring of boundaries and responsibilities for tackling social and economic issues" (p. 18). Similarly, we observe that economic and social missions are being reassembled within the existing institutions, resulting in the blurring of boundaries between the public and private domains. This not only involves changes in the nature of the role of the state as executor of public interests and social missions, but also of the market, including its logics, rationale, and agents.

An increasingly influential group of behavioral economists in the field of development policy are advocating evidence-based design for more effective development solutions (see, for example, Banerjee et al., 2011; Cartwright & Hardie, 2012; Karlan & Appel, 2011). According to Banerjee et al. (2011), development projects fail due to the "three i-problem," that is, ideology, ignorance, and inertia. In the academic literature too, we observe a strong ideological slant, where debates on governance and development continue to be driven by states versus markets distinctions.

Previous efforts to bridge the dichotomy, such as the mixed-economy compromise between states and markets (e.g. the Bretton Woods accord or the Keynesian welfare state) between the 1940s and the 1970s, have been criticized as the failure of either the state or markets. Stiglitz (2007), for example, attributes the failure of effective global economic governance to the absence of political solutions. In the 1980s, states began entering into public–private partnerships (PPPs),[1] driven by the "Washington Consensus" and its call for "public sector reform" by

---

[1]   There is no widely accepted definition of PPPs. Typically, they refer to "medium to long term arrangements between the public and private sectors whereby some of the service obligations of the public sector are provided by the private sector, with clear agreement on shared objectives for delivery of public infrastructure and/or public services" (World Bank Group, 2015a).

"reinventing governments" to eliminate inefficiency and corrupt processes in the public sector, and to limit the role of the state to ensuring the smooth functioning of markets (Heeks, 1999).

In the 1990s, Giddens advocated the "Third Way," which was a call to revitalize support for the social democratic left in response to the perceived threat of neoliberalism. The Third Way focused on reconstructing and modernizing the state, by advancing democracy, recovering its legitimacy and improving its administrative efficiency. He advocated the mixed-economy, to "seek synergy between the public and private sectors, utilizing the market but with the public interest in mind" (Giddens, 1998, p. 100). But this was a top-down vision whose preferred instruments were, "a combination of regulation and deregulation" (p. 100). Aside from state action, there were ambiguities on how to achieve "a balance between economic and non-economic life in the society" without jeopardizing individualism (p. 100). Furthermore, globalization was problematic for the advocates of the Third Way, and it was never dealt with adequately in their conceptualization despite extensive discussion. The pressures of globalization and rescaling on the one hand, and a call to reinvent and revitalize governments on the other, not only signaled an end to state monopoly over the responsibilities for collective well-being but also to a conceptual emphasis on "governance" (Mohan, 2014).

2.1.2   Problems with Public Goods

Public goods have been an essential conceptual vehicle in economics to explain the division of labor between the public and the private sector. Thus, a first step in generating a framework for contemporary governance is to re-examine the concept of public goods.

Public goods were conceptualized by Hume as non-rival and non-excludable, and range from concrete (infrastructural) examples (e.g. street lights) to intangible ones (e.g. law and order), to those that occur naturally (e.g. air). Public goods are defined as one of three instances of market failure; some public goods are collective goods or assets that cannot be exchanged, and others are undervalued in the market. While "the market was seen as the optimal institution for the production and exchange of private goods" (Ostrom, 2010a, p. 642), it was deemed unsuitable for public goods provision. Adam Smith believed that public goods are best provided by public authorities. The condition of natural monopoly, whereby the largest supplier has an overwhelming cost advantage over competitors, is another instance that necessitates interventions by non-market (primarily state) actors (Samuelson, 1954; Weisbrod, 1964). State intervention to public goods has traditionally been viewed as a means of limiting rent-seeking behavior, and to curb the market power conferred by natural monopolies (Rodrik, 1997).

Although broadly accepted and widely used, the concept of public goods is criticized on many fronts. First, public goods are ideal types and in reality, few pure public goods exist (Bodansky, 2012). For example, goods with positive externalities ("merit goods") are often labeled as public goods (e.g. knowledge, cyberspace, human rights) and various governments refer to all types of social well-being as public goods (Rioux & Zubrow, 2001), although they may not be purely non-excludable and non-rival in reality. Education, for example, is often considered a public good although it is excludable in many instances and partially rival. The conceptual ambiguities of public goods have long been recognized (see Arrow, 1970), and have led to rhetorical contrasts with "public bads," introducing normative ambiguities to what used to be primarily a technical concept. Air pollution, for example, has been used as an example of a public bad (see Kindleberger, 1981; Sonnemans et al., 1998) although it is more appropriate to consider it as a negative externality. In addition, to accommodate the reality of goods that fall within a broad spectrum of pure public goods and private goods, a variety of hybrids has been recognized, including club goods (excludable and non-rival) and common pool resources (non-excludable and rival).

Second, the ambiguous definition of public goods weakens the justification for state interventions in their provision. For one, the private provision of public goods is theoretically conceivable under public choice theory (see Bergstrom et al., 1986), leading to a possibility of PPPs. For another, while the state is assumed to be the ideal provider, it can be imprecise, clumsy, and often irrational (Lindblom, 1977). Thus, in instances of market failures, interventions by non-market actors will not necessarily help achieve Pareto-efficiency (Ostrom & Ostrom, 1999). Ultimately, because the public sector's options in providing public goods boil down to either make or buy (produce, or outsource production and then provide/allocate), states and markets must work together in most circumstances.

Third, the neo-classical conceptualization of public goods assumes Pareto-efficiency, with rational actors maximizing utility under competitive market environments. Consequently, most discussions of public goods revolve around issues of price (i.e. the free-rider problem) and quantity (i.e. shortages), which often translate into the narrow question of "who decides, who pays," and establishing decision making over financing, allocation and provision (Ferroni & Mody, 2002; Sandler, 1997, 1998).

Behavior such as collaboration, altruism, and philanthropy among actors is also described purely in economistic terms. Individuals are understood to collaborate with others only when they believe that they are better off than without doing so. Similarly, but on a different scale, states are believed to collaborate with one another only when the terms are favorable to further their economic competitiveness vis-à-vis other states. While compromises can be reached between competition and collaboration, long-run systemic stability is difficult to achieve, as experimental studies have shown that competition can lead to an erosion of collaboration (Barker et al., 2012). As long as the economy is viewed as being governed exclusively by competition among market-rational actors, it is implausible to reconcile the co-presence of competition and collaboration. In reality, however, the boundary between competition and collaboration is likely to be drawn, contested, negotiated, compromised, abandoned, and re-drawn.

2.1.3 From Local to Global Commons: Global Merit Goods

Traditionally, the commons have been conceptualized at the local scale. Geographic access is assumed to place boundary and proximity constraints on both the provision and consumption of public goods. Ostrom's example of a police force, Samuelson's example of the military, and Hardin's example of the grazing land all involve territorial boundaries. It is also worth noting that trading public goods across national borders is not within the scope of its conceptualization. At the regional scale, Scott (2002) conceptualized the "regional economic commons," a complex socio-economic collective which "benefit[s] all but the property of no one" (p. 152) and serves as an arena of joint action by states, corporations, and civil society organizations. By contrast, the global commons have been conceptualized primarily to address climate change (see, for example, Nordhaus, 1994).

The concept of global public goods has been most actively discussed in international relations and public finance (see, for example, Bodansky, 2012; Kaul, 2012; Kaul et al., 2003; Kaul et al., 1999; Maskus & Reichman, 2004; Stiglitz, 2007; Stoll, 2008), and is applied primarily to global economic stability, global environmental sustainability and global public health. However, both public goods and global public goods are conceptually problematic, particularly because it is unclear who is best suited to govern their production and delivery. As we show, the concept of global public goods is still in development at best (Stiglitz, 2007), and at worst, it suffers from conceptual deficiency (Stoll, 2008).

A good is considered globally public when its non-rival, non-excludable benefits impact "more than one group of countries and does not discriminate against any population group or generation" (Kaul et al., 2003, p. 95). Global public goods reflect some of the ideological and conceptual weaknesses of public goods, however. A rescaling of public goods to the global cannot be achieved through a simple expansion of the geographical boundaries for the following reasons. First, the rescaling of public goods to the global challenges the concept of non-excludability. As geographical distance and national regulatory boundaries inevitably shape accessibility to the site of public goods provision, access will not be uniformly distributed across the globe. Second, rescaling also challenges the assumption of non-rival consumption. Societal risks, such as financial instability, sea level rise, depletion of offshore fisheries, deep-sea mineral resources, can all be considered globally rival. Therefore, non-excludable and non-rival consumption cannot serve as suitable conceptual underpinnings for global public goods. Third, when public goods are freed from their territorial constraints, a discrepancy arises between the production and consumption of global public goods. The conceptual origin of public goods hinges upon the nature of consumption and the impossibilities of market provision. Markets for public goods are assumed to correspond with national boundaries (e.g. utilities). Rescaling therefore renders global public goods ungovernable.

We argue that addressing collective action challenges can be conceptualized as attempts to rescale positive externalities to achieve global merit goods, while mitigating the cross-border effects of negative externalities. But, under the accepted conceptualization of market failure, both positive and negative externalities are assumed to be largely contained within national borders. Externalities are also assumed to be non-tradable, and cross-territorial transfer is not within the scope of conceptualization. In reality, the impacts of negative externalities (e.g. communicable diseases, carbon emissions) increasingly cross national borders, and their sources have become diffuse and ubiquitous. In contrast, positive externalities are not uniformly distributed/allocated over a territory, and can be subject to a significant distance decay function from the site of provision. Thus, the production of global merit goods (e.g. carbon emission reduction, poverty eradication) would involve mitigating cross-territorial negative externalities and enhancing productivity and cross-territorial transfers of positive externalities.

As today's collective action problems, such as climate change, public health, and poverty alleviation, have been rescaled in an inter-connected global economic system, institutional design at the level of the nation-state is no longer proving effective in balancing social, environmental and economic objectives (see, for example, Bruni & Zamagni, 2007; Bruyn, 2000; Castells, 2005, 2008; Dees, 1998b; Mittelman, 2011; Porter & Kramer, 2006; Reich, 2008; Scholte, 2011; Swyngedouw, 2005). There is recognition that "people and their governments around the world need global institutions to solve collective problems that can only be addressed on a global scale" (Slaughter, 2004, p. 8). If a collective objective is to access and deliver global merit goods as ubiquitously as possible, the discussion in the previous section suggests that, provision by a single entity, in particular, the state, is no longer feasible conceptually or in reality. It requires, at the very least, some form of multi-stakeholder governance. In the context of the existing political power structure, economic hierarchy and institutional path-dependence, how can we redesign global governance to address the challenges of the twenty-first century?

2.2 POLYCENTRIC AND NETWORK FORMS OF GOVERNANCE

The provision of global merit goods and the mitigation of cross-border negative externalities not only forces us to confront the question of territory and sovereignty but also to engage with long-running debates around the two-sector view, or the functional division of labor and interaction between the political (state) and economic (market) systems (Bruni & Zamagni, 2007; Drache, 2001; Farnsworth & Holden, 2006; Maskus & Reichman, 2004; Polanyi, 1944; Stiglitz, 2007; Weintraub & Kumar, 1997). The challenges in developing a conceptual framework for global governance involve dealing with the complexities of cross-scalar relations that range from entrepreneurial practices at the micro level, community actions at the local level, to macro-level institution-building. The rescaling of problem identification leads to a rescaling of both institutions and solutions through reconceptualization of the governance mechanisms.

In this section, we examine existing models of multi-stakeholder governance, namely, polycentric governance, network forms of governance, heterarchies, and bricolage and explore their potential to deliver global merit goods effectively.

2.2.1 Polycentric Governance

We were inspired by Ostrom's conceptualization of polycentric governance, which involves the following features. First, according to Ostrom

(1996), the oppositional conceptualization of markets and states, or the government and civil society, is an academic construct that "is a conceptual trap arising from overly rigid disciplinary walls surrounding the study of human institutions" (p. 1073). The theory of coproduction, in her view, is in need of further development not only because it is relevant to the study of synergy and development, but also because it can potentially "change the views of social scientists toward the hypothetical 'great Divide'" (p. 1073) between states and markets.

Second, Ostrom (2010b) envisions a system in which diverse public and private agencies function, not simply as independent decision makers, but also act "in a coherent manner with consistent and predictable patterns of interacting behavior" (p. 3). While these stakeholders may be formally independent, they take into account each other's presence and activities, in some instances through contractual agreements and, in others, cooperative undertakings. Polycentricity is governed by well-established rules, with distributed autonomy that gives incentives to nurture trust while maintaining local autonomy to produce local solutions. A level of redundancy combined with a "trial-and-error" approach in devising solutions reinforces the robustness of the larger system even if small systems within them fail (Ostrom, 2000).

Third, Ostrom calls for "configural approaches" to better understand factors that contribute to "self-organized efforts within multi-level, polycentric systems" (p. 2). Ostrom's framework draws from concepts of collective action proposed by Olson (1965), and is useful in analyzing, to use the language of Schelling (1978), how micro-motives at the level of the individual translate into macro-behavior. Such a cross-scalar framework is critical in ensuring that the debates over governance do not remain abstract.

Yet, our conceptualization diverges from Ostrom's polycentric governance in many ways. First, polycentric governance was conceptualized to manage consumption of common property resources, with examples in the management of natural resources such as forestry and fisheries. It remains unclear how it applies to incentivizing innovation and producing common property. Second, polycentric governance is limited by its adoption of the original assumptions of the collective action framework, which are based on self-maximizing stakeholders facing a prisoners' dilemma, resulting in free-rider problems as the major source of contestation. Third, the collective action framework has largely assumed natural monopolies in the provision of public goods, associated with high initial capital costs, but various technological advances (e.g. ICTs, distributed power grids) today are altering such assumptions. Finally, territorial boundaries define and determine the limits of the resources as well as the populations who have access to those resources. Ultimately, the framework stops at acknowledging the diversity of stakeholders, while organizational effectiveness relies on the coherence between the "rules of use" (i.e. norms and conventions) and the structure of the specific common property resource in question.

2.2.2   Network Forms of Governance

We were also inspired by theorists who advocate network forms of governance. Organizational theorists acknowledge that it is the various combinations of the two governance modes identified by economists, market/price versus hierarchies/authority, that leads to the wide variation in empirically observed organizational forms (Adler, 2001). The tendency to place all forms in a "swelling middle" (Zenger & Hesterly, 1997) between the two ideal types, however, is being challenged. In the context of the proliferation of ICTs and the knowledge economy, a set of new actors has emerged. For example, Adler (2001) highlights community/reflexive trust as a third ideal type of governance. Whereas Adler's analytical distinction is limited to the role of trust within and between corporations, we follow sociologists who have pursued the idea more broadly in the form of networks.

For example, organizational forms have gone beyond well-specified state-led PPPs to "working arrangements based on a mutual commitment (*over and above that implied in any contract*) between a public sector organization with *any organization outside of the public sector*" (Bovaird, 2004, p. 200, emphasis added). As such, governance is no longer reducible to intermediate forms of markets and hierarchies (Powell, 1990) but increasingly involve collaboration across the public and the private domains.

Mohan (2014) draws parallels between networks, and what Burns and Stalker (1961) referred to as organic organizations. While a mechanistic organization is akin to a centralized Weberian hierarchy that achieves coordination through command-and-control, an organic organization is decentralized and relies on mutual adjustment for the demands of coordination made by constantly changing conditions. Organic organization comes close to Ostrom's self-organized polycentricity, but does not require *ex ante* coordinations and predictable patterns of interactions.

2.2.3   Heterarchies

Another concept that broadly falls under the network mode of governance is "heterarchies." According to Jessop (1998), heterarchies involve the coordination of distinct and operationally autonomous – but mutually interdependent – nodes across different institutional systems and domains. Heterarchies are distinct from the hierarchical and market modes of coordination in at least two ways (Mohan, 2014). In terms of the functional relationship between the various nodes, heterarchies are pluricentric, while their operational relationship is based on reflexive rationality, that is, informed by continuous dialog, information processing and knowledge sharing. This is in contrast to the unicentric system of state rule that operates on the basis of substantive rationality using administrative fiat and bureaucratic routine. Markets, by contrast, are multicentric and operate on the basis of procedural rationality with the backing of legal systems.

While heterarchies, like polycentric governance, have broadened the debate on governance, they also raise unanswered questions. First, if the state is to become another node, the literature is silent on how the command-and-control bureaucratic state will become less hierarchical to achieve pluricentricity (Mohan, 2014). The empirical forms of the reconfigured state are neither specified nor is the relationship between the state and other nodes adequately described. Second, although any node can facilitate the coordination essential to establish a shared vision and the mechanisms for collective learning among the various systems in a heterarchy, the state assumes the role of network "centrality" or "meta governance" (Jessop, 1998). This is because of the state being the guarantor of social cohesion in the last resort even if it is no more than another social system. While meta governance does not imply creating another hierarchical layer, and the state may be justified in undertaking meta governance, it is unclear why the centrality of the state will not provide opportunities and incentives that undermine its reflexivity and put it on the slippery slope to hierarchical control. More broadly, it points to the absence of a theory of heterarchical failure, akin to state or market failure. Finally, although heterarchy is situated as a response to unstructured complexity arising out of a proliferation of scales in governance (Cleaver, 2002; Jessop, 1998), it is still very much an attempt by the state to tame globalized capitalism. As such, heterarchy may further accentuate the "scalar mismatch" between the globalized market economy and national states.

Thus, while network forms overcome simple public–private domain conceptions, and go beyond the state–market dichotomies in the provision of global merit goods, they are not without limitation. It is to overcome those limitations that the next chapter discusses the hybrid domain.

2.2.4 Institutional "Bricolage"

The original meaning of the term "bricolage" refers to "making do" or a "do-it-yourself" assemblage of knowledge or institutions. It was originally used by the structural anthropologist Claude Lévi-Strauss to refer to make-shift or make-do aspects of work, as opposed to systematically trained knowledge or skills in describing the mythical nature of "primitive" cultures (Lévi-Strauss, 1962). "Bricolage" has come to be used in many conceptual settings, ranging from innovation and entrepreneurship to institutional theory. In innovation, Garud and Karnøe (2003) contrast bricolage with "breakthrough" innovation, and argue that, in the context of distributed agency, co-innovation by multiple actors occurs in a non-linear manner. In entrepreneurship research, bricolage is defined as "making do by applying combinations of resources already at hand to new problems and opportunities" (Baker & Nelson, 2005, p. 33). In particular, social entrepreneurs are constrained on many fronts, in terms of resources, regulations, and a particular customer base, which makes bricolage a key feature of their activities (Desa, 2012; Di Domenico et al., 2010) (see Chapter 3).

For institutional theorists, bricolage refers to a self-regulated, "do-it-yourself" form of governance. Mittelmann (2013) uses the term "global bricolage" to refer to recent emerging country groupings (e.g. BRICs, the Group of 20) to suggest an unsystematic yet shifting power base in international politics. Cleaver (2002), by contrast, discusses institutional bricolage in the context of natural resource management, and argues that the concept signifies an important acknowledgment of the "complexity, diversity, and ad hoc nature of institutional formation" (Cleaver, 2002, p. 11) that involves multiple actors, frequent cross-cultural borrowing, multi-purpose institutions, and long-term cooperation and reciprocity.

On the one hand, it is difficult to assess bricolage as its conceptualization is still fluid and in evolution, and each application subtly shifts its meanings. Its conceptual weakness in part derives from its largely accidental and anecdotal emergence. On the other hand, bricolage does not appear to be confined within the statist imaginary of governance. Furthermore, while heterarchy, network mode of governance and organic organization all acknowledge the role of self-regulation as an important aspect of its governance, bricolage appears to come the furthest in embracing it as a defining characteristic.

2.3 CONCLUSION

The existing paradigms of governance reviewed in this chapter suggest various attempts to incorporate emerging institutional transformations in the theory of governance. Nevertheless, they have their limitations in explaining contemporary realities. For one, globalization challenges concepts that assume territorial boundaries and a simple rescaling – from public to global public goods, for example – and renders them ineffective as conceptual tools. For another, frameworks that seek to cross territorial boundaries – such as network governance and associated concepts of heterarchy – still largely rely on state centrality. Finally, polycentric governance and institutional bricolage acknowledge multi-stakeholder engagements, but are in need of implementable frameworks in the era of globalization. These issues at least partly explain why heterarchy and bricolage are currently largely conceptual, with their usages restricted to an almost exclusively academic audience.

   In the subsequent chapters, we build on these efforts and develop a case for acknowledging the burgeoning space, which we call the "hybrid domain." The hybrid domain encompasses a variety of stakeholders, involved in the space between states and markets, with blended logics and developing new norms that better balance social and economic missions.

3. The hybrid domain: bridging the state–market divide

The debate over governance requires a better incorporation of the shifting assumptions, the blending rationales, and the multiple rescaling that are redefining and shaping the public and the private domains. We observe the rise of the "hybrid domain" as an emerging organizational arrangement with a goal of generating better solutions. Whereas Polanyi (1944) emphasized the "double movement" between state and markets, we propose to conceptually revise the scope of governance to triple movement (state, markets, and civil society), partly to fill the ideological chasm, and partly to fill the governance void that has emerged. The hybrid domain is not just the tensions between state, markets, and civil society, however. It represents an increasingly hybridized logic in economic governance, manifest in growing overlaps, spillovers, and even redundancies across public–private sectoral boundaries in fusing economic and social missions.

The hybrid domain emerges out of the limit of the two-sector model, combined with the need to deliver merit goods under rescaled governance. The hybrid logic in economic governance we observe is neither state-driven nor developed as an outcome of partisan politics and ideologies. The hybrid domain is distinguished by significant bottom-up characteristics, in which stakeholders, initially uncoordinated and disparate, gradually articulate a highly pragmatic, solution-oriented agenda. Stakeholders, who previously were characterized primarily by their public or private interests, or alternatively, their for-profit or non-profit orientations, are coming together to coordinate actions in a manner that is neither state-directed nor administered. The hybrid logic we observe today is a new form of collective action, one that aims at developing solutions and resolving issues that have broad societal implications. This form of collective action leverages global reach, using technologies, accessing financing, and transferring knowledge and skills that are crucial in scaling up solutions.

3.1 THE RISE OF THE HYBRID DOMAIN

The hybrid domain sits on the boundary of, and overlaps with, the public and private domains. Since the public and private domains represent public and private interests, both of which shift over time with changing societal norms and values, the boundary between the public and private domains not only moves constantly, but its location also varies across cultures and societies. Although the modern state has largely been the guardian of the public domain, and markets serve as the purveyors of the private domain, the distinction between the public and private domains does not correspond perfectly with the distinction between the public and private sectors (states–markets). The public interest may be represented by non-governmental entities (e.g. NGOs) or even by market actors (e.g. renewable energy providers). The hybrid domain arises out of the blurring of the boundaries between public and private interests, and the blending of social and economic missions observed in various organizational forms today. The blurring and blending are intertwined and proceed alongside the growing transnationalization of various interests and stakeholders.

The hybrid domain is constituted by the constellation of actors and technologies that produce formulations of novel designs and solutions, with a new blend of economic and social missions. The hybrid domain is not confined to a particular scale; rather, it coordinates knowledge and technologies globally, and leverages multiple national regulations. In addition to various hybrid organizations, the hybrid domain not only involves conventionally hierarchical actors of governance, such as the state and corporations, but also the grassroots, and the participation of individuals as political actors, economic agents, producers, and consumers. While power and information asymmetries exist in the hybrid domain, the characteristics of actors do not *a priori* determine the asymmetries. The hybrid domain is a necessary organizational framework to produce social innovation.

The process of the rescaling and hybridizing of the public domain invariably necessitates organizational flexibility, as observed in the blurring and mixing of boundaries between public, private, and civil society organizations. The increasing popularity of various instruments such as CSR initiatives, corporate foundations, cross-sectoral collaboration involving corporations and NGOs, and the growth of entities such as strategic and leveraged NGOs and social enterprises, point to the growth of the hybrid domain. The hybrid domain emerges out of intra-sectoral and cross-sectoral transformation to pursue a new combination of social and economic missions. We observe a gradual transition from bilateral negotiations between the state and the markets to hybrid missions and heterarchical complexity. In some cases, this can be observed in subtle shifts in objectives or articulations of multiple objectives in existing institutions. In other cases, this can be observed in cross-sector collaboration between existing institutions, or the rise of new hybrid institutions that straddle the public and private domains.

The hybrid domain blends aspects of market and non-market principles to generate various hybrid forms of coordination and organizations. For one, civil society organizations (i.e. NGOs) have challenged the two-sector view of governance by increasingly representing aspects of the public interest, at times with more credibility than the state bureaucracy and the politicians.[1] For another, the private sector is also undergoing transformation in embracing social missions. With the growing attention to global reputation as a corporate asset, corporations often voluntarily adopt social standards and codes of ethics (Haufler, 2001). Corporations and NGOs are increasingly considered distinct, yet equally important, stakeholders shaping global governance (Millar et al., 2004; Ottaway, 2001; Warhurst, 2005). These partnerships are viewed as "an inescapable and powerful vehicle … for achieving social and economic missions" (Austin & Seitanidi, 2012, p. 728).

Hybrid organizations are emerging in multiple forms. Not only have corporations become more involved in social causes (Farnsworth & Holden, 2006; Moon et al., 2011; Utting & Marques, 2010), some are even being established specifically to fulfill societal objectives. One example is the rise of benefit corporations in the United States, which no longer hold managers accountable for maximizing profits on behalf of shareholders (see Section 3.3.1). Another example is the growing popularity of social enterprises among the millennial generation.[2] Social enterprises typically combine private sector management practices with social objectives, although no consensus has yet emerged on their definition (Chell et al., 2010). These hybrid entities are increasingly instrumental in combining public and private interests and simultaneously achieving economic and social objectives.

The hybrid domain in the early twenty-first century is based on the notion of egalitarianism combined with pragmatism, and the breakdown of the division between the public and the private domains established

---

[1] See, for example, Edelman Trust Barometers Annual Global Survey (2016) which ranks NGOs higher than governments.

[2] The Millennials, otherwise known as Generation Y, refers to those born between 1980 and 2000.

under the dominant form of capitalism in the twentieth century. The disenchantment with purely state-driven and market-driven solutions is prompting a redrawing of the boundaries of the public domain. It is also replacing arms-length, contractual cross-domain partnerships with more intricately blended and synergetic collaboration that adequately and appropriately produces solutions.

3.2 DOMAIN AND SCALAR FLEXIBILITY

Governing the hybrid domain necessitates what we call hybrid governance. Hybrid governance involves complex interactions between two axes of transformation; one, a geographic rescaling from the sub-national to the global, and another a functional hybridizing between the public and the private domains. On the former, rescaling makes state-centered approaches to governance increasingly obsolete, as the scale of governance requires flexibility ("scalar flexibility"). Notwithstanding the existing institutional diversity across states and economies, a resolution to the "scalar mismatch" between (national) states and (global) markets requires a fundamental reconceptualization. In arguing for the hybrid domain as a potential solution that serves rescaled public interests, we seek to shift the states versus markets debate, and reconceptualize governance to incorporate the evolving global civil society. On the latter, newly emerging hybrid norms and values that combine economic and social missions, influenced by twenty-first sensibilities such as social value creation (Austin, 2010) and "shared value" (Porter & Kramer, 2006), require "domain flexibility" – a less rigid division of labor between the public, private, civil society, and various hybrid organizations.

With scalar flexibility, establishing institutional coherence becomes a formidable challenge, as rules and conventions no longer hinge upon a local community, but on global, heterogeneous populations and institutional diversity. While not the sole determinant, scalar flexibility in large part has prompted domain flexibility to cope with such heterogeneity. The hybrid domain involves partially de-territorialized beneficiaries, as it leverages multi-scalar collaboration and spillovers of positive externalities across territorial boundaries, even though each effort may focus on specific groups (e.g. women in urban slums; rural "tribal communities" in India). This aspect makes the hybrid domain distinctive from the traditional notion of cooperatives which seek to benefit their members and employees, thus representing a closed system. As the geographical spillovers of negative externalities redefine the boundary of public interest, a global public interest becomes socially constructed, shifting the demarcation between the public and private domains. Geographical spillovers of negative externalities are often dealt with by improvised solutions on a case-by-case basis, either by reterritorializing negative externalities to suit the existing governance structure, or developing collaboration or hybrid organizations to produce mitigation strategies. A global public interest redefines the boundary of the public domain in some instances, and creates a hybrid domain in others.

Governance in the hybrid domain is conceptualized by foregrounding social innovation which, on the one hand, necessitates multi-sectoral involvement to induce innovation, and, on the other, emphasizes delivering dual missions which require new approaches to governance. To date, debates over innovation have seldom intersected with debates over governance (Swyngedouw, 2005), and organizational innovation has been discussed almost exclusively at the level of the corporate organizations (Christensen & Bower, 1996; Godoe, 2000; Miles, 2000). The hybrid governance framework reflects a shift of emphasis from consumption and management to the production and innovation of commonly shared resources, as in the case of global merit goods discussed in Chapter 2.

Hybrid governance is neither driven nor coordinated by the state, but it is not state-less. The state is not a dominant node of the network, but its role is not by any means insignificant. States vary in their power, effectiveness, and legitimacy, which in turn results in how they shape the needs and opportunities for social innovation. Instead of governing, by rule and diktat, states increasingly have to engage in dialog and respond, in varying degrees, to the economic and social demands of actors from both the public and the private domains, and to adapt/alter regulations and provide contracts. Actors in the private domain are no longer simply subordinate to the state. Hybrid governance is based on cross-scalar reflexive rationality, which is only beginning to emerge in the world where sovereignty is increasingly tenuous as a conceptual underpinning of governance.

In sum, hybrid governance addresses the complexities of balancing social and economic objectives at multiple scales. A key feature of hybrid governance is cross-domain multi-stakeholder involvement. Whereas polycentric governance involves public and private agencies at various scales as independent decision makers, and heterarchic governance involves the state, the private, and non-profit sectors, with the state providing meta governance, hybrid governance involves newly emerging actors. Actions within the hybrid domain today represent an aspect of collective action combined with durable goals. They are at times experimental, at times marginal (or at the very least, not dominant), at times overlapping, and at times duplicating, and involve many combinations of existing and newly emerging actors. As Sassen (2006) observes, "today, we see public–private partnerships for mixed public–private goals that result in entities that are neither fully public nor fully private" (p. 198). In effect, hybrid governance is an effective way to address the "scalar mismatch" without reterritorializing the political domain, and domain flexibility addresses the governance gap.

3.3   ACTORS IN THE HYBRID DOMAIN

Who are the key actors in the hybrid domain? In conceptualizing the "business ecosystem," Moore (1993) adopted an ecological metaphor to signify the importance of adaptation to changes in the economic climate and competitive dynamics, by various stakeholders, including corporations, customers, and others who constitute an economic community. The hybrid domain can be understood as a knowledge ecosystem, in which cross-sector learning takes place and knowledge for social innovation is synthesized and shared among the stakeholders.

In this section, we cover existing actors in transition, and newly emerging actors who combine for-profit and non-profit motivations. It is worth noting that existing actors perform multiple roles and functions in the hybrid domain. Notable functions of for-profit organizations in the hybrid domain include R&D for social innovation, leading CSR initiatives and philanthropy, while non-profit organizations are no longer limited to advocacy roles. The blurring of the boundaries between for- and non-profit entities has broken new ground with the emergence of NGOs as collaborators in innovation, the blending of R&D and CSR initiatives and the rise of TSE. Particularly in the context of the Global South, this collaboration suggests emerging forms of, and opportunities in, combining economic and social objectives.

It is important to recognize that existing actors have evolved in their missions and organizations. While corporations have become increasingly involved in social causes (Farnsworth & Holden, 2006; Moon et al., 2011; Utting & Marques, 2010), NGOs have come to seek revenue-generating activities, recruit staff with professional credentials, and in some instances have gone global. As a result, some NGOs bear "an uncanny resemblance to transnational corporations" (Smillie, 1995, p. 212) in organizational features and territorial coverage. Known as leveraged NGOs, these NGOs strive for financial accountability and transparency. Finally, newly emerging actors, such as social entrepreneurs and social finance investors play an important role in shaping the evolution of the hybrid domain.

3.3.1   Corporations: From Shareholder to Stakeholder Governance

Corporations play a crucial role in the hybrid domain by contributing technological and managerial expertise. The role of corporations in society has seen a transformation in the late twentieth century. For one, some believe that the global reach of MNEs, combined with the unmatched capacity to make and implement decisions faster than states or international agencies, may allow them to build broader social capacity and even "fill global governance gaps and compensate for governance failures" (Ruggie, 2004, p. 24). For another, whereas concepts such as business ethics and corporate citizenship have a long history, the nature, substance, societal expectations, and magnitude of public responsibilities and accountability have risen sharply in recent years (Findlay & Whitmore, 1974; Waddock, 2000, 2004).

On the one hand, the decline of collective bargaining and the increase in offshoring has given large MNEs considerable power and leverage along with a *carte blanche* in many aspects of their operations. Corporate citizenship has been interpreted politically, and concerns over the growing role of powerful corporations in dictating political outcomes through lobbying, financing and the media have led to various legal battles.[3] On the other hand, corporate citizenship is a reflection of growing societal pressures on corporations to behave ethically. Business–society relations vary by country (Amsden, 2001; Evans, 1995; Hall & Soskice, 2001; Johnson, 1982) ranging from the corporatist (e.g. the Scandinavian countries, Germany) to the liberal (e.g. US, UK). In Asia, the post-World War II growth was facilitated at least in part by an export-led industrialization strategy with administrative guidance and strong state intervention in the economy (Amsden, 2001; Johnson, 1982). China was a relative latecomer to economic reform (1978), and India's reforms began even later (1991). In general, however, environmental concern and social protection of workers has been weak in many parts of Asia and regulatory compliance, if any, is relatively recent.

Even in the United States, considered the paragon of liberal ideologies for much of the twentieth century, a profound transformation on the role of corporations in society is observable over time. Since the 1960s, businesses have been increasingly expected to serve as conscientious "corporate citizens" by taking on greater social and environmental responsibilities. The 1970s saw a proliferation of regulations for labor

---

[3]   A prominent recent case in the United States is Citizens United versus Federal Election Commission, 2010.

conditions, consumer safety, and health. Both the Environmental Protection Agency (EPA) and the Occupational Safety and Health Administration (OSHA) were established in 1970, enforcing many new regulations.[4] These did not, by any means, eliminate corporate misconduct; but public expectations pressure corporations to alter their practices and develop technologies that are more socially responsible and intergenerationally sustainable.

The twenty-first century has been characterized as an era of industry self-regulation, as corporations become increasingly subject to environmental risks and political uncertainties. Most publicly traded corporations today have a committee devoted to corporate citizenship at the Board of Directors level, and some adopt practices such as internal social audit and stakeholder governance (Freeman, 1984). An overwhelming majority of corporate leaders believe that social expectations of corporate conduct has risen in recent times.[5] Various corporate experiments today attempt to fuse economic and social missions, including collaboration with the non-profit sector (Boddewyn & Doh, 2011; Dahan et al., 2010a; Dahan et al., 2010b; Webb et al., 2010). Unlike shareholder governance, in which corporate objectives are measured by maximizing returns to shareholders, stakeholder governance seeks to promote a better balance among the interests of stakeholders, including employees, consumers, suppliers, states, financiers, shareholders, and civil society organization representatives. The rise of stakeholder governance suggests that capitalism itself may be in transition. Some corporations conduct collaborative self-regulation by developing stakeholder dialog or by forming industry coalitions (Burchell & Cook, 2013; Mohin, 2012).[6]

More recently, legal structures are emerging in the Global North that permit hybrid organizations to combine social and economic missions.

---

[4] Key regulations implemented by the EPA include the Water Quality Improvement Act (1970), Clear Air Act Amendments (1970), Federal Water Pollution Control Act Amendments (1972), Federal Insecticide, Fungicide and Rodenticide Act (1972), Noise Control Act (1972), Safe Drinking Water Act (1974), Toxic Substances Control Act (1976), and Comprehensive Environmental Response, Compensation, and Liability Act (CERCLA) (1980).

[5] Ninety-five percent of CEOs participating in a survey conducted by McKinsey (Bonini et al., 2007) believed societal expectations have risen in the last five years.

[6] For example, the Electronics Industry Citizenship Coalition was founded in 2004 by eight MNEs to set industry-wide standards for social and environmental practices and to create a unified approach in the industry supply chain. It was run with volunteers drawn from the employees of the MNEs until a full-time professional administrator was appointed nine years after its inception.

Examples include the community interest company (CIC) in the United Kingdom, and the low-profit limited liability company (L3C) in the United States. Both CIC and L3C were established to accommodate social enterprises without sacrificing the tax benefits of the non-profit organization (Battiliana et al., 2012). The L3C was created to make room for foundations to fund social enterprises in the United States and, to date, is in operation in ten states.

Benefit corporation legislations in the United States are a movement designed to counteract "shareholder primacy" established in US law. First enacted in the state of Maryland in April 2010, 30 states have followed suit. The need for regulations for benefit corporations arose due to the US legal decision in 1919, which held the directors of corporations legally liable for shareholder profit maximization, which effectively precludes them from engaging in social and/or environmental missions.[7] The benefit corporation status was established to allow commercial enterprises to strengthen social missions in their business practices. The status offers legal protection to directors when considering non-financial interests in their decisions; helps affirm and maintain the corporate mission over time; and creates marketing opportunities as a differentiation strategy.[8] Regulations for benefit corporations ensure that the legal framework does not constrain "mission-oriented" for-profit entities, and allow corporations to seek the double-bottom line – social and profit considerations (Gaffney, 2012). Although the benefit corporation legislation does not affect the tax status, it affects the requirement of corporate purpose, accountability and transparency.

While Canada and the United Kingdom have also enacted similar legislations (known as community interest or community contribution companies), to date, other countries have not followed suit. In some countries it is believed that legislation is unnecessary, given that shareholder primacy has not been legalized. Yet, interests in corporations that combine economic and social missions are on the rise worldwide, as indicated by the growth of certified B-Corps. Not to be confused with benefit corporations, B-Corps certifications are issued by B Lab, a non-profit organization established in Philadelphia in 2006, which evaluates and certifies corporations on the basis of certain social and environmental parameters. Since certification by B-Corps does not confer a legal status, it can be applied to corporations worldwide. As of April 30, 2016,

---

[7]   There are disagreements on the interpretation of this law, however. For details, see Storper (2015).

[8]   For indepth legal discussions of hybrid organizations, see Esposito (2013), Murray (2012), Battilana et al. (2012), and Sabeti (2011).

there were 1,704 certified B-Corps in 50 countries, up 32 percent from the previous year.[9] Although still miniscule in numbers, in comparison with the total number of corporations around the world, the growth of certified B-Corps suggests that the movement to alter corporate practices is on the rise across many countries, and will likely grow further in the future.

3.3.2 Corporate Social Responsibility (CSR) Initiatives

While objectives and actions vary, corporate social responsibility is defined as "actions that appear to further some social good, beyond the interests of the firm and that which is required by law" (McWilliams & Siegel, 2001, p. 117). CSR represents an extension of what is traditionally understood as charity, designed to enhance corporate and product brand images. In addition, developing progressive human resource management programs, non-animal testing procedures, pesticide-free produce, and abating pollution can all fall under CSR activities.

From the perspective of the theory of the firm, CSR is yet another strategy that contributes to profit maximization (Jensen, 1988; McWilliams & Siegel, 2001), and a cost–benefit analysis can be conducted to determine the appropriate level of CSR activities. Views are divided, however, about how CSR affects business performance (Crets & Celer, 2013; McWilliams & Siegel, 2001). Corporations that embrace CSR value the recognition they generate among multiple stakeholders.[10]

CSR spending has risen, reaching USD 18.5 billion in 2014, according to a survey among 271 corporations, including 62 of the Fortune 100 (CECP The Conference Board, 2015). Evidence suggests that CSR initiatives are becoming increasingly important for corporate leaders and employees alike (*The Economist*, 2008). Direct impacts on the bottom line notwithstanding, it is clear that corporations are no longer able to ignore the importance of CSR. One report found that the overwhelming majority of the millennials "would deliberately seek out employers whose CSR values matched their own" (88 percent of the respondents) (PricewaterhouseCoopers, 2011). Another survey suggests that more than

---

[9] Data provided by B-Lab (www.bcorporation.net). There were 1,287 certified B-Corps in 41 countries as of May 18, 2015.
[10] For competing views on the impacts of CSR on corporate performance, see McWilliams and Siegel (2001).

40 percent of a corporation's reputation is derived from its CSR activities (Mohin, 2012).[11]

In India, CSR is mandated by the state. The government issued guidelines in 2009 urging firms to allocate specific budgets for CSR and to work in partnership with local authorities, business associations and NGOs.[12] This voluntary code of conduct became mandatory with the passage of the Companies Act 2013.[13] Section 135 of the Act requires corporations to spend at least 2 percent of their net profits on CSR and articulate a CSR policy.[14] As a result of these regulations, CSR spending in India was projected to grow four-fold to USD 2.5 billion in 2015 (*The Economic Times*, 2015).

The growth of CSR notwithstanding, views on the motivation and efficacy of CSR are highly divided. As we shall show in subsequent chapters, CSR is being actively experimented with, as many corporations view the socio-economic/environmental impact of straightforward charity as being limited or unsustainable.

3.3.3   NGOs in Transition

In recent decades, the non-profit sector has begun to represent public interests in many ways alongside the state. NGOs are important civil society organizations that started off as outsiders in local and global policymaking, but have increasingly become insiders and active partici-pants in shaping policies in various arenas. The active presence of non-state actors in the public domain has "created the possibility of 'non-nationalist' action for greater social justice across the world" (Harris, 1986, 2005; Kitching, 2010; Rangan, 2007), which Foucault (1991, p. 103, emphasis in original) termed as the "*etatisation* of society." Today, NGOs are increasingly considered to be distinct, yet equally

---

[11]   The significance of CSR for employees proves not to be recession-proof, however. The same share dropped to 59 percent in 2015 (Pricewaterhouse-Coopers, 2015).

[12]   The guidelines are available at http://www.mca.gov.in/Ministry/latestnews/CSR_Voluntary_Guidelines_24dec2009.pdf (accessed July 5, 2015).

[13]   For more details, see (Government of India, 2013a). Schedule 7 of the Act specifies the activities (such as eradicating poverty, improving health and promoting education), which may be included by firms in their CSR policies.

[14]   More specifically, the Act requires firms with a net profit of INR 50 million or more during any financial year to spend at least 2 percent of the average net profits of the three immediately preceding financial years.

important, stakeholders along with corporations in shaping global governance (Millar et al., 2004; Ottaway, 2001; Scholte, 2004; Warhurst, 2005).

The relationship between corporations and NGOs has evolved from being adversaries, to fulfilling contractual obligations, and finally, to becoming partners. In the initial adversarial engagements with the for-profit sector, NGOs represented civil society interests and often served as watch-dogs of private sector activity. Then the primary role of the NGOs became one of advocacy, filling the "trust-void" (Argenti, 2004; Marano & Tashman, 2012; Yaziji & Doh, 2009), conducting factory audit, and/or implementing certification programs across the corporate value chain (Gereffi et al., 2001; Teegen et al., 2004).

However, with the growth of CSR initiatives, NGOs increasingly receive grants from the private sector to support their social missions (Doh & Guay, 2006; Hess et al., 2002; Rondinelli & London, 2003; Vogel, 2007; Winston, 2002). For NGOs, corporations have therefore become a target of criticism as well as sources of funding. On the one hand, the NGO sector welcomes the expansion of CSR as an additional source of support for their social missions. On the other hand, it poses a moral dilemma for NGOs attempting to balance their missions with the need for resources. While some corporations use the RFP (request for proposals) model to seek NGOs that best correspond to specific CSR missions, most corporations are highly selective in choosing NGOs to carry out their missions, in part due to the risks and transaction costs of searching, verifying and working with unknown NGOs. This confounds the already asymmetrical power relations between corporations and NGOs, where NGOs are not only the recipients but also the contractors, providing access to communities in some instances and delivering products/services in others.

NGOs are experimenting and expanding their scope in various forms of cross-sector partnerships to create social value (Austin & Seitanidi, 2012). Corporations no longer view NGOs solely as a means to garner social legitimacy, but increasingly as critical sources of knowledge to serve their triple-bottom lines. From a resource based-view of the firm (Penrose, 1959), NGOs bring to the firm crucial resources, in the form of the knowledge of the needs of users/consumers, to break through the "glass floor," an impenetrable market threshold experienced by many MNEs that confines them to premium markets. As corporations find NGOs to be increasingly essential collaborators, NGOs can no longer be understood either as recipients of corporate charity (Dees, 1998a; Doh & Guay, 2006; Hess et al., 2002; Rondinelli & London, 2003; Vogel, 2007; Winston, 2002) or playing merely an advocacy role.

Civil society organizations have become insider rather than outsider critics in global policymaking, and are well-established stakeholders in the structures and mechanisms of global governance (Scholte, 2004). BRAC (est. 1972), headquartered in Dhaka, Bangladesh, for example, is the largest NGO in the world with over 100,000 employees. Not only do they draw the majority of their resources from their for-profit entities in dairy/food production, they also partner with private philanthropic foundations (such as Nike and MasterCard Foundations) to pursue developmental objectives. BRAC provides a number of basic services, such as education and healthcare, besides running agricultural cooperatives.[15] Coupled with expanding global foundations (described in the following section), these trends culminate in the scalar and domain flexibilities that characterize the hybrid domain.

3.3.4 Social Enterprises

Some corporations are being established specifically to fulfill social goals. Social enterprises have grown in numbers in recent years, and are generally characterized as for-profit organizations with the dual objective of increasing social value as an outcome of product/service delivery, while remaining sustainable financially (Weerawardena et al., 2010). Social enterprises typically combine private sector management practices with social objectives, although a consensus has yet to emerge on a definition (Chell et al., 2010).[16] Situated between the non-profit organization on the one hand and commercial enterprises on the other, social enterprises are heterogeneous and fall within a broad spectrum (Austin et al., 2006). As a result, the social entrepreneurship literature today is drawn from business strategy and entrepreneurship, and community development and non-profit management (Sharir & Lerner, 2006; Weerawardena & Mort, 2006).

Social enterprises are not just profit-seeking corporations with social impacts; rather, they are driven with a vision of prioritizing the social objectives of stakeholders. The organizational manifestations of social enterprises are context-specific and vary across countries. For example,

---

[15]   When Balaji observed the ubiquity of BRAC services in rural Bangladesh in 2011, a local researcher commented that the only difference between BRAC and the government was that the latter had an army!

[16]   Austin et al. (2006) note the challenges of developing appropriate performance measures for social enterprises, as social value is not only difficult to measure quantitatively, but also involves issues of multi-causality, perception differences, and temporal dimensions.

organizational entities that are recognized to serve a combination of economic and social missions in Europe include various institutions in the so-called "third sector," such as limited guarantee companies (UK), co-operatives (Italy) and associations (France, Belgium). In the UK, social enterprises that cater to social and/or environmental goals have emerged as an outcome of state withdrawal from various public services (Shaw & Carter, 2007). Early research on social enterprises focused on areas of social welfare where government services fall short (Leadbeater, 1997), such as healthcare (Campbell, 1998). The differences across countries in social service provision have led to what Bacq and Janssen (2011) call the "trans-Atlantic divide" in conceptualizing social enterprises. In most European countries, social enterprises are situated as alternatives to charities, while in North America, social enterprises represent a bolder change in the corporate sector, with some envisioning them as the "fourth sector" (Battilana et al., 2012; Esposito, 2013; Sabeti, 2011; Valor, 2005).

Social enterprises differ from commercial enterprises in terms of their sources of funding and the expectations of pecuniary versus non-pecuniary compensation. Social enterprises are defined by several characteristics, such as 1) emphasis on production of goods and services (not relying on advocacy or grants as with NGOs), 2) risk-taking, 3) dependence on paid work (versus volunteers in NGOs), 4) clear community beneficiaries, 5) representation of some kind of collective action/objectives, 6) limited profit maximization, 7) autonomy from state action, 8) emphasis on stakeholder over shareholder and 9) participatory management style (Defourny & Nyssens, 2013). Social enterprises also differ from cooperatives, as they do not serve membership-based "closed commons" of sorts, but instead, cater to "open-commons," in which membership is not required and services are not territorially bound.

Social entrepreneurship is not confined to social enterprises, as it can be practiced through for-profit or non-profit organizations. Some include CSR initiatives as a form of social entrepreneurship (see Murphy & Coombes, 2009), while others view social entrepreneurship as operating an NGO (Gomez & Helmsing, 2010). The context-specific organizational attributes associated with social entrepreneurship, combined with multi-disciplinary interests, have led some scholars to claim that social entrepreneurship suffers from conceptual ambiguities (Chell et al., 2010; Martin & Osberg, 2007). As individuals, social entrepreneurs are defined as those who aim to create social value by employing market-based strategies (Austin et al., 2006; Bacq & Janssen, 2011; Dees & Anderson, 2006; Sommerrock & Sommerrock, 2010; Zahra et al., 2008). The business entrepreneurship literature emphasizes the entrepreneurial orientation of individuals who serve as agents of change, recognize new opportunities, and combine resources creatively to produce products and services with social value. In contrast, the non-profit management literature views social entrepreneurship as a sustainable funding strategy to seek out revenue-generating activities to support a social mission. From this standpoint, social entrepreneurship is a response to the reality of a competitive funding environment particularly during recessions, as non-profits are disproportionately affected by austerity measures (Simms & Robinson, 2009).

The ambiguous conceptual basis of social entrepreneurship is further amplified by its dual entrepreneurial identity. Simms and Robinson (2009) argue that social entrepreneurs combine the identities of the activist and the entrepreneur – and this duality leads them to discover, define, and exploit two types of opportunities – issue-based and value-based – with the ultimate objective of enhancing social wealth. In this view, the identity of the social entrepreneur is a juxtaposition of opportunities and conflicting views over how the self operates. Austin et al. (2006) suggest that resolving the tensions that arise from the dual activist-entrepreneur identity may become the ultimate mission of their activities, and their social commitments may induce "strategic stickiness" (p. 12), preventing them from switching markets and products/services to protect their emotional commitment to the social mission.

So far, the social entrepreneurship literature mostly relies on evidence from the Global North. In the Global North, social enterprises are largely an outcome of the devolution of the state, and have grown particularly since the global financial crisis of 2008. Recently, however, it has been acknowledged that a growing number of entrepreneurs are crossing borders to engage in poverty alleviation (Alvarez & Barney, 2014; McMullen, 2011). The success of the Ashoka Foundation in coining the term, and the work of Grameen Bank in Bangladesh and its role in servicing micro-credit for the poor, have also contributed to the international recognition of social entrepreneurship in the Global South.

Social entrepreneurship has been known to deliver social innovation in areas such as ethical banking, work integration, and environmental services, including recycling (Defourny & Nyssens, 2013). Sommerrock and Sommerrock (2010) argue that social entrepreneurs serve a specific role as providers of public goods that typically involve multiple actors, such as the state, state-run corporations and non-profit organizations. Social entrepreneurs function as catalysts in the economy by creating markets for products and services, which are characterized by either people's unwillingness to pay (i.e. free-rider problem) or their inability to pay (due to poverty). The latter is a particularly acute problem in the Global South where poverty, combined with deficient physical infrastructure, is widespread. Therefore, the potential of social entrepreneurship in developing novel designs that help overcome the constraints of underprivileged populations is significant in the Global South.

3.3.5   Transnational Social Entrepreneurs (TSEs)

Our recent observations from India add yet another layer to social entrepreneurship: an emerging group of highly-skilled entrepreneurs originating from the Global North and relocating to the Global South seeking to further entrepreneurial objectives with social missions. Thus far, the literature on transnational entrepreneurship has been concerned almost exclusively with commercial entrepreneurs, primarily in such forms as ethnic/diaspora entrepreneurship (Bhachu, 2003; Ioannides & Minoglou, 2005; Kloosterman et al., 1999; Kyle, 1999; Light et al., 1993; Zhou, 2004), and returnee/argonaut entrepreneurship (Chrysostome & Lin, 2010; Saxenian, 2006; Wright et al., 2008). TSEs refer to an emerging group of skilled immigrants from the Global North, relocating to select locations in the Global South to launch enterprises with a strong social mission. TSE start-ups in the Global South represent a new combination of transnational resources – human capital, social capital, technology, and knowledge of needs – for entrepreneurship that combines social and economic missions. Aside from media reports on this topic (see Vaidyanathan, 2012), scholarly writing on the global aspects of social entrepreneurship is sparse, and there are even fewer studies empirically documenting these TSEs in emerging economies.

Zahra et al. (2008) speculate on the significance of the role model effect by technology entrepreneurs, such as Bill Gates (Microsoft), Jeffrey Skoll and Pierre Omidyar (eBay), and Larry Page and Sergey Brin (Google), engaging in social causes. TSEs are very active in contemporary India in sectors where social and economic values intersect, such as health, renewable energy, and education. TSEs leverage "mixed embeddedness" (Kloosterman et al., 1999) with a new combination of Global North–Global South knowledge and resources, and seek to expand their activities to other areas of the Global South. They bring a new perspective to longstanding local problems, and serve as catalysts of social innovation, by drawing from transnational access to financing, technologies and business know-how. Their transnational access to resources helps them overcome some of the inherent constraints of social entrepreneurship.[17] Contemporary TSEs bridge transnational access to technology, business models and financing, and markets where unmet social needs are acute.

As we shall demonstrate in Chapters 7 and 9, our interviews revealed the significant role of elite institutions in engaging with various social innovation projects, and inspiring students to become social entrepreneurs. They include: in the US, Brown University, Harvard University, Massachusetts Institute of Technology (MIT), Stanford University, University of California, Berkeley, and University of Wisconsin, Madison; in the UK, Cambridge University and the London School of Economics and Political Science; and in India, the five original campuses of the Indian Institutes of Technology (Kharagpur, Bombay, Madras, Kanpur, and Delhi).

3.3.6 From Traditional to Venture Philanthropy

Although official development assistance (ODA) by states is by far the largest source of funds for development in the Global South, at USD 167 billion in 2013 (OECD, 2015), philanthropic organizations are playing an increasingly active role in innovating and producing global public goods. For example, global public–private partnerships (GPPPs) are funded by ODA and led by the United Nations, but philanthropic organizations are increasingly important funders of these projects. Unlike public charities, that receive broad public support and contributions, private philanthropic foundations are funded with endowments given by one or a few sets of individuals, and their missions and objectives largely remain in private hands.[18] A greater involvement of philanthropic organizations in development is leading some to claim the emergence of "philanthrocapitalism" (Bishop & Green, 2008; Edwards et al., 2014), which signals "the effort by a new generation of entrepreneurial philanthropists and business leaders to drive social and environmental progress by changing how business and government operate" (Edwards et al., 2014, p. 550).

Financing that straddles the for-profit and the non-profit sectors is a key feature of the hybrid domain. Acs (2013) argues that strong philanthropy driven by private foundations is a uniquely American capitalist

---

[17]   Since their business models are generally neither global nor international (covering multiple markets) at the outset, we prefer to use the term "transnational" to demonstrate the complex manner in which they combine resources and markets.

[18]   Private foundations often do appoint a Board of Directors and trustees who give guidance, advice, and feedback to the foundations.

tradition that connects opportunities with entrepreneurship, as distinguished from social democracy or market socialism in which the state plays a key role in directing redistribution and providing basic needs.[19] The United States is the largest source of philanthropy in the world, contributing 1.67 percent of its GDP in 2006 (Charity Aid Foundation, 2006).[20] Since 1990, when there were 32,401 private foundations registered in the United States, the number grew more than 2.5-fold, to 87,142 foundations with USD 798 billion in combined assets (The Foundation Center, 2014).[21] The 1,000 largest foundations gave 153,000 grants in 2010 totaling USD 22.4 billion, of which about 5,000 grants totaling USD 1.9 billion went to recipients abroad.

Venture philanthropy is a form of grant making by private foundations that uses market-based strategies to overcome the limitations of traditional giving, and typically involves equity investment in the private sector. Much like venture capital, it provides support in areas such as business plan development, ensuring efficiency, and reporting progress. Unlike venture capital, however, venture philanthropy involves an exit plan once the target objective is accomplished. Unlike traditional philanthropy, venture philanthropy expects a financial return to investment. While views are divided as to whether venture philanthropy is revolutionary (Salamon, 2014), one notable aspect of emerging venture philanthropy is collaboration among philanthropists themselves. Entrepreneurial "philanthropreneurs," such as Warren Buffet and Bill Gates, have led an initiative called the Giving Pledge,[22] which is "a revival and a reinvention

---

[19]   Private foundations in Europe are concentrated in the United Kingdom. We speculate that philanthropy may not have taken strong roots in continental Europe due to a stronger welfare-state and social democratic tradition. Data on European foundations is sparse, although some sources claim that there were an estimated 85,000 private foundations in Europe around the start of the twenty-first century (OECD, 2003; Schlüter et al., 2001).

[20]   The United States was also ranked number 1 in the World Giving Index, tied with Myanmar in 2014 (Charity Aid Foundation, 2014). Top ranked countries included Canada, Ireland, Australia, New Zealand, Malaysia, and the United Kingdom. India was ranked number 67 among 160 countries surveyed. The World Giving Index is based on three primary criteria: giving money, helping strangers, and volunteering, and is conducted by Gallup.

[21]   The data includes all US independent, corporate, community and grant-making foundations that gave out grants. Does not include public charities other than community organizations.

[22]   The Giving Pledge (givingpledge.org) currently lists 138 individuals/ families who have pledged to dedicate the majority of their wealth to philanthropy (August, 2015).

Table 3.1 *Private foundations in the United States*

Rank	Foundations	Assets (in Billion USD)	Rank	Foundations	Total Giving (in Million USD)
1	Bill & Melinda Gates Foundation (WA)	37.2	1	Bill & Melinda Gates Foundation (WA)	3,200.0
2	Ford Foundation (NY)	11.2	2	Ford Foundation (NY)	593.8
3	J. Paul Getty Trust (CA)	10.5	3	Walton Family Foundation, Inc. (AR)	423.8
4	Robert W. Woodruff Foundation, Inc. (GA)	9.5	4	The William and Flora Hewlett Foundation (CA)	381.2
5	W. K. Kellogg Foundation (MI)	8.2	5	The Susan Thompson Buffett Foundation (NE)	367.2
6	The William and Flora Hewlett Foundation (CA)	7.7	6	Silicon Valley Community Foundation (CA)	294.0
7	Lilly Cares Foundation, Inc. (IN)	7.3	7	Robert W. Woodruff Foundation, Inc. (GA)	292.9
8	The David and Lucile Packard Foundation (CA)	6.3	8	W. K. Kellogg Foundation (MI)	259.9
9	The John D. and Catherine T. MacArthur Foundation (IL)	6.0	9	The Andrew W. Mellon Foundation (NY)	258.1
10	Gordon and Betty Moore Foundation (CA)	5.7	10	Foundation to Promote Open Society (NY)	257.9

Source: The Foundation Center (2014). *Key Facts on US Foundations*

of an old tradition that has the potential to solve many of the biggest problems facing humanity today" (Bishop & Green, 2008, p. 2). Some private foundations are also teaming up and combining their resources to make a larger impact. Big Bang Philanthropy is one such example, in which 12 foundations combine resources to maximize impact.[23]

While philanthropy from the United States is sizable, it is by no means the only source of financial support for social innovation in the Global South. The Wellcome Trust from the United Kingdom, for example, encourages research in health, and grants over GBP 700 million annually to scientific research, commercialization, and dissemination in health/ medical fields. The Wellcome Trust also supports initiatives to develop affordable healthcare solutions, and has forged a cross-domain partnership with the Indian state in the area of biomedical research.[24]

Health is by far the largest category of overseas giving, constituting 38 percent of total grant-giving in 2012. The Bill and Melinda Gates Foundation is a particularly important foundation for international grants, contributing 38.7 percent of total grants to overseas recipients in 2010 (The Foundation Center, 2012). In the area of global public health, grants from the Gates Foundation amounted to 76 percent of total international grants in health from the 1,000 largest US foundations. The Gates Foundation combines advocacy with schemes to induce innovation and to support new social enterprise start-ups, while encouraging market-based strategies, financial accountability, and transparency among the NGOs. The Foundation has been instrumental in creating collaborative financing schemes for product development partnerships (PDPs) to support R&D for vaccines of "neglected" diseases, such as malaria and tuberculosis, which are prevalent in the Global South and are not adequately served by the private sector. The Gates Foundation's most recent initiative is a Vaccine Discovery Partnership (VxDP) with GlaxoSmithKline and Sanofi. Announced in late 2013, the partnership provides financial incentives for vaccine manufacturers to conduct early-phase research and to accelerate the development of affordable new vaccines in the Global

---

[23]   Big Bang Philanthropy includes the Barr Foundation, Bohemian Foundation, Child Relief International Foundation, David Weekley Family Foundation, Dietel Partners, Draper Richards Kaplan Foundation, Greenbaum Foundation, Jasmine Social Investments, imago dei fund, Montpelier Foundation, The Mulago Foundation, Open Road, Peery Foundation, Pershing Square Foundation, Planet Wheeler Foundation, and Segal Family Foundation (www.bigbangphilanthropy. org).

[24]   The DBT/India Alliance is a GBP 160 million alliance between the Wellcome Trust and the Government of India's Department of Biotechnology. Equally funded by both partners, the alliance was established in 2008 to build an Indian biomedical scientific community, and to offer various fellowships to encourage research in the field.

South. In India, the Gates Foundation has been critical in supporting social entrepreneurship for the medical devices and diagnostics industry.

It should be noted that foundations originating from the Global South are in many ways forerunners in the hybrid domain in combining for-profit and non-profit activities. The Aga Khan Foundation, for example, is part of the Aga Khan Development Network which operates a variety of for-profit operations in areas of education, health, rural development, humanitarian/disaster relief, micro-credit, and architecture/ planning mainly in South Asia, Africa, and the Middle East.[25] Although privately-held, the organization is non-denominational in most respects and works toward the betterment of humanity. It is known for its long investment horizons (50 years) and offers patient capital in many development projects.

Although venture philanthropy is new to India, the country is not without a long tradition of charity, primarily by religious organizations (such as *mathas* or *ashrams*) and industrial conglomerates (e.g. Tata Trust, founded by India's oldest and largest industrial groups) taking the lead in areas such as education and livelihoods.[26] Today, new sources of funding have emerged, primarily from the new wealthy class of individuals (high-net-worth individuals – HNWIs – and their descendants).[27] As a result, over 70 percent of donors in India today had less than three years of history in grant making (Spero, 2014). In addition, newer industrial conglomerates are establishing Indian corporate foundations. Examples include the Bharti Foundation by Bharti Enterprises (telecommunications/retail/financial services), the Shiv Nadar Foundation by HCL (ICTs), and the Azim Premji Foundation by Wipro (primarily ICTs). At the moment, however, Indian philanthropy has stayed largely within the realm of traditional charity, while global foundations are increasingly involved in "venture philanthropy," with a strong emphasis on innovation that generates profitable solutions to social problems.

---

[25] The foundation was established in 1967 by a Shia Muslim clan of Ismailis who migrated from pre-independence India/Pakistan to East Africa. The organization is now headquartered in Geneva, Switzerland.

[26] An analysis conducted by Charity Aid Foundation (2014) suggests that India's philanthropy is mature and gives disproportionately more than those in other countries with similar GDP per capita based on purchasing power parity.

[27] HNWIs are typically those individuals with an investable asset of over USD 1 million. They are concentrated in the United States (4,006 in 2013), followed by Japan (2,327), Germany (1,130), and China (758). India is ranked sixteenth with 156 HNWIs. https://www.worldwealthreport.com/Largest-HNWI-Populations-2013-by-Market (accessed December 29, 2015).

3.3.7   The Rise of Impact Investment

Investors take on a social mission by adopting this newly emerging vehicle of financing that bridges social and economic missions. The phrase "impact investment" was coined by a group of entrepreneurs, investors, and philanthropists at the Rockefeller Foundation's Bellagio Center in Italy to refer to investments that are "intended to deliver both financial returns and social and environmental benefits" (Rodin & Brandenburg, 2014, p. vi). The rise of impact investment, in part, stems from the tradition of American philanthropy that links entrepreneurship with the spirit of equal opportunity (Acs, 2013).[28] Some founders of philanthropy are more familiar with the world of finance than the world of grant making and, in some instances, are genuinely lost when it comes to structuring and developing grant-making strategies (Rodin & Brandenburg, 2014). In addition to the recognition of the limits of traditional charity in generating sustainable solutions that empower the poor, impact investment emerged as a mode of intervention that effectively leverages, and gives due credit to the vast and thriving presence of micro-entrepreneurship on the ground. An avenue to nurture micro-entrepreneurship is viewed as a far more empowering and sustainable strategy over the continuation of traditional charity.

Impact investment is still emerging as an empirical phenomenon and evolving as a concept; its intentions, objectives, and outcomes have been criticized for being too broad, too vague, and difficult to assess. Salamon (2014), for example, defines impact investment as an effort that seeks social and/or environmental value creation, by promoting health, well-being and quality of life improvements, particularly among the disadvantaged. Impact investment does not take a single form, and can be structured as equity, debt, cash deposits, or other hybrid forms, and also vary by asset class, return expectation, sector and geography (Rodin & Brandenburg, 2014).

---

[28]   Social finance and impact investment are distinct from investor/shareholder activism, which is characterized by highly interventionist shareholders (as opposed to "lazy" investors) seeking to influence and shape corporate decisions broadly. Emerging in the United States in the 1980s, investor activism has grown in the past decade (*The Economist*, 2015). With its origins among "corporate raiders," investor activism does not, by default, involve social missions. But it has been adopted occasionally as a strategy to influence corporate decisions with social or environmental impacts, such as those on climate change and supply chain sustainability.

Actors in impact investments take many organizational forms. It is worth noting that early pioneers, such as the Acumen Fund (est. 2001 in the United States) and Social Finance (est. in 2007 in the United Kingdom) were established as non-profit organizations. The Acumen Fund was established through an initiative of the Rockefeller Foundation, while Social Finance pioneered the issue of Social Impact Bonds in 2010, to generate financing for projects that involve social benefits. The Omidyar Network (est. 2004 in the United States by an eBay founder) takes a hybrid organizational form, operating a for-profit and a non-profit organization, to provide grants as well as to invest in a variety of areas. Some foundations also participate in impact investment by making program-related investments (PRIs). Increasingly, traditional financial agencies, such as banks and pension funds, are expanding social investment portfolios. Various financial intermediaries, who are active in funding social enterprises, are involved in the development of social capital markets (Kaplan & Grossman, 2010).[29] Sources of impact investments are therefore many and do not only include venture philanthropy and HNWIs, but also such entities as social-impact capital aggregators (which assemble capital from HNWIs and serve as intermediaries), social-impact secondary market operators (which securitize bundled loans as collaterals to issue bonds), social stock exchanges (which serve as platforms where funds are matched with seekers of funds),[30] and quasi-public investment funds (e.g. the International Finance Corporation of the World Bank, Multilateral Investment Fund established by the Inter-American Development Bank, Big Society Capital funded by the UK lottery).

In the Global South, impact investment is still emerging. Aavishkaar (est. 2001) in India, and Abraaj Capital (est. 2002), a private equity firm established by an expatriate Pakistani with broad operations in the Global South, were among the early examples. The Global South has been the dominant destination, rather than the origin, of impact investment, and its potential as the source of capital is not yet fully evident (Rodin & Brandenburg, 2014). In India, impact investment is led by international foundations, HNWIs, and angel investor networks. While domestic

---

[29] Examples included are EMCF, New Profit, Robin Hood, United Way, Combined Jewish Philanthropies, and the Boston Foundation.

[30] Examples offered by Salamon (2014) include the Chicago Climate Exchange, the European Climate Exchange (both trade carbon credits), the Bolsa de Valorous Socioambientains (Brazil), Mission Markets (USA), Impact Partners (Singapore), Artha (India), Social Stock Exchange (UK), Impact Exchange (Mauritius), and Impact Investment Exchange (Singapore).

foundations currently only offer modest support, focusing instead on providing technical assistance to small and medium-sized enterprises (SMEs), international foundations such as the Rockefeller Foundation, the Michael and Susan Dell Foundation, and the Gates Foundation dominate as funding sources. HNWIs are the primary source of seed-funding for new start-ups, but compared with foundations, HNWIs expect higher returns on their investment. Established angel networks, such as the Intellecap Impact Investment Network (I3N), Mumbai Angels, and the Indian Angels Networks, also provide resources to impact investment. In contrast, large business conglomerates focus on either purely commercial investments or traditional philanthropy (Global Impact Investing Network, 2015). Notably, the recipients of impact investment also have considerable international backgrounds. As we shall show in Chapter 8, TSEs are active and important aspects of social entrepreneurship in India.

Recognizing the sluggish growth of early impact investment funds due to lower financial returns, efforts are underway to encourage the growth of the pool of funds available for social enterprises. The Social Success Note (SSN) is one such example, where a private investor offers a loan at a below-market rate with a pre-determined social outcome. Once the social outcome is met, a philanthropic payer offers an additional "impact payment" to close the gap between below-market and market rate return (Kohn & Bruysten, 2016).

Even though the impacts of the current reorientation may thus far be modest, impact investment and the rise of ethical investing more broadly signal a transformation of capitalism, and a growing community interested in solving social challenges. Funds serve as intermediaries between investors and social entrepreneurs, providing knowledge and pooling resources for social causes. As such, it can be considered a movement involving bankers, philanthropists and individual investors, and compliments existing efforts that combine economic and social missions, such as microfinance and the fair trade movement.

3.4 CONCLUSION

The emergence of many new actors, and the changing character of existing actors, are in part outcomes of regulatory constraints that bind the for-profit and non-profit branches of our economy separately. They suggest that, on the ground, the complementarity supersedes the dichotomous antagonism between the for- and non-profit spheres that is often portrayed in the academic literature. As public and private interests are fused in a new manner, as evident in the changing roles and objectives of these actors, capitalism itself is adapting to the new social demands, arising out of rescaled consciousness. Despite the conceptual ambiguities, and the blurred boundaries, the diverse actors in the hybrid domain can be best understood as falling along a spectrum between the bipolar conceptualization.

Actors in the hybrid domain increasingly serve as stakeholders of social innovation. Collaborations that involve states, foundations, and social finance that serve as private equity funds promoting social innovation and entrepreneurship are becoming increasingly common, to the point where the collaborative model is emerging as the "new normal" in the field of development (Salamon, 2014). These stakeholders are broadening the scope of the hybrid domain, generating diversity in institutional forms and variety in resources. While maintaining institutional diversity, the hybrid domain emerges as a key arena that directs efforts toward innovation and production of merit goods, some of which now transcend national borders (i.e. global merit goods). As we shall show in the following chapters, these institutional diversities are allowing new possibilities for social innovation.

4. Social innovation in global contexts

What is social innovation, and what is behind the interest in the phenomenon? In this chapter, we seek to develop a geographically nuanced definition of social innovation that is conceptually useful in the contemporary global context. The chapter includes an overview of the debates on social innovation, which primarily relies on evidence from the Global North where the imperatives are state devolution, privatization, and austerity measures. Social innovation in the Global South differs in features, orientations and emphases due to its distinctive context, including instances of state failure. We also discuss controversies over social innovation, and how competing paradigms conceptualize knowledge resources for social innovation as market intelligence for corporations on the one hand, and community assets for empowerment on the other.

4.1 SOCIAL INNOVATION

The term "social innovation" warrants some specificity. Simply put, social innovation refers to innovation for social change (Michelini, 2012), designed to satisfy unmet social needs (Van Dyck & Van den Broeck, 2013). Following this definition, social innovation is an outcome of the juxtaposition of social mission with market logic, and enacted either by, or in collaboration with, the private sector.

4.1.1 Defining Social Innovation

Long before the term social innovation became popular, Moulaert et al. (2013) discuss how Drucker (1987) defined social innovation, as "innovation in meeting social needs of, or delivering social benefits to, communities" and conceptualized it broadly as institutional design that generates social benefits. To Drucker, social innovation in the nineteenth century was primarily led by the state (e.g. the social security system by Bismarck), whereas the key initiators of social innovation in the twentieth century were in the private sector (e.g. corporate research laboratories, mass media, and farm agents[1]).

Today, social innovation is more narrowly defined; Moulaert, et al. (2013) define social innovation as "the creation of new products, services, organizational structures or activities that are 'better' or 'more effective' than traditional public sector, philanthropic or market-reliant approaches in responding to social exclusion" (p. 1). Contemporary examples of social innovation include, but are not limited to, micro-credit financing, micro-franchising, clean/alternative sources of energy, and new modes of health-care delivery using the Internet. In our research, we observed that social innovation often involves novel technology design, and is aimed at mitigating socio-economic exclusion of various kinds, ranging from issues such as employment and environmental sustainability, to public health.

To broaden the scope of the debate over social innovation, we situate it as an outcome of the double-edged impact of globalization in the twenty-first century.[2] At one level, contemporary globalization, which Sassen (2006) refers to as an "epochal transformation," is being driven by ICTs to produce an "informational, global and networked"[3] economy that is capable of applying "its progress in technology, knowledge, and management to technology, knowledge, and management themselves. Such a virtuous circle should lead to greater productivity efficiency, given the right conditions of equally dramatic organisational and institutional changes" (Castells, 2000, pp. 77–78). However, the impacts of ICTs have been highly uneven, and manifest themselves in social inequalities and uneven geographies. The resulting network is highly selective in "connecting localities throughout the planet, according to criteria of valuation

---

[1] Julius Rosenwald of Sears & Roebuck Co. provided philanthropic support for the US Department of Agriculture to launch the Farm County Agent program, to address what he viewed as the widespread social problems of ignorance, poverty and isolation among American farmers.

[2] The World Development Report (World Bank, 2008) defines globalization as the progressive integration of the world's economies, which requires national and international partners to work together and manage changes relating to international trade, finance and global environmental issues.

[3] It is informational as the productivity and competitiveness of its units is dependent upon their capacity to "generate, process and apply efficient knowledge-based information." It is global as "its core activities of production, consumption and circulation are organized and generated on a global scale either directly or through a network of linkages between economic agents." It is networked as "its productivity is generated through and competition is played out in a global network of interaction between business networks"(Castells, 2000, pp. 77–78).

and devaluation enforced by social interests that are dominant in these networks" (Castells, 2002, p. x).

We define social innovation as a combination of the following features. First, social innovation refers to a basket of solutions which create social value and, in the twenty-first century, involve actors in the hybrid domain in one form or another. Second, technological innovation plays a significant role in social innovation today, either through new technological development or, more typically, new applications of existing technologies. Although there are many technologies that catalyze social innovation by enabling access to otherwise infrastructure-deficient, difficult to service areas and populations, ranging from the rural poor, the disabled, and the elderly, it is argued that ICTs have had the most significant impact on social change (Castells, 2000; Jessop, 1998; Sassen, 2006).

Third, social innovation may involve new micro modes of delivery, resolving the issues of economic, social, and geographical accessibility which often result in the "last-mile" problem. Micro modes of delivery range from financing (e.g. micro-credit), packaging (e.g. micro-sachets for shampoos) to servicing (e.g. micro-charging for mobile phones). New business models may be conceived for micro-delivery and micro-franchising. In health services, for example, a recent buzz word is "social-franchising," which is designed to replicate delivery formats as a way of amplifying social impacts across multiple geographies (Hanson et al., 2008; Montagu, 2002; Tracey & Jarvis, 2007).

Fourth, social innovation is an outcome of "double failures," of both market and non-market forces. In some cases, social innovation is perceived as a need when market solutions fail. In such cases, the involvement of civil society organizations or state interventions is sought. In other cases, interest in social innovation arises out of state failure to meet social needs, such as education and infrastructure, prompting involvement by the private sector and civil society organizations.

Fifth, the need for social innovation varies by the territorial and institutional context (Moulaert & Nussbaumer, 2005; Van Dyck & Van den Broeck, 2013). By focusing on how the variation in supply-side institutions shape innovation, the "national system of innovation" literature (Freeman, 1995; Freeman & Perez, 1988), points to how contexts frame social innovation. Ideas that are novel, solutions that have social impacts, and designs that work on the ground, are all specific to the context in which social innovation is generated and applied. As we shall elaborate in the subsequent sections, contexts for social innovation vary considerably between and within the Global North and the South. The significance of "contextual learning" for social innovation in the Global South today suggests the need to reorient our conceptualization of learning, from the accumulation of tacit knowledge that leads to productivity gains (Arrow, 1962), to communities of practice that emphasize the role of tacit knowledge in shaping intra- and inter-organizational learning (Brown & Duguid, 1991; Lawson & Lorenz, 1999; Nonaka, 1994; Wenger, 1999). Context learning shifts the emphasis from a productivist orientation to a market orientation to a social solution orientation, one that focuses on understanding latent needs and developing new solutions, with the participation of the users/consumers. Contextual learning drives design engineering research to deliver solutions for perceived social needs. As such, contextual learning generally cannot be accomplished effectively through conventional market research.

Moreover, social innovation requires institutional change, formally and/or informally. In combining social and economic missions, corporations have reconceptualized the ideal locations for innovation, altered knowledge sourcing strategies and, in some instances, changed the logic of operations to support the new hybrid missions. To remedy non-market failure, states and civil society organizations have also altered their justification, *modus operandi*, and forms of engagements with the stakeholders of social innovation. For instance, since delivering social innovation requires additional access to financial resources, it is often combined with a novel financing scheme. Some institutional transformations may be gradual and subtle, but possess the potential for systemic change that fundamentally alters the forms and logics of governance.

Thus, social innovation involves a combination of technologies and hybrid socio-economic logics, often mobilizing resources from both the for-profit and non-profit sectors, to enable the production of novel products and services and to provide access to those products and services for underserved populations.

4.1.2　Context in Social Innovation

In social innovation, context plays a significant role in defining what is considered novel, what can work as a solution, and what can generate social impacts. In the Global North, the literature on social innovation is associated with the growth of the social sector outside the state, including the non-profit sector (the "third sector") and social entrepreneurship (the rise of the so-called "fourth sector"). The rise of the fourth sector is understood as an outcome of the retreat by the state from social service provision, and the absence of sustainable models in the NGO sector. Some include CSR activities, and new forms of collaboration that differ from traditional "arms-length" partnerships, in social innovation (Crets & Celer, 2013; Kanter, 1999).

Emerging markets offer an opportunity to tackle rich, "wicked problems" which involve strong social dimensions and require non-linear, multi-disciplinary, multi-stakeholder design solutions. Wicked problems were first defined as a "class of social system problems which are ill-formulated, where the information is confusing, where there are many clients and decision makers with conflicting values, and where the ramifications in the whole system are thoroughly confusing" (Churchman, 1967, p. B-141). Wicked problems are characterized by multiple interdependencies and, from a social planning perspective, are not amenable to scientific solutions (Rittel & Webber, 1973). Confronting wicked problems in the Global South induces social innovation by challenging stakeholders to design solutions that solve complex and multi-dimensional problems. In the Global South, novel designs are being developed to overcome the constraints facing underprivileged populations. The constraints combine infrastructural deficiencies with difficult-to-meet price-points, and require technological innovation, detailed contextual intelligence, learning, and access to financial resources. Notably, contexts in the Global South have inspired "resource constraint-innovation" (Ray & Ray, 2010), "frugal innovation" (Zeschky et al., 2011) or "value engineering" (Sharma et al., 2011), all of which emphasize affordability and accessibility of technologies primarily through de-featuring, that is, stripping down of functions to the bare bones. The Indian context in particular inspired the notion of *jugaad* (Radjou et al., 2012).[4]

In India, our evidence suggests that social entrepreneurship almost always combines technological and business model innovation and collaboration, to develop products and services that fuse cutting edge technologies with new-to-the world design and usage. State failure, the prevalence of poverty, and inadequate infrastructure on the one hand, and the availability of English-speaking talent in urban areas on the other, make India a fertile location for social innovation.

4.1.3 Proximity in Social Innovation

Proximity in innovation is the essence of what economic geographers call "local buzz" or "geographical contexts" (Asheim et al., 2007; Gertler, 1995; Gertler, 2003; Storper, 2009; Storper & Venables, 2004).[5] In

---

[4] Frugal innovation and *jugaad* are not always driven by social missions and social impacts, however, and they can be driven by economic missions in for-profit organizations.
[5] Design is seen to have a particularly "sticky" geography (Leslie & Rantisi, 2006; Patra et al., 2009; Vinodrai, 2006).

general, most innovation occurs in domestic corporations for home markets (Håkansson, 1989), and distance typically increases "noise" in communications and raises cultural and institutional barriers (Zaheer, 1995), although geographical proximity alone does not guarantee innovation (Boschma, 2005). For corporations, the lack of knowledge of the demand side is often cited as a key reason for the failure to launch a new product (Chenier & Prince, 1990; Chonko et al., 1991; Cornish, 1997; Fletcher & Wheeler, 1989) or a new retail format overseas (Aoyama, 2007; Aoyama & Schwarz, 2006). Thus, proximity to markets becomes essential for corporations as geographic distance raises cultural barriers.

Knowledge required for social innovation is "tacit" and context-specific, and thus has strong geographical implications, as the most effective "learning-by-interacting" requires face-to-face interactions. A mechanism of inter-organizational coordination is required to effectively transfer "tacit knowledge" for innovation, and to develop an "innovation regime" that allows knowledge sharing (Carson et al., 2003; Gambetta, 1988; Godoe, 2000; Krasner, 1985). By contrast, R&D in emerging economies has long been seen primarily as a means of technology transfer (Amsden, 2001; Fromhold-Eisebith, 2002), with MNEs engaging in secondary marketing (selling existing and often obsolete technologies to customers) (OECD, 2008). R&D activities outside the Global North have been understood as being limited to "localization" (adaptation of existing products to local markets) and "asset exploitation" (use of existing technologies), at the expense of "asset-seeking" (technology-creating basic research) activities (Chen, 2008).

R&D activities by corporations have taken place largely in key markets in the Global North, that is, where "lead users" and "lead markets" for new products/services are to be found.[6] As a result, studies typically presuppose lead users in the developed world (see Gerybadze & Reger, 1999; Grabher et al., 2008). Consumers in the Global South, and particularly the poor, have not been the main target segments for R&D intensive corporations, many of which are from the Global North. For most MNEs, poorer consumer segments in the Global South constitute unfamiliar markets about which there exists no knowledge base within the corporation.

Today, some areas in the Global South have become favored R&D locations for MNEs whose interests lie in expanding the scope and the geography of the markets they have covered traditionally (Aoyama &

---

[6] In the business and management literature, most studies stop with offering classifications and typologies of R&D facilities, which may include market-driven R&D as one of the categories; see, for example, Kuemmerle (1999a, 1999b), von Zedtwitz and Gassmann (2002), and Chen (2008).

Parthasarathy, 2012; Dunn & Yamashita, 2003; Hitt et al., 2005; London & Hart, 2004; Parthasarathy & Aoyama, 2006). Moreover, "reverse innovation," a reversal of technological transfer, from the conventional North to South, to South to North, is increasingly a reality (Govindarajan & Trimble, 2012). Combined, these trends demonstrate the innovative capacity in some emerging economies (e.g. China and India), and an increasing openness among MNEs to incorporate new product/service development designs originating from the Global South.

Social innovation demands a new conceptual framework that explicitly recognizes innovation as emerging from interactions between perceived social needs, market opportunities, technological knowledge, and organizational forms. Multiple strategies are employed by corporations to effectively learn and conduct social innovation. One is to establish R&D units with a specific mandate for social innovation with dedicated teams that bring together expertise from many disciplinary backgrounds, including not just science and engineering, but also from the social sciences, to develop solutions that respond to multi-dimensional problems. Given the relative scarcity of knowledge, proximity to markets also offers opportunities for learning through collaborating with the state and civil society organizations. As we shall demonstrate in Chapter 6, India serves as a learning laboratory for social innovation, where technical knowledge intersects with unmet social needs. Yet another is to find local partners who can effectively source knowledge and facilitate access to users and consumers. Collaboration with local NGOs, social entrepreneurs, or other entities that collect accurate, contextual and appropriate data for the underserved are indispensable for many MNEs.

4.1.4 Technology in Social Innovation

Social innovation is not technology-specific, but the role of the Internet in contemporary social innovation is significant. The Internet has dislodged the previously sharp boundaries between public and private goods and challenged the boundary between common property and private property for knowledge. The consumer is now the "last worker on the production line" (Humphreys et al., 2005; Leadbeater, 2000). The Internet has not only made possible the public sharing of private goods, but has also enabled collective innovation. In the new system, the realm of the public goods has expanded and, in some cases, encroached upon those realms which were earlier exclusively private. The knowledge and its spillover is no longer restricted to the producers (i.e. the firm and the industry) but also flows to users and consumers. The barriers and the division of labor that existed between the producer and the consumer are breaking down (Hartley, 2004; Humphreys et al., 2005).

Knowledge for social innovation can be divided into: 1) indigenous knowledge, or effective use of particular local resources (such as medicinal herbs); 2) institutional knowledge, of agency and stakeholders; and 3) contextual knowledge, such as habits, norms, power relations, and culture. Designing user-friendly interfaces is particularly critical for the widespread adoption of devices such as mobile phones by lower-income segments in the Global South (Donner, 2008; Prahalad, 2006). This suggests a need to cultivate local expertise that effectively combines technical solutions and marketing strategies. Market-capture R&D represents a deeper form of localization by MNEs than previous forms, namely, the localization of products, decision making, and human resources. Whereas product localization essentially involves technology transfer with minor product adaptations that are either cosmetic, or meant for regulatory compliance (e.g. voltage requirements, safety standards), localization of innovation is a process that involves not only an in-depth understanding of the markets, but also an ability to capture new markets that were previously beyond the scope of MNEs especially when deploying general-purpose technologies like ICTs.

4.1.5   Sustainability in Social Innovation

Sustainability in the context of social innovation has many meanings. One refers to innovation that aims at achieving environmental sustainability. Sometimes known as "eco-innovation," innovation in areas such as energy, biodiversity, and conservation can yield significant positive social impact and simultaneously contribute to environmental sustainability. Another refers to innovation that promotes sustainability of livelihoods for both the producers and consumers. For example, as we discuss in later chapters, a model that contributes to livelihood sustainability involves the creation of economic opportunities for micro-entrepreneurs to take part in the production and micro-delivery of services. Furthermore, environmental and livelihood sustainability are not mutually exclusive; for example, both are relevant for farmers who use environmentally sustainable fertilizers to produce internationally certified agricultural crops.

Finally, sustainability may refer to organizational models intended to ensure resilience of social missions, typically through resource diversification strategies intended to reduce dependence on grants from the state or foundations. As the subsequent chapters will show, some believe that the rise of social finance is a key aspect of sustainability in social innovation.

4.2 COLLABORATIVE GOVERNANCE FOR SOCIAL INNOVATION

How is the interaction between the providers and consumers of innovation understood in the literature, and how is it relevant for social innovation? This section reviews the literature on the significance of demand-side knowledge and the role of users in innovation, and examines its relevance for theorizing social innovation. We explore how and why corporations engage with social innovation, how proximity matters in social innovation, how user/consumer participation is conceptualized in the innovation process, and how NGOs organize the needs of users to contribute to social innovation.

4.2.1 Corporations

In general, the role of demand-side knowledge in innovation has been neglected at the expense of technical, scientific, or organizational knowledge. Innovation has traditionally been understood largely as a technology (scientific knowledge)-driven process, and is typically measured by supply-side factor inputs (technical labor force) or outcomes (patent applications) (Almeida & Phene, 2004; Audretsch & Feldman, 1996; Cantwell & Piscitello, 2005; Feldman, 2000; Feldman & Massard, 2002; Frost, 2001).

Factor inputs from the demand side have remained under-theorized in the innovation literature. Traditionally, locations of R&D activities are understood to follow the supply-side logic, namely the availability and affordability of skilled engineers and scientists (Kuemmerle, 1997; Malecki, 1987; Serapio & Dalton, 1999). Research on the knowledge on the demand side is dominated by the literature in marketing. Labeled as "market intelligence" by Cornish (1997), it refers to "information about customer needs, preferences, attitudes, and behaviors, plus potential changes in the business environment that may affect buyers" (p. 454). Innovation in marketing strategies, namely product differentiation and market segmentation, prompted the increasingly sophisticated collection and analysis of demand-side information (Cornish, 1995). Today, market decisions often precede, rather than follow, decisions to conduct R&D, highlighting the importance of demand-side knowledge in contemporary production processes.

An important organizational implication for the hybrid domain alters the role of corporations in innovation. The Internet played a major role in shifting the traditional advantages of internal R&D facilities (the "closed innovation" model) from the perspective of both the transaction costs (Williamson, 1981, 1985, 1993) and the knowledge-based theory of the firm (Barney, 1991; Penrose, 1959). A transactions cost perspective points to how the absence of trust leads to "hazards in R&D cooperation" (Oxley & Sampson, 2004), particularly when intellectual property (IP) is weakly protected, whereas the knowledge-based theory emphasizes the strategic importance of mobilizing internal technological assets. More recent theories have emphasized the value of mobilizing external assets by relying on "open innovation." To be effective, organizational strategies of the open innovation model involve partnering or acquiring start-ups to exploit resources external to the firm (Chesbrough, 2003, 2004; Chesbrough & Crowther, 2006). Therefore, open innovation typically requires an environment characterized by the strong presence of external-to-the-firm ideas, active venture capital, numerous start-ups, and high labor mobility (Chesbrough & Crowther, 2006). In emerging economies, weak institutional and IP regimes have posed difficulties in implementing the open innovation model (Quan & Chesbrough, 2010).

In the context of the Global South, innovation from a strictly neo-classical paradigm was always problematic, as innovation was assumed to always reside in the Global North and as something that could be transferred costlessly to the Global South (Lall, 1992). Although innovation in the Global South was a largely abstract idea for corporations until a decade ago, recent evidence suggests that new opportunities for innovation are emerging in some markets (Dunn & Yamashita, 2003; London & Hart, 2004). China and India have becomes alternative R&D destinations, initially driven by the availability of low-cost R&D personnel (Parthasarathy, 2000; Reddy, 1997).[7]

In India, MNEs express growing interests in the BOP market, which offers a potentially vast and, yet largely untapped new market (Prahalad, 2002, 2006; Prahalad & Hammond, 2002; Whitney & Kelkar, 2004). Asia

---

[7] According to Farrell et al. (2005), India had the lowest labor cost for university-educated workers in 16 countries in the early 2000s and they also worked the longest hours (2,350 hours/year, compared to 1,700–1,900 hours in Germany/US). At the time, cost savings came not only from lower salaries of engineers (roughly 20 percent of the US counterparts), but also from lower support staff salaries and lower construction costs. The most recent salary figure of mid-career level IT staff shows that India's salary is 31 percent of that of the US in dollar terms (Sugden, 2015). Early MNE entrants to India, such as IBM and Texas Instruments, followed by GE and Intel, were all drawn to the attractive quality–cost ratios, particularly in the context of shortages of skilled labor in the developed world.

is the location of the largest BOP population in the world, and India's rural population is considered to be 100 percent BOP (Hammond et al., 2007). The saturating markets, both of the Global North, and the more affluent segments of the Global South, combined with the increasing recognition for heterogeneity of ideas as a basis for innovation in various niche areas of the market, contribute to the interest in BOP markets. For these reasons, R&D decentralization to emerging economies gains strategic importance for successful innovation and to promote diverse business models within the firm.

For social innovation, knowledge of the demand side is crucial in making a social impact by successfully appropriating technology, deploying and implementing products and services in a sustainable manner, and ensuring that innovation translates into social benefits. Furthermore, given that the underserved populations in the Global South have not traditionally been conceptualized as lead users by MNEs from the Global North, it often demands a radical reworking before a technology, management practice, or service can be successfully adopted. Khanna (2014) laments the general neglect in management literature of "contextual intelligence," which includes knowledge of local conditions, including economic development, physical geography, educational norms, and language and culture. Contextual intelligence is all the more important for social innovation, given the importance of institutional contexts that shape the social dimension of innovation.

To conceptualize social innovation, we need to overcome the productivist bias of the innovation literature. How do we incorporate knowledge from the recipients of technologies, that is, the users and the consumers? Recent efforts by MNEs to globalize R&D activities to the Global South reflect the effort to capture newly emerging markets, by learning about users and consumers, and developing effective products and services that address consumer needs. MNEs are not only seeking geographic expansion, but also using the emerging markets to expand across the silos of industrial specialization (see Chapters 6 and 7). The perception of BOP products and services as targeting monolithic markets and functions is currently being challenged by their multi-industrial orientation, heterogeneity in innovation processes, and multi-stakeholder organizational strategies. The use of mobile phones to provide information to raise productivity in the agriculture sector is but one example. This suggests, for one, that firms may exploit partnerships to acquire knowledge of the market, particularly new and unfamiliar industries.

4.2.2   Users and Consumers

Why should users and consumers participate in innovation? User incentives for innovation are problematic, since corporations capture most revenues from innovation while users volunteer their time and efforts. Innovation is considered as a market failure because of the presence of positive externalities, and some view innovation as non-excludable and non-rival (i.e. public goods). Since it is difficult to restrict the gains from innovation, innovation becomes a form of common property, inherently subject to the deficient incentives, resulting in the free-rider problem (Ostrom, 2012). An argument for IP protection would claim that, as the market fails to provide sufficient incentiveş, policy intervention is necessary to effectively capture returns on investment in innovation (Martin & Scott, 2000).

Whereas corporations view users and consumers as sources of market intelligence, NGOs seek to meet the needs of the communities they serve. The business innovation literature is largely concerned with the former, in which the users are an essential source of information in product development (Lundvall, 1988; Lundvall, 1992; von Hippel, 1976, 1977, 1989, 2001; von Hippel, 2005). User demand shapes innovation (Porter, 1990; Porter & Sakakibara, 2004), and with the onset of the Internet, users have also taken on the role of active producers (i.e. open-source programming, crowdsourcing, and user toolkits) (Franke & Piller, 2004; Jeppesen, 2005; von Hippel, 2005). User-led innovation is particularly effective in reducing the costs of gathering "sticky" information about user preferences, because some information is costly to acquire, transfer, and use (Riggs & von Hippel, 1994; von Hippel, 2001; von Hippel, 2005).

Communities are formed through the sharing of resources in production and distribution when users embark upon the release of products on their own. Users and consumers earn a more powerful "voice" when they express their views to firms to alter the direction of innovation activities. While users and consumers are largely synonymous in the context of the Global North, this is not necessarily the case in the Global South, and particularly for social innovation. The inability to pay for technologies/ services frequently relegates the act of consumption upward to an organization (e.g. state, NGO, or social enterprise) which acts as a purchaser and then offers the product/service either free or at a subsidized price to the consumers/users.

The sociology and development literatures offer a needs-centered perspective, and are generally critical of the business/management literatures that encourage corporations to combine economic and social missions. In the development literature, consumers are not necessarily viewed as communities, and communities are not viewed as consumers. In particular, the concept of BOP markets is contested on both ethical and pragmatic grounds – that it is both ethically offensive and economically unrealistic to help the poor profitably (Davidson, 2009; Karmani, 2007; Schwittay, 2011). For one, it has been argued that the market is too small for corporations to operate a profitable business. For another, profit creation and poverty alleviations do not mix easily as the functioning of the for-profit sector is inherently at odds with helping the poor, given the existing power asymmetries between corporations and communities. Finally, a critique of various revisionist narratives of capitalism, from the "inclusive" (Prahalad, 2006) to the "creative" (Gates, 2008), is that they only result in the marketization of poverty, rather than its eradication.

Although most needs remain latent and are articulated by individuals and households, NGOs serve as important intermediaries, translating, aggregating, articulating, prioritizing and communicating the needs of the population to states and markets. The clientele of the NGOs, however, are not typically conceptualized as consumers, even though they may well use and consume products and services provided by the state, markets, and civil society organizations, either free-of-charge, subsidized, or at market prices.

4.2.3 Incentivizing Social Innovation

The literature on commercial innovation suggests that the incentives for user participation can be strong in certain circumstances. In a market characterized as demand–pull rather than supply–push (Neale & Corkindale, 1998), where demand is heterogeneous rather than homogeneous, where demand for customization is high, and where product life is short and there is a high level of product turnover, users are more likely to participate in innovation. Furthermore, information that can be easily shared or disseminated facilitates the ease of user-involvement. Because of this, user incentives are high amidst user-to-user reciprocity and when peer-to-peer reputation is at stake, as is the case for hobby products with a user community of dedicated enthusiasts.

Understanding user incentives for social innovation is a new area of research, and the literature that evaluates social innovation from the user's perspective is sparse. Yet, it is not difficult to imagine that user incentives work differently for social innovation. For one, participatory development – community involvement and active participation are known to be crucial for the success of development projects (Choguill, 1996; Korten, 1980; Mansuri & Rao, 2004; Paul, 1995; Platteau &

Gaspart, 2003; Schuler & Namioka, 1993; Stiglitz, 2002), and the voice of the community plays a crucial role in sustainable and inclusive development. Given that greater attention is paid to participation in the field of development, and that users of social innovation can expect returns on their investment more directly for themselves, one would not expect a large gap between provision and adoption of social innovation, rendering concerns about user incentives unnecessary.

Yet, researchers and practitioners in development have long struggled with the reality of failed development projects and how and why, in many instances, the uptake of technologies, products and services by the underserved population have failed to meet the expectations of the providers (see, for example, Kottak, 1985; Kumar & Corbridge, 2002). Questions remain over the extent to which community involvement is linked to empowerment. Empowerment has been an elusive outcome of community participation in development projects (Fraser et al., 2006; Tosun, 2000). Moreover, relevant measures of empowerment have been notoriously difficult to specify, especially in areas such as education and health (Fawcett et al., 1995; Israel et al., 1994; Laverack & Wallerstein, 2001).

In reality, the needs of low-income users in the Global South remain the least well understood. The politics of participation, that is, whose voices are heard, and who is included and excluded, plays a role in perpetuating power relations and shapes developmental outcomes (Cornwall, 2004; White, 1996). What is viewed as irrational action in the long run from the outsiders' perspective, may turn out to be perfectly rational for an insider in the short run. For example, agreeing with Hardin's notion of the "tragedy of the commons," Rangan (1996) has shown that the rational actions of communities may prompt overconsumption, instead of the preservation of common resources.

The role of communities in development has traditionally been discussed in the context of natural resource preservation (see, for example, Agrawal & Gibson, 1999; Ostrom, 1999). Various efforts are underway in behavioral economics to better understand the types of incentives that best facilitate socio-economic practices (Thomas, 2016). Banerjee et al. (2011) advocate the use of randomized controlled trials to pinpoint correlations between incentives and adoptions, while Karlan and Appel (2011) claim that a traditional deductive model-based understanding of decision making can be improved when combined with an observation-based method in identifying problems and finding effective solutions.[8]

---

[8] It is worth noting that randomized controlled trials have been criticized by others, including Deaton (2010) who argues that the method only achieves

The very features of innovation that makes it problematic from the neo-classical perspective are important advantages for social innovation. In seeking social impacts, social innovators seek to not only take advantage of knowledge spillover, but also to amplify social impact by scaling and replicating social innovation, and thereby encourage use and the generation of revenues through market expansion. As such, social innovation serves as a vehicle through which actors in the hybrid domain fuse economic and social missions.

4.2.4 The State in Social Innovation

Although the state is not a lead actor in the hybrid domain, it still matters in various indirect ways in promoting social innovation. An important role of the state is to provide regulatory frameworks and tax incentives for actors in the hybrid domain, including promoting and supporting CSR, NGOs, private foundations, and social enterprises. Regulations vary by states and, while some already have robust legal frameworks, others are only emerging (see Section 3.3). Another important role of the state is facilitating social innovation through public R&D, including university research laboratories and national research institutes, to offer technical support and to train suitable talent. In effect, the state plays a role in institutionalizing the "national system of social innovation."

Theoretically, no systems of innovation can exist under state failure. In such cases, a weak or non-existent national system of innovation generates a need for social innovation. In India, the national system of innovation exists in the conventional forms of national research institutes, university research centers, and a small but growing pool of research funding to support innovation (see Chapter 5). However, what is clear is that India's national system of innovation has failed to deliver basic public goods, such as education and infrastructure, and particularly in rural areas. The absence of inclusiveness in the national system of innovation is unlikely to be the result of internal factors, but rather lie external to the system.

Where states have failed to provide basic services, traditionally, international aid agencies and public and private charitable organizations have played a major role in facilitating the support provided for the poor, at times directly (e.g. emergency relief) and at times indirectly (i.e. awarding grants to NGOs to execute programs on the ground that fulfill

---

quasi-randomization, and therefore does not fundamentally resolve the methodological issues.

social missions). Of the total flow of USD 445 billion to ODA recipient countries, development assistance committee (DAC) countries contributed USD 167 billion to ODA in 2013, whereas private flows amounted to USD 164 billion.[9] The growth of non-DAC donors notwithstanding, international aid agencies are aware that their budgets are unlikely to grow in the coming decade. They believe that the future of development will be more realistically supported by alternative sources of funds, as they observe the growth of private sector donations (CSR, foundations) and remittances (from international labor migration). There is a growing interest among actors in the hybrid domain in India on leveraging scarce funding sources to maximize social impact.

4.3 CONCLUSION

While social innovation is still an emerging field of study with contested definitions, several features stand out as essential in understanding its significance. First, institutional contexts are vital in both defining and generating social innovation. Second, institutional contexts have evolved with the onset of the Internet, and the shift from closed to open innovation facilitated institutional innovation across various entities for collaboration. Third, social innovation knowledge combines market intelligence on the one hand, and social needs, and particularly of the economically disadvantaged segments of society, on the other. This combination is where the greatest opportunities, both economic and social, as well as controversies, are found. Given the nature of the hybrid domain, it is imperative that we examine the context, the dynamics of collaboration, and where power lies within the collaboration. As a starting point, we must first look at various cases of social innovation, to understand what it is that is being innovated, who the stakeholders are, and how this collaboration emerged. The subsequent chapters offer insights into these questions in depth, taking the case of social innovation in India. We first explain how and why both states and markets failed in providing basic needs for the poor (Chapter 5), followed by how the private sector is designing solutions (Chapter 6), case studies of social innovation (Chapter 7), and emerging organizational forms (Chapters 8 and 9).

---

[9]   The figures are for disbursement of total flows (ODA, other official flows and private) by DAC countries in current USD prices, based on the figures provided by OECD Query Wizard for International Development Statistics.

5. Social innovation in India

In this chapter, we provide the context for social innovation we observed in India. Among the BRICs, not only is India the poorest country in relative terms (per capita Gross National Income) but also in an absolute sense (people living below USD 3.10 a day) (Table 5.1). Yet, the Global Innovation Report 2015 also classifies India (along with China) as an outperformer, relative to other countries with similar levels of development in innovation inputs and outputs.

To place in historical perspective why India lags the BRICS on many indicators, and to also understand why it is considered an innovation outperformer, the following section will provide a brief overview of economic development policies in India. It will then explain how the policies have created opportunities and spaces for social innovation in the hybrid domain.

Table 5.1   Macro-economic indicators: BRICS countries

	India	Brazil	China	Russia	South Africa
Per capita GDP 2014 (in current USD)	1591.7	11384.6	7593.9	12735.9	6477.9
Population earning below USD 3.10/day (a) (%)	58	11	27 (b)	0.6	n.a.
Net FDI inflows (as a % of GDP) 2013	1.5	3.4	3.1	3.3	2.2
Rank in Global Innovation Index 2015	81	70	29	48	60

Notes: (a) In 2011 Purchasing Power Parity which corresponds to USD 2/day in 2005; (b) data for 2010

Source: (i) World Bank (2015b) for data on per capita GDP and population earning below USD 3.10/day; (ii) Dutta, et al. (2015) for the Global Innovation Index

5.1 FAILURE OF THE STATE TO PROVIDE PUBLIC GOODS

To claim that the Indian state has failed would be inaccurate, as the country has seen a measure of political and economic success since independence in 1947. Thus, India cannot be compared with states such as Afghanistan, Bosnia, Syria, Somalia, and Congo, which are deemed to have failed.[1] Yet, the Indian state has struggled to provide adequate basic infrastructure, that is, clean water, reliable electricity, roads, basic education, and healthcare services, and particularly so for the poor in rural areas. Among the BRICS, India has the lowest levels of adult literacy and public spending on education. Similarly, in health, India has the lowest life expectancy (with the exception of HIV-ravaged South Africa), the lowest per capita spending, and the lowest level of public expenditure (see Table 5.2). Ironically, the shortfall in public spending on health is made up mostly by the out-of-pocket expenditure of citizens. This makes greater demands on private expenditure in a relatively poor country and, not surprisingly, per capita spending on health is much below those in other countries.

While the state has undoubtedly facilitated India's emergence as an important location in the current ICT revolution, its success continues to be narrowly confined to a certain segment of the economy. In contrast to the growth of the ICT and pharmaceutical industries, and FDI since 1991 in major cities, the state's inability to provide basic infrastructure has constrained India's otherwise considerable economic growth in recent years.

Why has the state failed on infrastructure while developing the largest and most continuous democracy in the Global South (for 70 years with the exception of two years), the IT industry and even a nuclear weapons program? The answers are complex, and the analysis would require a book on its own to cover this in its entirety. We limit our focus to explaining how different economic ideologies, the Nehruvian and Gandhian, guided policymaking in the country for nearly half a century. But as the implementation of these ideologies confronted political barriers, and an inefficient (and often corrupt) state bureaucracy, it only exacerbated longstanding and institutionalized social and spatial inequalities. Growing acknowledgment of the limits of post-independence economic policies has provided the circumstances for a shift to policies that have emphasized inclusive development, which, in turn, has led to the

---

[1] See, for example, Carment (2003).

Table 5.2   *Education, health and infrastructure indicators, BRICS countries*

	India	Brazil	China	Russia	South Africa
Education					
Adult literacy rate 2010 (a) (%)	69	90	95	100	93
Government expenditure on education (% of GDP, 2010)	3.30	5.60	n.a.	4.1 (b)	5.70
Health					
Life expectancy at birth (in years, 2013)	66	74	75	71	57
Public health expenditure (% of total health expenditure, 2013)	32.2	48.2	55.8	48.1	48.4
Out-of-pocket expenditure (% of private expenditure on health, 2013)	85.9	57.8	76.7	92.4	13.8
Health expenditure per capita (in current US dollars, 2013)	61	1085	367	957	593
Infrastructure					
Electric power consumption (in kWh, 2012)	744	2462	3475	6617	4405
Mobile cellular subscriptions 2014 (per 100 people)	74	139	92	155	150
Internet users 2014 (per 100 people)	18.0	57.6	49.3	70.5	49.0

Notes: (a) refers to literacy rate among those 15 years and older; (b) 2008 data

Source: World Bank (2015b)

increasing engagement of various hybrid domain stakeholders in improving social welfare in India.

5.1.1   The Nehruvian Ideal of Scientific and Technological Self-sufficiency

Innovation policy has been identified as a crucial vehicle for long-term development for late industrializers. It is imperative that these countries develop effective national systems of innovation and knowledge clusters (Freeman, 1995; Hershberg et al., 2007; Lundvall et al., 2011), which lead to "strategic coupling" between regions and firms (Yeung, 2016), to ultimately situate themselves firmly in global innovation networks (Liu et al., 2013).

Despite a long scientific tradition and a history of technological achievements, India's infrastructure for science and technology (S&T) at the time of independence was limited to a few universities, and laboratories of the Council for Scientific and Industrial Research (CSIR), which was founded in 1942 (Tyabji, 1989). Since independence, policy frameworks in India broadly prioritized technological self-sufficiency, and the need to develop indigenous technology to solve India's many "wicked problems."[2] The first Prime Minister Jawaharlal Nehru declared that "... in an underdeveloped country like India, science must be made the handmaiden of economic progress, with scientists devoting their work to augmenting productivity and ending poverty" (Guha, 2007, p. 215). A number of public sector research institutions were established to promote scientific research,[3] and to complement Nehruvian import substitution-led industrialization (ISI) policies.[4] To implement these policies, the state was assigned a central role in coordinating the development process since it was believed that allowing the market to take over would lead to distributional inequities and uneven spatial and industrial development (Chakravarty, 1987). The Industrial Policy Resolution of 1956 allowed the public sector and public sector enterprises (PSEs) to occupy the "commanding heights of the economy." But the pay-off from India's S&T and ISI policies was limited. As shown in Table 5.3, between the 1950s and the 1980s, India's economic growth averaged little more than 3.5 percent, which the economist Raj Krishna pejoratively termed a "Hindu" rate of growth (Ahluwalia, 1985).

There were at least two reasons for the limited pay-off of relevance here. First, protection of domestic industries under ISI served as a disincentive for technological innovation, as evidenced by the Indian electronics industry (Sridharan, 1996). This only contributed to making Indian products uncompetitive in the global market, and India's share in world trade declined from 2 percent in 1950 to 0.4 percent in 1990 (Ahluwalia, 1996, p. 21). The disincentives for innovation were exacerbated by mandatory state licensing for all industrial production. While licensing was intended to direct resources to industries of national

---

[2]   See Technology Policy Statement of 1983, at http://www.nstmis-dst.org/TPStatement.aspx (accessed December 29, 2015).

[3]   For the policy framework, see the Scientific Policy Resolution of 1958, at http://unesdoc.unesco.org/images/0015/001543/154344eb.pdf (accessed December 29, 2015). For a description of the research institutions that were established, see Parthasarathy and Ranganathan (2010).

[4]   ISI involved high tariffs to protect domestic products from imports, both to conserve foreign exchange and for infant industry promotion.

Table 5.3   Average annual GDP growth rate in India

Plan	Years	Growth Rate (%)
1st Plan	1951–1956	3.5
2nd Plan	1956–1961	4.2
3rd Plan	1961–1966	2.8
Annual Plans	1966–1969	3.9
4th Plan	1969–1974	3.2
5th Plan	1974–1979	4.7
Annual Plan	1979–1980	–5.2
6th Plan	1980–1985	5.5
7th Plan	1985–1990	5.6
Annual Plans	1990–1992	3.4
8th Plan	1992–1997	6.5
9th Plan	1997–2002	5.5
10th Plan	2002–2007	7.7
11th Plan	2007–2012	8.0

Source: Planning Commission (2008, 2013a)

importance, it only created an ineffective state intervention, contemptuously referred to as the "license Raj," with an array of controls, implemented in an ad-hoc fashion with little coordination (Mohan & Aggarwal, 1990).

Second, as Lall and Rastogi (2007) explain, slow economic growth was both a cause and a consequence of inadequate investment in infrastructure, all of which were run by public sector monopolies. While investment in physical infrastructure was positively co-related with GDP growth (Table 5.4), it also reflected political priorities. When Nehru was Prime Minister until the mid-1960s, the emphasis was on large-scale multi-purpose projects to generate power for industrialization and to irrigate agriculture. But most projects suffered from years of delay and cost over-runs because of poor implementation. Under Nehru's daughter, Indira Gandhi, the focus of infrastructure investment until the 1980s shifted to giving farmers the means to benefit from the Green Revolution. For instance, emphasis was placed on ground water irrigation with pumps powered by extensive rural electrification programs. However, in a climate of political populism, state-owned power utilities were directed to give power free to agriculture. As the practice left the utilities with mounting financial deficits, their ability to generate enough power to meet demand declined, and farmers' access to the grid increasingly meant little. In the 1980s, the emphasis was on using technology for socio-economic change, especially when Nehru's grandson Rajiv Gandhi was Prime Minister from 1984–1989. Rajiv Gandhi pushed through the early policies that enabled the growth of the Indian ICT industry.[5] He also backed NRI Satyen Pitroda, who brought years of experience in the US, to transform India's dysfunctional telecommunication system by designing new equipment to suit local operating conditions (Pitroda, 1993). This backing came after Pitroda drew attention to the high correlation between prosperity and telephone density worldwide to emphasize that, contrary to Indian thinking, it was the telecommunications infrastructure that created the wealth.

Table 5.4   Infrastructure spending as a share of GDP, India

Period	GDP Growth (%)	Spending on Infrastructure (%)
1950–1967	3.6	4.2
1967–1984	4.2	4.1
1984–1991	5.9	5.2
1991–2004	6.0	4.5
2002–2007	7.7	5.0
2007–2012	8.0	7.2

Source: Lall and Rastogi (2007, p. 4); Planning Commission (2013a, p. 87)

The 1980s also saw the gradual dismantling of ISI and self-sufficiency, although the gains from faster industrial growth, and a near 3 percent annual increase in manufacturing total factor productivity, were blunted by deteriorating public finances and, in mid-1991, a balance of payments crisis forced the government to turn to the IMF for a fiscal stabilization

---

[5]   The policies explicitly rejected the ISI and self-sufficiency, as India aspired to become to software what Taiwan and Korea were to hardware (Lakha, 1990). The Computer Policy of 1984, and the Computer Software Export, Development and Training Policy of 1986 (Subramanian, 1992), and the Software Technology Parks (STPs) in 1990, were radical departures from previous policies, as the government was to provide only promotional and infrastructure support. Indian firms responded by pioneering a Global Offshore Delivery Model, by establishing software factories with the technology, quality processes, productivity tools, and methodologies of the customer workplace (Parthasarathy, 2010).

plan.[6] This plan was accompanied by a structural adjustment program to increase the efficiency and international competitiveness of industrial production by attracting foreign investment and technology. The goal was to increase the productivity of investment, improve the performance of the public sector, so that key sectors of the economy became globally competitive.[7] A new Statement of Industrial Policy of 1991 emphasized the "encouragement of entrepreneurship, development of indigenous technology through investment in research and development, bringing in (from abroad) new technology, and dismantling of the regulatory system." To that end, licensing was abolished for all but 18 sectors where strategic or environmental issues were involved, and industries exclusively reserved for the public sector were reduced to six. The new Science and Technology Policy announced in 2003, called for promoting close interaction between private and public institutions in science and technology.[8]

Ironically, as rapid economic growth in the 1990s demanded more infrastructure, investment declined. Fiscally constrained and politically weak coalition governments of the 1990s had little option but to favor spending on subsidies and other current consumption rather than invest in infrastructure for the long run (Lall & Rastogi, 2007). However, spending became more targeted and efficient, and structural reforms began to attract private investment, especially in telecommunications services. In the new millennium, there has been greater urgency to improve infrastructure by mobilizing PPPs as evident, for instance, in the National Highway Development Program (Planning Commission, 2013a). Recognizing the need for better governance, and to raise an estimated USD 1 trillion to overcome the infrastructure gaps, the government has established regulatory and tariff authorities for the civil aviation, ports, power and telecommunications

---

[6] For an extended discussion of the factors leading to the crisis, see Joshi and Little (1994).

[7] Budget 1991–1992, Speech of Shri Manmohan Singh, Minister of Finance, July 24, 1991. Available at http://indiabudget.nic.in/bspeech/bs199192.pdf (accessed December 28, 2015). Changes included the devaluation of the Rupee by 24 percent and making it convertible on the current account. On the trade front, a single negative list replaced import licensing, and, by 1994–95, the import-weighted tariff came down from 87 percent to 33 percent. A new Statement of Industrial Policy was also issued on July 24, 1991 (see http://siadipp.nic.in/publicat/nip0791.htm for full text of the policy [accessed December 28, 2015]). The policy permitted FDI in most sectors of the economy and India demonstrated its seriousness in this pursuit by joining the Multilateral Investment Guarantee Agency in April 1992.

[8] See http://www.dst.gov.in/stsysindia/stp2003.htm for the full text of the policy (accessed December 28, 2015).

sectors to encourage more private participation (Xu & Albert, 2014). Despite such efforts, there are gaps in implementation. For instance, there is considerable skepticism and opposition surrounding land acquisition, even after the passage of The Right to Fair Compensation and Transparency in Land Acquisition, Rehabilitation and Resettlement Act, 2013 by the Lok Sabha (lower house of Parliament).

5.1.2 The Gandhian Ideal of Decentralized Self-reliance

In contrast to the Fabian socialism that guided Nehru, Gandhi advocated *swaraj*, or self-rule, which emphasized self-reliance and people organizing to manage their affairs locally and pragmatically to meet real needs (Jenkins, 2010; Tellis, 2006). In economic terms, this meant an economic structure based on traditional, rural household enterprises, such as *khadi* (homespun cloth), to produce what is in demand locally, using local raw materials, tools and processes, without any displacement of labor. While the Nehruvian ideal prevailed, explicit support for micro, small and medium enterprises (MSMEs) was a concession made to the Gandhian faction of the ruling Congress party.[9] The political rationale for promoting MSMEs was buttressed by a Ford Foundation report in 1954, which emphasized the importance of small firms in the industrial structure. By 2005, MSMEs accounted for 75.0 percent of all enterprises in manufacturing and services while contributing to 49.9 percent of non-agricultural gross-value added (NCEUS, 2009, pp. 255, 260).[10] It is in recognition of their significance for employment and the economy, that MSMEs have long received political and institutional support in addition to various incentives.

---

[9] For the politics of MSMEs, and a history of their institutional support structures, see Tyabji (1989) and Gupta et al. (1995). MSMEs also receive a number of incentives. They are exempt from licensing procedures and are provided fiscal incentives, including limited excise duty and sales tax and price preference in government purchases. Concessional credit became available, especially after bank nationalization in 1969. A set of protective measures complements the promotional measures. The key protective measure was the reservation of products for exclusive manufacture by MSMEs. Starting with 47 items in 1967, the number increased to 836 by 1980.

[10] Although MSMEs are defined in terms of investment rather than employment, the National Commission of Enterprises in the Unorganised Sector (NCEUS, 2009, p. 255) points out that 98 percent of MSMEs had an investment of less than INR 2.5 million that is, they were micro enterprises. Further, since these MSMEs also had fewer than ten employees, they were in the unorganized sector.

Yet, MSMEs have faced many constraints over the years that have pushed them toward informality. Thus, despite their significance, 98 percent of MSMEs were in the informal sector in 2005.[11] The most severe constraint is the lack of capital, which limits their ability to access technology and skills to upgrade their capabilities. The lack of knowledge and access to markets constrain most MSMEs to local markets in the scale of their operations and scope of their product markets. To compensate for the lack of capital and knowledge, MSMEs resort to alternative forms of innovation; thus it should come as no surprise that amidst such a large informal sector *jugaad* is so prevalent. MSMEs often chose not to grow in order to avoid losing tax benefits and the benefits of product reservation.[12]

The limited success of MSME policies, at least partially, highlights the challenges faced in implementing the Gandhian ideal, despite it being propagated by influential post-independence leaders such as Vinobha Bhave. With the failure of elite politics and development policies to meet socio-economic needs, a growing number of voluntary efforts, invoking Gandhi's vocabulary of self-reliance, began to proliferate from the 1960s to fill the gaps in government service provision (Jenkins, 2010). Multiple and overlapping formal organizations, such as dairy farmers cooperatives to grassroots groups, such as informal village councils and women's self-help groups (SHGs), were widespread and, by 2008, India was home to an estimated 3.2 million NGOs (see Table 5.5 for growth by decade), approximately one for every 400 people, compared to one policeman for every 709 people (Godfrey, 2015).[13] As Tables 5.5a and 5.5b show, it is NGOs that provide social services for the household sector that are

---

[11] The NCEUS uses the terms "informal" and "unorganized" interchangeably. This chapter will do likewise. According to NCEUS (2009, p. 3), "The unorganized sector consists of all unincorporated private enterprises owned by individuals or households engaged in the sale and production of goods and services operated on a proprietary or partnership basis and with less than ten total workers." Unorganized workers refers to "those working in the unorganized sector or households, excluding regular workers with social security benefits provided by the employers and the workers in the formal sector without any employment and social security benefits provided by the employers."

[12] In a partial attempt to overcome these challenges, product reservation for MSMEs was scrapped on April 13, 2015, on the grounds that it only inhibited investment in new technologies and reaping economies of scale, and competitiveness, especially against imports.

[13] There are many legal options to establishing an NGO in India. These include the Societies Registration Act 1860; the Indian Trusts Act 1882; the Charitable and Religious Trusts Act 1920; and under Section 8 of the Indian Companies Act 2013.

dominant. This "institutional thickness" makes India unique, particularly in comparison to sub-Saharan African states, which have long been aid-dependent.

Table 5.5   Registered NGOs in India

a: By date of establishment and location as percentage of total NGOs

Registered NGOs in 2008	Total (%)	Rural (%)	Urban (%)
Total	100.0	58.7	41.4
Established:			
Before 1970	4.5	2.3	2.3
1971–1980	5.6	3.1	2.5
1981–1990	17.4	11.1	6.3
1991–2000	35.6	21.2	14.4
2001–2008	35.7	21.0	14.8
Unknown	1.3	0.2	1.2

b: By primary activity and date of establishment as percentage of total NGOs

Primary Activity (%)	2008	Before 1970s	1971–80	1981–90	1991–2000	2001–08	Unknown
Total	100.0	4.4	5.6	17.4	35.6	35.7	1.3
Social Services	40.5	1.3	2.3	7.6	14.9	14.3	0.1
Education and Research	19.4	0.7	0.9	3.0	6.9	7.7	0.2
Culture and Recreation	11.7	0.4	1.0	2.9	4.0	3.3	0.1
Associations, Unions	7.2	0.2	0.4	1.2	2.6	2.8	n.a.
Development and Housing	4.9	0.1	0.2	0.6	1.9	2.1	n.a.
Religion	4.2	1.0	0.3	0.7	1.1	1.1	n.a.
Health	1.9	0.1	0.1	0.2	0.5	1.0	n.a.
Others	9.7	0.1	0.4	1.2	3.7	3.4	0.9

Note: Numbers do not add up to 100% in both directions due to rounding

Source: CSO (2012, pp. 29–31)

Table 5.6   Sources of funding for NGOs in India

By sources of funding and primary clientele as a percentage of total funding received by NGOs, 2009–2010

Sources of Funding (%)	Total	Primary Clientele (a)		
		Government	Industry	Households
Total	99.7	31.6	3.2	64.9
Grants	53.5	29.1	1.7	22.7
Donations and offerings	16.4	0.4	0.2	15.8
Income/receipts from operations	16.2	1.0	1.0	14.2
Other income/receipts	8.1	0.7	0.3	7.1
Interest/dividend/rent	3.5	0.3	negligible	3.2
Membership subscription	2.0	0.1	negligible	1.9

Notes: Data drawn from a sample of 694,186 NGOs surveyed in 2009–2010; (a) government = providing services and implementing projects for the government; industry = serving businesses and industries, such as chambers of commerce, trade and professional associations, market federations, etc.; households = including trade/labor unions, consumer associations, resident welfare associations, parents–teacher associations, charities, relief, and aid organizations

Source: CSO (2012, p. 55)

But tensions continue to exist between the state and the NGOs in India (Jenkins, 2010). NGOs have historically been viewed as politically suspect by the state, as their mission inherently involves challenging the *status quo*. In particular, ever since NGOs played an active role in opposing the state of emergency between 1975 and 1977, the state has closely monitored funding sources, especially from international donors, claiming potential threat to national sovereignty and integrity.[14] Alongside the tensions, however, there has been growing mutual acknowledgment and collaboration, as described in the following section.

---

[14]   The instrument to do this is the Foreign Contribution (Regulation) Act which was originally passed in 1976, and later repealed and replaced in 2010.

5.1.3 Inclusive Development

The initial adoption and the subsequent distancing from the Nehruvian model since the late 1980s, along with limited impact of the Gandhian tradition, has led the state to increasingly articulate and adopt the language of inclusive development in its policy objectives, and to refocus the state's role in public goods provision. For instance, the Mahatma Gandhi National Rural Employment Guarantee Act (MGNREGA) 2005, is described as the "the largest and most ambitious social security and public works program in the world." It guarantees one hundred days of unskilled manual work in a financial year to adult members in every household, by providing employment on projects to create durable assets (such as flood control works).[15] The MGNREGA is overseen by the Ministry of Rural Development, and reinforced another ongoing asset-building initiative; the *Pradhan Mantri Gram Sadak Yojana* (the Prime Minister's Rural Roads Program or the PMGSY) launched in 2000 to provide all-weather road connectivity to all habitations with more than 250 persons.[16] While MGNREGA and the PMGSY addressed the in-adequacies of physical infrastructure, the National Rural Health Mission (NRHM) was launched on 12 April 2005, to make the public health delivery system functional and accountable, and thereby provide accessible, affordable, and quality healthcare to the rural population.[17] An example in education is the launch of the *Sarva Shiksha Abhiyan* (SSA – or the Education for All Movement) program, following the passage of the Right to Education and Free Education Act, 2009. The Act is meant to achieve universal elementary education as mandated by the 86th amendment to the Constitution of India which makes free and compulsory education to children, between the ages of six and 14 years, a fundamental right.[18]

NGOs play an important role in the agenda on inclusive development. The state had begun to acknowledge the role of the NGOs in development since the 1980s, although sections of the NGO community remained skeptical and wary of being co-opted by the state into supporting a neoliberal agenda and market fundamentalism (Jenkins, 2010).

---

[15]   The full text of the Act is available at http://nrega.nic.in/rajaswa.pdf (accessed January 10, 2016).

[16]   For details, see http://pmgsy.nic.in/ (accessed January 10, 2016).

[17]   For details of the NRHM, see http://nrhm.gov.in/images/pdf/about-nrhm/nrhm-framework-implementation/nrhm-framework-latest.pdf (accessed January 10, 2016).

[18]   For more details, see http://ssa.nic.in/ (accessed January 10, 2016).

However, with the state's emphasis on inclusive development in the new millennium, both the state and the NGOs have come to expect an even greater role for NGOs in economic development. Not coincidentally, India has seen a proliferation of NGOs since the 1990s (Table 5.5), with the government providing almost 30 percent of all funds to NGOs in 2009–2010 (Table 5.6).

NGOs became active in the implementation of MGNREGA projects, especially in the social audits that the Act mandates to check corruption. Similarly, the Ministry of Health proclaims, "involvement of non-governmental sector organizations is critical for the success of the NRHM." As a result, not only have NGOs become less dogmatic in their views of the state, but also gained knowledge and experience of working with the state in implementing development projects. The involvement of NGOs was sought not merely to help implement the expanded social agenda of the state, but also in the role that was expected of the corporate sector. As explained in Chapter 3, CSR is legally mandated for for-profit organizations, and they are expected to work with NGOs, among others, to achieve the goals of a publicly articulated CSR policy. This collaboration provides fertile ground for nurturing active involvement in collective action, and a culture of collaboration among multiple stake-holders for social welfare, across public, private, and civil society organizations.

The 11th Five Year Plan (2007–2012) explicitly acknowledges the need to "reduce poverty and creates employment opportunities, access to essential services in health and education especially for the poor, equality of opportunity, empowerment through education and skill development." The 12th Five Year Plan (2012–2017) continues with the theme of inclusion but with two notable enhancements. First, its goals are "faster, more inclusive and sustainable growth" (Planning Commission, 2013a). It also acknowledges, "… quality infrastructure is important not only for faster growth but also to ensure that growth is inclusive" (p. 15). Second, the plan called for different stakeholders to work together to achieve broad consensus on key issues. These stakeholders include not just different levels of the government (national, state and rural/urban local bodies) but also the private sector, including large corporations and MSMEs, citizens' groups and the voluntary sector, to help improve the efficacy of government action with people's participation.

The election of a new government headed by Prime Minister Narendra Modi in 2014 saw a boost in spending on infrastructure, especially in segments such as roads and railways, in the hope that increased public expenditure would stimulate growth and "crowd in" private investment (Vaishnav, 2015). Inclusiveness has remained a theme although there is a shift in programmatic emphasis. The Prime Minister's *Jan-Dhan Yojana* (the People's Wealth Scheme) for financial inclusion was launched in August 2014 as a national mission to ensure that every household had a bank account and access to needs-based credit, remittances facility, insurance and pension.[19] In October 2014, a major sanitation and public health initiative, the *Swach Bharath Abhiyan* (Clean India Mission), was launched with the goal of eliminating, by October 2, 2019 (Gandhi's 150th birth anniversary), the scourge of open defecation by 7.9 million urban households without access to indoor plumbing. The construction of toilets was to be funded from various sources including CSR.[20] However, the 30 percent share of the central and state government of spending for the mission came at the expense of existing programs such as the NRHM and the SSA, which witnessed a 7.5 percent and 3.6 percent decline in spending in the first two years of the new government.[21]

5.2 FAILURE OF THE MARKET TO PROVIDE PUBLIC GOODS: THE MYTH OF THE BOP

While the infrastructure and developmental outcomes provided by the Indian state are far from adequate, the promise of private sector solutions to serve the BOP market to improve the lives of the poor has also been disappointing. Our field research revealed the profound influence of the late C. K. Prahalad's mantra, "serving the world's poor, profitably," as a call for a more active involvement of the private sector – particularly MNEs – in solving the challenges of global poverty. Although there is considerable interest expressed by the private sector to engage with the BOP market, our survey findings and interviews suggest that it is often unable to generate sufficient revenues to maintain product/service lines for the BOP market, never mind solve the problems of poverty on its own.

Our survey suggests that interest in the BOP market is an important factor in determining why MNEs conduct R&D in India. As shown in Table 5.7 below, among 158 respondents, a little over a third claimed that they had undertaken R&D for the BOP market in the last two years (2011–2013). This figure is surprisingly high as it refers to only the last

[19]   For details, see http://www.pmjdy.gov.in/ (accessed January 23, 2016).

[20]   For details, see http://swachhbharaturban.gov.in/writereaddata/SBM_Guide line.pdf (accessed January 23, 2016).

[21]   For details see http://www.indiaspend.com/cover-story/centres-health-education-spending-declines-over-2-years-13686 (accessed January 23, 2016).

two years and BOP consumers are not relevant for all industrial sectors.[22] The reasons for doing so were high growth potential, compatibility with the corporate brand image, and availability of specialized R&D staff with knowledge of BOP markets. Over a quarter of the respondents reported that products/services developed had been introduced to other parts of the world.

Table 5.7   Results from the survey questionnaire: R&D for BOP markets

"Have you undertaken R&D for BOP market in the last two years?"	Yes	37.3%
Reasons given: (multiple responses)	High potential	19.9%
	Compatibility with the corporate brand image	15.4%
	Availability of specialized R&D staff with knowledge of BOP markets	14.7%
Have the products/services been introduced to other parts of the world?	Yes	27.8%
Destinations: (multiple responses)	To a developed country	36.7%
	To a developing country outside South Asia	34.7%
	To another South Asian country	28.4%

Source: Based on the survey conducted by the authors

Given the lack of comprehensive data on the profitability of BOP-focused initiatives, we interviewed social innovation stakeholders to probe this question. The influence of Prahalad's work was almost unanimously acknowledged across both for-profit and non-profit stakeholders of social innovation. Some of the MNEs we interviewed launched social innovation initiatives that were directly inspired by his work. For example, one executive in a European MNE in pharmaceuticals (M54) described the company's involvement in social innovation as follows:

> *Where did this idea really generate from? We were attending [a] global seminar by late Professor C. K. Prahalad from Michigan, [known for] his*

---

[22]   In fact, there may have been a positive selection bias on the part of respondents who volunteered. It is difficult to completely eradicate such biases, however, in survey responses.

*book on the Fortune at the Bottom of the Pyramid. Our Chairman was
chairing this forum where he heard some **very thought-provoking innovation
that were sustainable, yet making big social impacts** in the Bottom of
Pyramid. And I think, that's where we got inspired ... why haven't we tried
doing something more from a sustainable business angle rather than philanthropy? You can achieve a far bigger impact, make a magnitude of social
difference, rather than probably using hundreds of millions in charity. There
are 4 billion people out there who lack access to medicine and healthcare,
and charity alone is not going to solve their problems. What can we do that
can accelerate access to medicine, and with some sense of a business growth,
may be in the mid- to long-term ...? This was just an exploratory idea way
back in 2006 and early 2007.*[23]

Even when MNEs did not attribute their initiatives to Prahalad's work, it
was clear that their perspective has broadened beyond the single bottom
line. Profound as Prahalad's influences have been, most for-profit organizations (including MNEs and social entrepreneurs) we interviewed were
reluctant to use the term BOP, or to conceptualize their customers as
BOP.

5.2.1   The Myth of Profitability

While the reasons behind their reluctance to use the term BOP varied, the
biggest reason was the unrealistic expectations for profitability. As an
executive from an American MNE in ICTs commented (M7):

*[Providing BOP solutions] are very, very important, but very difficult to sell
and even break-even, **forget about making money**. There are other opportunities [that make big business and social impacts].*[24]

The reality of consumers in the BOP market was also described by an
executive from another American MNE in ICTs (M1), who acknowledged that their product and service offerings were largely irrelevant to
the BOP market.

*Looking at people in slums or farmers, etc. as end-users of technology ... one
of the things that we have had to come to terms with is the fact that many of
these people have so many problems already, that **technology is really kind of
meaningless** for them ... if you are trying to help them to do things ... they*

---

[23]   Interview, July 16, 2013.
[24]   Interview, June 12, 2012.

have such small amounts of money in the first place and they are not going to be spending that money on IT typically.[25]

The original definition of the BOP population included those "living on less than USD 2 a day" by Prahalad and Hart in 1999, or more recently, those "who are living on about USD 3.50 a day."[26] In reality, most products and services offered remain out of reach for the target population.[27] Corporations readily corroborated the difficulty in reaching out to the BOP population, with some challenging Prahalad's conceptualization. For instance, an executive from a European MNE in electronics (M9) commented:

> *The book by Prahalad ... what he is describing is not really the BOP ... these people have many needs and [for] many of them, our products do not play a role. Their aspirations are not buying a TV or to be examined by MRI (magnetic imaging resonance), even if they may be helped by having a TV or coffee maker ... **they have other priorities** in life.*[28]

An executive of a European MNE in medical devices (M47) described that, realistically, they are unable to address the BOP market:

> *Now **I don't think we have the cost structure nor the organization which can go below a certain tier** ... as a product development organization we look at models which are sustainable ... There needs to be a balance between what you provide and what it tells you to get out of.*[29]

It should be noted, however, that the BOP market may well be viable for smaller corporations. In particular, start-ups may find ample opportunities, as observed by one executive in a European MNE, in pharmaceuticals (M54):

> *A SME cannot compete against a MNE, or even mid-size companies. But they find **niche segments like BOP** to start with, where there is no overcrowding in the market, and they create a space for themselves, generate enough [revenues], and they move upwards. Without naming names, **I know at least***

[25] Interview, May 28, 2012.

[26] These figures are based on current US dollars. Measured by Purchasing Power Parity, these figures are roughly equivalent.

[27] Some NGOs focus on the ultra-poor, who are defined by BRAC as those living on "less than half of the $1.25-a-day poverty line, and eat below 80 percent of their energy requirements despite spending at least 80 percent of their income on food" (McMillan, 2013, p. 3).

[28] Interview, June 13, 2012.

[29] Interview, July 3, 2014.

> *two very successful organizations which are amongst the top ten players in India, which actually started their journey in BOP.*[30]

Most importantly, the ethical issue surrounding the emphasis on consumption over livelihood production in the conceptualization of BOP markets has also made private sector involvement controversial. As a founder of a longstanding and reputed grassroots NGO in health (N3) commented:

> *The private sector [opportunities in BOP] are growing, definitely ... huge markets ... [and] there is growing interest ... but **I only get hurt when they use the word – bottom of the pyramid – to further exploit people.** That should not happen. There may be some genuine people ... I would not [deny] that. There are good people as individuals, but as a company policy [questions remain] ... if any company can declare [they are] pro-poor, that would be great. They can [innovate on] low-cost technologies that are useful for the poor, and it can matter. The digital x-rays, ultrasound, dialysis machines – companies are [making efforts to] bring down the cost for the middle class, but not enough for the poor.*[31]

Similar sentiments are echoed by a social entrepreneur in ICTs (S7) who commented that *"the fundamental ethos should be ... you should **make their lives productive.** Making them consumers is not [the same thing as] making them productive."*[32]

With a few exceptions, the myth of the profitable BOP market is now widely acknowledged by social innovation stakeholders in India. Given this recognition, some corporations have opted to reorient their customer base from individual consumers to NGOs which, in turn, provide products/services free to BOP end-users. An American MNE in ICTs (M1) has adopted this approach, as described by its executive:

> *One of the things that we started doing is ... looking into **how can we help NGOs** or other organizations that have a little leverage already and have a little bit more money to do their jobs better on behalf of these people that we are trying to help ... from a development point of view.*[33]

By providing technological solutions to the NGOs and social entrepreneurs who engage with end-users, these corporations indirectly engage with development issues in India, improving access to education and

---

[30] Interview, July 16, 2013.
[31] Interview, June 15, 2012.
[32] Interview, July 24, 2012.
[33] Interview, May 28, 2012.

healthcare. However, this approach is limited to certain industrial sectors in which NGOs are active. This is because the choice of NGO as collaborator and customer on the part of corporations may well be driven not by their non-profit status but their insider status. The same executive (M1) situated the NGO as follows:

> *I think whether it's an NGO or just a local partner ... it's more the local partner – it's the insider part [that's important] ... when we tend to be trying to do development-type projects, they tend to be NGOs. But if you are trying to do something else ... then an NGO could be useless ... The main point is* **the insider**.[34]

5.2.2 Opportunities and Challenges

The interests of corporations in the BOP market segment are, in part, a result of market saturation in the Global North and the phenomenal growth of markets in the Global South. On the first, an executive from a European MNE in medical devices (M47) made the following comment:

> *Those MNEs that always considered premium market segments, and focused on developing expensive, premium products saw* **the premium segment starting to get saturated**, *and the mid-segment becoming bigger and bigger and bigger ... [which got them wondering] how do we start getting there?*[35]

On the second, MNEs seek to expand in the Global South by moving beyond their traditional focus on the top-tier markets. Even if it is a simple by-product of economic interests, this has implications for social impacts. As an executive working for a European MNE in medical devices (M56) commented:

> *You cannot claim to be a leading social healthcare provider in a country like India by targeting only the top 200 million people. So if you really want to position yourself you really need to understand* **how to add technologies and target the next few million** *customers.*[36]

It is, therefore, a result of the limited affluence of the market in the Global South. Yet, various entry barriers exist for MNEs targeting BOP segments. The need for scale is paramount for large corporations, without which it is difficult to justify product development. While everyone recognizes the potential size of the market, transforming the potential to

---

[34] Ibid.
[35] Interview, July 3, 2014.
[36] Interview, July 27, 2010.

reality is another matter. As an executive in an American MNE in ICTs described it (M13):

> *We do a lot of experiments, but the efforts largely need to be boiled down to one or two things. A lot of [product development for emerging market] is,* **boiling down 50 ideas to 2** *... [for us] it [has to pass] rigorous strict criteria ... five hundred million users have to use it. They should be able to afford it ... and it should make sense for them when they have never used information ever in their life ... It has to be compelling enough, so that they spend that extra money or effort or whatever it might be to go online and use it. And if you apply that criteria, all kinds of good ideas fall apart.*[37]

In addition, targeting the BOP segment involves a business risk, for corporations seeking to protect brand images as providers of premium goods and services. As an American MNE in ICTs noted (M7):

> *[Customers in emerging markets] are very value-conscious ... we have to* **worry about the company brand** *as well, not to have things in the press about products that are not up to the quality or not providing good support/ maintenance. So large companies are typically reluctant.*[38]

Another executive from a European MNE in medical devices (M47) also discussed the problem of brand expectations.

> *The big thing is our customers look at [our products] with certain expectations ... premium products ... with products coming out of China and India, there is a little bit of mixed optimism cum pessimism [about] quality ... it* **should not in any way erode our brand.***[39]

Furthermore, a considerable cost is associated with any new product development, and emerging markets today require time and investment before corporations begin to accrue financial returns. The same executive above (M47) noted that the cost of developing a product for an unfamiliar and unpredictable market for which little data exists is a significant deterrent.

> *We would have to build prototypes, test them, then throw them away.* **There is a lot of cost involved in developing [a product] – the same talent could be developing some other products for the Western world where you will get a much larger ROI (return on investment).** *You have positioned it for a particular market segment, you know the exact size, purchasing power,*

---

[37] Interview, June 21, 2012.
[38] Interview, June 12, 2012.
[39] Interview, July 3, 2014.

whether they are going to buy it, all that information is out there. In emerging markets, you don't have that kind of data or the data are not very reliable. So why put people on these projects?[40]

Similarly, short-termism inherent in corporations may hinder their conducting social innovation in emerging market contexts. An executive in an American MNE in ICTs (M13) observed:

*[T]hese things take time … something that I am doing might take 2 years to do. Nobody wants to wait for 2 years. They want quick successes, show results … **patience is not a virtue of corporations.***[41]

Furthermore, business opportunities at the top- and mid-tier segments may distract corporate objectives away from lower segments of the market. According to the previously quoted executive (M47):

*From a distance, these markets are attractive and you see a sizable opportunity, whereas at the same time, there's **so much untapped [demand] even at the top**, and the middle of the pyramid … and [an] organization with limited resources probably would then try and maximize their returns on a shorter time frame, rather than doing something that takes you about 5 to 7 years to get your financial returns.*[42]

Almost paradoxically, abundant opportunities and growth potential can also pose a business challenge. The challenge of engaging with a market with too many opportunities was described as follows:

*The biggest challenge that we all face in India is that you can pick anything and there is a [business] opportunity. Right from toilet paper to anything you can think of … **how do you prioritize?** You can't do everything, or you don't do anything. The process we followed is, we had presentations by the verticals and then we sat down and said – let's do some sanity check and see where the real opportunity is.*[43]

In sum, maintaining an organizational focus to cultivate emerging market consumers requires considerable determination and sustained efforts. However, unlike in the past, many corporations today believe that it is a worthy investment to position themselves well in emerging markets.

---

[40] Ibid.
[41] Interview, June 21, 2012.
[42] Interview, July 3, 2014.
[43] Ibid.

5.2.3 From BOP to "Emerging Market" Consumers

Another response to the challenge of meeting the needs of the BOP market is to seek a more realistic, so-called middle-of-the-pyramid (MOP) or "emerging market" segment. As an executive at an American MNE in ICTs (M13) described it, the emerging market segment has more education and disposable income than the BOP segment, yet differs significantly in its patterns of consumption from the middle class in the Global North.

> The **mainstream emerging markets users** are ... in USD 2,000 annual income range. They read a newspaper, not in English, don't use the Internet and they aspire to be moving upwards to middle class ... usually they make their money through blue collar or unskilled services.[44]

Similarly, a European MNE in medical devices (M47) distinguished between entry- and mid-segment for emerging markets versus their traditional markets in the Western hemisphere.

> We are very clear about going to mid-segment – we are not going to the entry segment in India. We are saying **mid-segment products in India and China**, which are entry-segment products in US and Western Europe.[45]

Depending on the industrial sector, customers can be other corporations, not end-consumers. An understanding of market characteristics, including the shape of the market pyramid and the context, matters, albeit differently in these cases. An executive from a European MNE in ICTs (M43) observed the need to cultivate customers in the mid-segment as follows:

> In the US, Germany, Japan, you'll find many companies over 10 billion dollars turnover and you could pretty much be very successful focusing on that [segment]. In India, you can count companies that make that kind of money in two hands, and the bulk of the companies are between 100 to 1,000 crores.[46] So, **the pyramid is very flat**. If you don't attune yourself to that characteristic of the market, then, you run out of customers to call very quickly.[47]

---

[44]   Interview, June 21, 2012.
[45]   Interview, July 3, 2014.
[46]   Crores are part of a commonly used Indian numbering system. One crore equals 10 million. A turnover of INR 100 to 1,000 crores equals USD 15 million to 150 million at the current exchange rate (August, 2015).
[47]   Interview, June 23, 2014.

Affordability therefore becomes a key issue, regardless of whether the clients are end-consumers or corporations. To cater to these markets and deliver on affordability becomes a key motivation for seeking innovation in general. For social innovation in particular, ensuring widespread acceptance and adoption is also essential, and, as such, other stakeholders have much to learn from the private sector in achieving this goal.

5.3 CONCLUSION

In India, the context for social innovation has been shaped by the pursuit of Nehruvian industrial and technological self-sufficiency and the Gandhian ideal of decentralized rural self-reliance. The pursuit of the Nehruvian ideal has facilitated some technological capabilities, and the Gandhian legacy is evident in widespread informality, vibrant local entrepreneurship, and an active civil society. However, if economic growth and inadequate infrastructure are any indication, the pursuit of these models for nearly 50 years met, at best, with limited success. The government's official pronouncement of inclusive development as a national policy in 2002 is an outcome of this history, acknowledging in part state failure in providing basic education, health services and infrastructure, which, in turn, has created an avenue for social innovation beyond the traditional social sectors. While there is widespread recognition that the state has largely failed in providing basic necessities, particularly to the rural poor, our interviewees also acknowledged that the social challenges are enormous and solutions are difficult to design. There was even a tacit acknowledgment that the shift in policies may indicate that the state may have finally woken up to the scale and magnitude of the challenges.

Our survey and interview results presented in this chapter serve as an important context for developments in cross-domain collaboration between for-profit and non-profit organizations, discussed in subsequent chapters. Active involvement of the private sector was called for by Prahalad and others, with the rhetoric of BOP markets, advocating that MNEs, in particular, profitably serve the world's poor. Yet, our interviews suggest that achieving profitability for these markets is an arduous task, if not unrealistic.

Simultaneously, however, in recognizing the limitations of conventional business approaches of the decades past, MNEs are seeking different ways to source knowledge and learn about the needs of emerging market consumers. Given the context in which these consumers live, with frequent power outages, water shutdowns, considerable air and noise pollution, and inadequate basic education, these corporations are inevitably engaging in, intentionally or otherwise, social innovation of sorts. The needs of these consumers are also harder to accurately discern through conventional market research, and often, special design or new technology is called for to devise solutions that overcome a variety of access issues.

6. Designing solutions for "wicked problems"

This chapter explains how the private sector is incorporating greater social missions in innovation activities. We focus on the role of design, which has become a prominent concept in the innovation literature (Goldberg, 2013; Utterback et al., 2006; Verganti, 2009). We begin with strategies to access the necessary knowledge to tackle "wicked problems" (see Chapter 4), such as de-featuring, frugal innovation, bottom-up design, design for constraints, and cross-sectoral solutions. We discuss social learning strategies within India, the exchange of knowledge within the Global South, and so-called reverse innovation, or knowledge flows from the Global South to the Global North.

6.1 DESIGNING SOLUTIONS

Our interviews in India showed how widespread wicked problems are, and how deep and abundant the needs for solutions. Devices with certain designs offer effective avenues to tackle wicked problems. An interviewee who runs a medical device firm (S19) described the role of design as follows:

> *Design is what sits between the technology and your solution. It's about how you configure your product. For example, if you know that there is limited electricity, people have limited skills, a device that requires high levels of training is unlikely to fly. If you know that availability to clean water is limited there will be hygiene issues, this has to be built into how you conceive a solution. Sometimes there may not be any technological breakthroughs, but it might be about design. Technology just enables the design.*[1]

Engaging with the emerging market segment is partly about reaching beyond the traditional market segment by designing for infrastructural constraints. The same interviewee observed that developing solutions demands a reconceptualization of needs.

---

[1]   Interview, June 25, 2013.

> *If we make a [product] cheaper, will this solve the problem? We don't think so, because of all these constraints of requiring trained manpower, spare parts, continuous electricity and so on. So we went back and looked at what the real problem is, and what the needs are.* **By reframing the problem and the need, you rethink the solution. People often confuse needs and solutions.**[2]

In this section, we examine current and emerging practices in developing solutions to wicked problems: de-featuring, frugal innovation, bottom-up design, design for constraints, and solutions that bridge multiple verticals.

6.1.1   De-featuring and Frugal Innovation

In the past, MNEs entering emerging markets typically used two strategies to cultivate domestic markets; de-featuring (eliminating functions to improve affordability) and secondary marketing (selling older models to emerging markets, often with obsolete technologies).[3] These strategies have proven ineffective in many instances. For example, contrary to common perception, de-featuring is complex and can result in adding rather than subtracting costs. An executive of a European MNE (M56) in electronics observed that *"De-featuring … will give you some kind of cost leverage, but only [up] to a point, because the moment you have frozen the design the* **cost gets [fixed]***."*[4]

Similarly, an executive from an American MNE in medical devices (M14) discussed how de-featuring cannot achieve true affordability:

> *If you start from the top, it's extremely difficult to remove features at the right value proposition, and at the optimal cost levels … You always hit … **a glass floor** – not a glass ceiling – it's very difficult to push the product down-market.*[5]

Secondary marketing also faces considerable challenges, as markets and consumer preferences are rapidly changing in emerging economies. According to an executive at an American MNE in ICTs (M12):

> *I was informed by [our UK team] that I've got it wrong, the market for [older mobile phone models] is actually the US right now. China and India want the*

---

[2]   Ibid.

[3]   An executive from an American MNE in medical devices (M14) observed *"Ten years ago, de-featuring was a big part of product development in the Global South …"* Interview, June 22, 2012.

[4]   Interview, July 27, 2010.

[5]   Interview, June 22, 2012.

next generation, **the latest and the greatest** ... *which is what is driving the emerging markets today.*[6]

The final misconception revolves around the notion of frugal innovation. The current usage of the term frugal innovation lacks analytical precision. Depending on the context, frugal innovation refers to cost arbitrage in conducting R&D, energy- or resource-savings through sustainably designed products/services, and/or low-priced product/services for consumers with limited resources, including USD 2,500 cars (e.g. Tata Nano), micro-financing, and marketing innovation (e.g. micro-packaging of shampoos to make them affordable for the poor by Unilever). Frugal innovation may involve user-friendly, maintenance free products that require little by way of supporting infrastructure. However, accomplishing frugal innovation may paradoxically require more technologies, not less. An executive at a European MNE in medical devices (M47) observed:

> *A lot of the [design] was driven by cost ... but **there were other constraints such as availability of continuous power ... then the amount of dust, moisture, parts go bad** and things like that. There are lots of components or IP which already exist in different products, but it has not been put to use [in BOP products].*[7]

6.1.2 Bottom-up Design

One approach to design gaining currency in India is bottom-up design, by starting at the base of the market and reaching upward, instead of the conventional approach of starting at the top and reaching downward. An executive from an American MNE in medical devices (M14) described bottom-up design as follows:

> *You start innovation right at the bottom. We are beginning to see everywhere, across competition ... people who start at the low-end market – they always find it **easier to move up-market**. If you design something which is extremely optimized for one of the most demanding of markets like India, it's very **easy to add features**.*[8]

---

[6] Interview, June 20, 2012.
[7] Interview, July 3, 2014.
[8] Interview, June 22, 2012.

An executive at a European MNE in medical devices (M47) drew a sharp distinction between bottom-up innovation and the earlier practice of localization.

> *The design would be from ground up, but we would steal ideas from the existing products. But* ***we should not start from existing products and try to customize it.*** *There is a big difference between the former and the latter.*[9]

Bottom-up design often generates disruptive innovation, such as a novel application of technologies, innovation in new materials, and/or a new combination of services. An executive from a European electronics MNE (M6) claimed that, *"in the process of designing products from ground zero, what comes out is* ***innovative thinking.***"[10] An executive from an American MNE in medical devices (M14) corroborated:

> *you can always talk about how to localize a particular product … The next stage is – what do we need to do uniquely from the technology standpoint that caters to the requirements of the customers here? That is really the next [phase] … it brings in* ***disruptive thinking, both from technology push [perspective] and it also forces you to think about market strategies*** *… the buying behavior of the customers, and the uniqueness of the different markets. It is highly stimulating, challenging and you learn. You really have to rethink a variety of things in India.*[11]

Thus, bottom-up design is intimately linked to learning and acquiring contextual knowledge, which in turn necessitates proximity (see Chapter 4). It is a process that incorporates knowledge of contexts, users, and markets. A European MNE in ICTs (M43) was emphatic that they were "creating ***absolutely new concepts and ideas based on very, very indigenous requirements.***"[12]

6.1.3 Design for Constraints

To develop effective designs that serve as solutions, various experiments are underway, many of which use existing technologies. An executive at an American MNE in ICTs (M13) described the objective of design for constraints as leapfrogging:

---

[9]   Interview, July 3, 2014.
[10] Interview, July 27, 2010.
[11] Interview, June 22, 2012.
[12] Interview, June 23, 2014.

*What that team is doing is trying to leapfrog ... is ... **how do you figure out technologies which are deployable in emerging markets [but] do not require a nitrogen cooled datacenter** and are cheap enough that it makes economic sense?*[13]

One example comes from the area of **healthcare using online video**. Using video for healthcare overrides constraints posed by multi-lingual environment and low literacy. As an executive at an American MNE in ICTs (M12) explained *"**video is a voice medium** – with video, you can have a conversation with somebody in whatever language that you want."*[14]

Another example from healthcare *involves teleradiology equipment designed to be operated by non-specialists.* While the health system in India suffers from insufficient doctors generally, specialists are especially scarce and their quality varies widely. To accommodate an acute shortage of radiologists,[15] a social entrepreneur (S4) developed a new cloud-based teleradiology platform that integrates the traditionally separate, Radiology Information Systems (RIS) and the communication systems known as Picture Archiving Communication Systems (PACS). The platform allows fast downloads of patient data with images in limited bandwidth environments, and comes with a training module to enable use by low-skilled medical assistants and non-radiologists, where qualified instructors and training materials are limited. Most recently, the social enterprise began collaborating with a US MNE to develop a new telemedicine platform that incorporates instrumentation (i.e. a heart and blood pressure monitor) for remote diagnosis along with images and videos.

India's inadequate infrastructure and its diverse socio-cultural environment serves as a laboratory for the challenges commonly faced in many multi-lingual and multi-ethnic countries of the Global South. An American MNE in financial software (M27) that runs an SMS service for farmers in India, designed the service so that illiterate farmers could decipher the contents of an SMS.

---

[13] Interview, June 21, 2012.
[14] Interview, June 20, 2012.
[15] While India's population is roughly four times that of the United States, the website of the Indian Radiological and Imaging Association (www.iria.in, accessed January 26, 2016), claims a membership of ~10,500 radiologists, compared to the American College of Radiology (www.acr.org, accessed January 26, 2016) which claims a membership of more than 30,000.

The challenge is ... [farmers] are not technology savvy. How do you even identify a right user experience in SMS, and create a SMS right for them? We did a lot of work around that, so that people can understand ... farmers are not literate. How will they read SMS? If you have a pattern and a structure, and you maintain the structure consistently, people start memorizing the pattern itself ... That's where we see working closely with customers.[16]

Another example was offered by an executive from an American MNE in ICTs (M16), on **voice-based applications**, using voice interaction technology. Although the technology itself is not new, considerable work went into designing the product that involves a voice protocol linking the technology with the Internet infrastructure.

Through logical deductions, we came up with – why not enable people to interact with information system by voice? **Voice interaction technology had already been developed several decades ago, but it never intersected with the Internet infrastructure.** *We had to advance the voice-based touch tone system, take the text protocol and make a voice protocol, and think of a parallel web which is all voice-based. I can set up my own voice home page and link it to your home page and you can drive traffic, transaction, as all those things on the Internet today are translated into voice. A lot of work had to be done on the interface side, on the usability side. We refined the system significantly through observations on usability and usage patterns. And we have had to think about how we provide security. How do you authenticate? How do you make sure somebody is not tampering with somebody else's ...? All these problems came up after launch. So you get practical experience from the deployments.*[17]

Initially, they had expected the service to be used for weather and crop information, and for local *panchayat* (self-government) meetings. A few pilot projects were run in collaboration with NGOs in Andhra Pradesh and Gujarat. Once the technology was in place, however, users adapted the application to suit their needs, including matrimonial ads.

Very interesting usage models started emerging out of this. *People would set up their voice sites to advertise their services ... [for example] I am a carpenter and this is my mobile number ... Others set up service to provide information, like bus arrival times. And as you would naturally expect in India, a whole bunch of things started. Matrimonial ads and exchanges started cropping up.*[18]

---

[16] Interview, January 8, 2013.
[17] Interview, June 28, 2012.
[18] Interview, June 28, 2012.

Cloud computing is a highly useful technology to bypass various infrastructural constraints and other access issues in India. As an executive of a European MNE in ICTs (M43) described it:

> *What we do is to really take the globally cutting edge [technology] and apply it to the Indian context. To me, cloud is meant for mid-market India. What are the advantages? [If you are a business owner], the risk is very low, you don't have to worry about hiring and retaining people for installation and updates, software doesn't become obsolete in 3 years, all that is taken care of. There is no capital expenditures, only operating expenses. Fast time to value. Instead of going through all the pain of actually acquiring the infrastructure, skills capable to run a software tool, now you can just get the benefits without the headaches. It's almost like a readymade solution for mid-market India.*

For an executive in a European MNE in medical devices (M47), *designing remotely connected devices* is crucial in overcoming many constraints inherent in the Indian context. Remotely connected and maintained equipment will self-install and self-test, thereby "building quality" into the product.

> *You can build your product in such a way that A) it is highly reliable in Indian conditions and B) if it fails, you will be able to remotely connect to it or you build certain error messages, and remotely tell the customer what they need to do … we are trying to build products which you don't have to come and install … that's a huge challenge for product development companies … India is not going to build its road infrastructure, power infrastructure as fast as we want them to. So we have to build quality into the products … customers should be able to unpack it and it should run, it should have self-test, blah, blah, all of that, and built-in remote connectivity pieces for remote maintenance … otherwise, the service personnel will first go, then do diagnosis, then will come back with the part and then, when that will not work, then you come back …[19]*

6.1.4 Cross-sectoral Solutions

Developing designs that overcome constraints is not simple. It requires cross-industrial contextual knowledge, an in-depth knowledge of user incentives, and often multi-disciplinary expertise. As an executive of an American MNE in chemicals (M42) described:

> *Innovation cannot be … what I call choreographed … in that sense, putting the R&D center here in its entirety where we get people from various disciplines together, and the real world problems are not very cookie cutter*

---

[19] Interview, July 3, 2014.

> *type of things, you are talking about a solution which might require drawing people from different kinds of background, different kinds of expertise together talking to each other and solving [problems].*[20]

Wicked problems often require solutions that require expertise in different "verticals," or industrial specialization, as the limited adoptions of many solutions is often attributed to problems outside the specialization. For example, the adoption of a technology may be facilitated by making a financing scheme available for end-users. A social entrepreneur in energy (S22) described how he developed and delivers **a micro-franchising model for solar lantern rentals** by devising financing solutions that work for both banks and end-users (see Section 7.5.2).

> **it was not technology, it was the financing** ... *the ability of the [stakeholders] to get [a loan]. How do you be that catalyst? A street vendor, ... [for] four hours of lighting on a daily basis in Bangalore, will say 300 rupees a month is expensive, but 10 rupees a day is fine. The bank will say ... we cannot create a [loan] system where I can go and collect on a daily basis. So, we created an entrepreneur who delivers light at six o'clock, comes back at ten to take the battery out. She is saving 5 rupees/day, and he gets 6 rupees/day. So, you have created a whole ecosystem, [provided for] an underserved entrepreneur and [the street vendor].*[21]

In another example, a **micro-automatic teller machine (ATM) software** is being developed as part of the point-of-sale (POS) cash registers for small retailers, to overcome the collective challenge posed by illiteracy and a limited road infrastructure and bank network. An executive in a European MNE in ICT (M46) described the product as follows:

> **The problem is you have to walk 18 miles to the nearest bank and you're afraid of the ATM machine because you're illiterate.** *[With our service] ... you don't have to go to the bank, you just walk to the nearest shop in your village, put your fingerprint on a POS machine. It identifies you and pops up a micro-ATM software which lets you deposit or withdraw up to $20 with the shopkeeper with the certification of the government.*[22]

An executive of an American MNE in ICT (M7) shared the example of an unconventional mix of industrial expertise to develop a system for **GPS with cargo temperature tracking**.

---

[20] Interview, June 20, 2014.
[21] Interview, July 12, 2013.
[22] Interview, July 2, 2014.

*Just to give you a very simple example … In India nowadays supermarkets have become really popular, people buying frozen potato chips and yogurt … These things have to be transported on refrigerated trucks. But truckers are trying to save fuel by turning off refrigeration, and then all the merchandise goes bad. **The insurance companies end up paying, so they are very interested in developing a solution that tracks cargo temperature with GPS.** We got the exposure from these different verticals and we had the bottom up ideas.*[23]

In sum, various constraints are inspiring innovation and cross-sectoral solutions, aimed at resolving wicked problems. Increasingly, these MNEs are developing a knowledge base for social innovation in India, employing cutting edge technologies and designing for constraints. These innovation projects are distinctive from appropriate technology movements, de-featuring or frugal (low-cost) innovation. As we shall show in subsequent sections, various forms of learning are taking place to develop solutions for wicked problems.

6.2 INDIA AS A LABORATORY FOR SOCIAL INNOVATION

India has emerged as a laboratory for social innovation in two stages: the first is the shift from the global to the domestic markets, and the second is the shift from the domestic to the markets in the Global South, as described in this section.

6.2.1 Learning for Social Impacts: Contexts and Proximity

For many MNEs, cost arbitrage was the initial reason for locating their R&D facilities in India. Increasingly, however, they have shifted their emphasis away from serving the global market to innovating for the Indian market. As an employee of an American MNE (M19) in medical devices summed up, "we came for the talent, we stayed for the market."[24] Another executive in an American MNE in ICTs (M18) corroborated:

Initially we came here specifically for just talent and to service mostly the Western markets. And that has changed dramatically in the last 4 to 5 years … we started very modestly in 1997 and developed our first product for a Western market out of India in 2003. In 2009 and 2010, we developed our

---

[23]   Interview, June 12, 2012.
[24]   Interview, July 5, 2012.

*first product for the world market that includes developing as well as developed markets. **Today, we are doing cutting edge technologies.***[25]

Many corporate interviewees argued that geographical presence is crucial to understand the needs of the lower-income consumers in emerging markets. According to a representative of an American MNE in ICTs (M13):

*What is obvious sitting in India is **not obvious in Mountain View, California.** And the same way, we need to have that **sense of obviousness** about all the emerging market regions. You have to be on the ground to really understand users.*[26]

To another executive in an American MNE in ICTs (M1), the most important role of R&D in India is invalidating ideas that come from the Global North.

*A lot of times our role is trying to ... maybe **debunk stupid ideas** that come up in West Coast America. You know, "don't spend 10 million dollars on this idea" ... we do that occasionally.*

Our survey findings show that MNEs used a variety of sources to access knowledge of the BOP market (see Table 6.1.).

Table 6.1   Results from the survey questionnaire: sources of knowledge for the BOP market

Most frequently used sources of knowledge (multiple responses)	Responses (%)
Internal marketing staff	10.5
Internal R&D staff	10.0
NGOs	9.2
Foundations	5.9
Market research firms	5.9
Universities	4.1
Government	3.7

Source: Based on the survey conducted by the authors

[25]   Interview, July 2, 2012.
[26]   Interview, June 21, 2012.

Local presence alone is insufficient to generate the contextual understanding necessary for innovation with social impacts, however. While conventional market research dwells on knowledge of competitors, deployment, supply chains, and macro-economic and regulatory contexts, knowledge required for social innovation often comes down to product/service/system design. According to a representative of an American MNE in ICTs (M1):

> *The kind of research we do is more of* **design or engineering research that is** **driven by perceived needs**. *We really care about demand through the point of view of – what do the people want? It's different from market research which has a very strong economic connection of understanding how you would design the entire market place, supply chain, distribution, etc.*[27]

Both for-profit and non-profit interviewees noted that a considerable knowledge gap exists between socio-economic classes in India. A social entrepreneur working with the urban informal sector (S11) observed:

> *People tend to think that they know about their neighbors, but in general* **people don't know about their neighbors** *at all ... you take my wife's Brahmin family. Living in this neighborhood for 400 years, she wasn't allowed to play with any schoolchildren outside ever ... they were from a different class ... Indians in a sense are very, very divided ... there's a sort of localized knowledge that I don't think an upper-middle-class Indian knows any more about – how a slum dweller lives here – than say, anybody in Boston.*[28]

A perception of an average educated employee in India is often far removed from reality. Our interview participants repeatedly mentioned that it is a misconception to assume "Indians know India." An employee of an American MNE in distribution (M1) commented that "*I think it's just ... when they don't see it, they don't realize it exists, like the difference in lifestyle and background and economic stuff.*"[29]

Similarly, a social entrepreneur in energy (S18) shared the following experience:

> *I have had people who have lived in Bangalore their whole life say to me,* **there is not a single person in Bangalore without access to electricity,** *and*

---

[27] Interview, May 28, 2012.
[28] Interview, June 12, 2013.
[29] Interview, June 13, 2012.

we are standing in front of one of the slums [without electricity], and it is just
like, oh, how can you say that?[30]

Turning a blind eye to social problems may well be a self-preservation
strategy for those who grew up side-by-side with poverty, as another
transnational social entrepreneur speculated. This leads to different
perceptions and insights generated by insiders versus outsiders, which
anthropologists have long recognized. According to him (S11):

> *when you are living in a society with lots of BOP needs, it is* **hard to try and**
> **feel for all** *of those, and you need to prepare yourself … but I do think that is*
> *where … coming in with Westerners who are open to the realities does help*
> *[face reality] in some ways.*[31]

The lack of knowledge and insight of the context, even by Indian
employees, translates into a number of practical problems. A director of a
local NGO (N1) gave the following example to illustrate how such
employer–employee knowledge gaps manifest themselves in everyday
work.

> **The upper-middle class has become westernized** *and assume a clean toilet is*
> *a dry toilet. For the poor, where domestic workers come from, a wet toilet*
> *means cleanliness – [because] water is scarce, so if you used water, then*
> *you've cleaned. That's very Indian … Now imagine a [middle class]*
> *employer simply giving an instruction – "clean" – with all of these electrical*
> *wires [in their bathroom] … or how do you clean a Faber chimney? If you*
> *use water to clean it, it will clog up, and you [assume] that she's done*
> *something stupid … but my [middle class] reality and her reality are exactly*
> *the reverse.*[32]

Although all organizations, including foreign MNEs with decades of
presence in the Indian market, domestic MNEs or local NGOs, are
subject to some measure of the knowledge gap, newly entering foreign
MNEs without familiarity of the Indian market conditions are clearly at a
particular disadvantage. To overcome the knowledge gap that emerges
from consumers/users belonging to populations that are "extremely
different from the investigator," ethnographers are increasingly called
upon to take part in social innovation projects. According to the
interviewee who works for an American MNE in ICTs (M1):

---

[30]   Interview, June 25, 2013.
[31]   Ibid.
[32]   Interview, June 4, 2012.

Companies are learning that many of their markets are different from the designers. *To the extent that [we are] selling to corporate America, we don't need any of these … But as soon as we try to sell to a businessman in Abu Dhabi or a mom in Tajikistan, then we don't have a clue about what we are having to design for. A lot of this is about* **bringing ethnographic practice, which is something new for corporate culture** *… but it's becoming much more fashionable now … anthropologists doing work for companies … ethnographic analysis is on the rise because it just happens to be the case that any enormous market is in these developing countries.*[33]

Another strategy used to narrow the knowledge gap is "amplification," which is to promote informal learning based on initiatives of employees and their involvement in CSR and other volunteer and training activities and put it to use in product/service design. An executive with an American MNE in ICTs (M13) described the process of amplification as follows:

[We have] an engineer who likes to work with orphans, and we have somebody else who is from rural Karnataka, and they live in a very well-to-do locality which is also adjacent to a slum of Bihari construction workers … I would encourage them to go out and reach out, and do more, just to understand what their lives are like. Maybe 40% of the team does that out of their own interest. **Encouragement would amplify their existing inclinations.** *You don't need everybody doing it, because that 40% tend to vocalize their experiences and [it] infects the whole team. You need enough as a bridge, and that has the largest impact.*[34]

CSR activities can serve as a vehicle to educate the workforce to narrow the knowledge gap and engage more effectively in social innovation. When the same MNE ran a mentor program with high-performing students from tier-2 and tier-3 colleges in India, the executive discovered that the impact on employees far exceeded that accruing to the mentees.

Two things came out, one is the impact on those 20 lives, [which] was extraordinary. They were almost in tears. And the other is … **all of our engineers were awestruck by what they learnt.** *They [realized that they] had no idea what our users were missing, what they needed … [including] two product managers specialized in emerging markets, one of them was at a loss of words when he was describing his experience. He was like: I did not know users, I don't know users … that's all he said, for something like two minutes. He actually does focus groups, and hangs out with users, goes to the user meet ups every time, and so on and so forth. But guess what, the users he's*

---

[33]   Interview, May 28, 2012.
[34]   Interview, June 21, 2012.

[used to] meeting were essentially self-selected power users and people like you and me.[35]

An important dimension of amplification is to let learning occur seren-dipitously and in an informal setting. This allows encounters with those who are typically not included in research surveys and focus groups. *"The key is not to institutionalize it ... because the moment you institutionalize in a large company, the structure takes over,"*[36] according to one executive (M13). *"I make it a requirement for my team ... **There is no substitute for spending time with random users**."*[37] To make his point, he shared a story of a visit to a village as part of the year-long training program for new hires from top business and engineering schools of the Global North. An impromptu visit in the first year yielded very different results from a repeat visit in the second year.

> *The first year, I took them to this village near Bannerghatta National Park (near Bangalore). What they saw was **very authentic** – we spent time with kids – it was both energizing and completely eye opening. [Normally] a very calm, very composed VP was not calm and composed that day. The following year one of the office managers went to these people and said "Look, they are coming" and organized it. They got prepared and formalized, and it became all show and tell.*[38]

6.2.2 South–South Knowledge Transfer and Reverse Innovation

The bottom-up design makes conducting innovation in the Global South attractive, as it can be used to address up-market users. In addition, the social and economic incentives are high, as some of the solutions designed for wicked problems in India are scalable and/or transferrable to other markets. While most interviewees agree that the model developed in India is not directly transferable to other countries in the Global South, they all argue that India is an ideal location from which to scale up to other areas of the Global South. First, India is an appropriate market for understanding user needs in the Global South. As an executive from an American MNE in ICT (M13) commented, *"**From Zurich to Bangalore is a jump ... Would it be the same kind of jump going from Bangalore**"*

---

[35] Ibid.
[36] Ibid.
[37] Ibid.
[38] Ibid.

to Rio de Janeiro? I think less so. And similarly in Africa."[39] Another executive of a European MNE in medical devices (M47) commented:

> [W]e found there are **many India-like markets** globally ... this whole Asia-Pacific region, Vietnam, Indonesia, Thailand ... South America, Sub-Saharan Africa, and many countries in Eastern Europe. They have the same needs and the same kind of products can fit in all of those places.[40]

Another representative of an American MNE in medical devices (M14) echoed a similar optimism. *"If you look at countries like Vietnam, Indonesia, a lot of the African countries, absolutely we are able to easily go in there."*[41] Among common contexts for the Global South is a specific example of the absence of uniform street address systems in many countries, including India, which causes a number of obstacles across sectors. As an executive of an American MNE in ICTs (M16) described the obstacles in India:

> [To] manage and process an unstructured address and put it into a common, structured form ... this turns out to be a significant problem at an enterprise level. Let's say, you are a bank, and you have two accounts with two different addresses, but in reality, they are the same address, the same individual who opened two different accounts. You are not able to tell ... [one address says] it is opposite to such and such a place and in another, next to something else. This is a major problem for a lot of institutions in India. And it turns out, **in many other countries, similar problems exist in terms of how addresses are specified and structured.** We had software products that could take unstructured addresses and standardize them, but it wouldn't work very effectively in India, because of the complexity of the different fields you have to deal with.[42]

Second, India's multi-ethnic, multi-lingual and multi-cultural environment allows innovators to anticipate a diverse market for subsequent transfer of products/services beyond India. As an executive of an Asian MNE in automobiles (M37) commented, *"India is highly diverse – for a country this size, there usually are 10 observation points to cover regional variations. In India you need 100 points of observation."*[43] Third, India is a demanding market, both from the perspective of prices and consumer demands. A social entrepreneur in renewable energy (S21)

---

39 Interview, June 21, 2012.
40 Interview, July 3, 2014.
41 Interview, June 22, 2012.
42 Interview, June 28, 2012.
43 Interview, June 13, 2014.

described how India serves as a useful point of departure to expand to other markets in the Global South.

> *[In India], you know customers are demanding, the willingness to pay is lower, and the regulations are tough, which ... **if we get it right here, it will be much easier anywhere else**.*[44]

Fourth, India, like many other areas of the Global South, has leapfrogged in some technologies. An executive at an American MNE in ICTs (M16) commented:

> *For example, how the telecom revolution has gone in India. The mobile is the predominant platform, not laptops ... now playing out in Africa, South East Asia and Central and Southern America, which is a very different and unique revolution. **You have to be here to understand that this is actually defining a new market in a new opportunity area.** There is an advantage of being in the forefront, being in the sort of ... in that neighborhood itself where those trends are actually taking place, and early visibility is an extremely important aspect as well.*[45]

Fifth, India's sheer market size makes technological innovation an up-front challenge, a useful experimental ground from which to antici-pate future problems and develop technologies accordingly. The same executive (M16) described how this challenge in the telecommunication sector can be useful in other applications, such as in environmental monitoring.

> ***How many telecommunications companies have 200 million subscribers?*** *Only five countries have 200 million people. It's very unique [in India], the volume of calls ... and very active number of calls, and they have to archive the call data records for both regulatory and enterprise purposes. We've now evolved our technologies and built processing capability to handle that kind of a volume. And the same technology is being used in many different applications around the world, like **in environmental monitoring**. If you have a large number of sensors to monitor water quality in a river in Ireland, because of the stream of data and real-time processing, [the problem] is very similar, although [with] lower volumes and faster response time. We can also use similar technology to do business intelligence applications, where streams of data are coming in and require fast processing.*[46]

---

[44]   Interview, July 3, 2013.
[45]   Interview, June 28, 2012.
[46]   Ibid.

Another executive from an American MNE in ICTs (M13) commented on potentially similar ways in which some countries adopt ICT. He shared his view on the significance of the need for information access after his trips to Afghanistan, Iraq, and Bangladesh.

Sixty percent of Afghanistan households have TVs, but only 30 percent have electricity. And 80 percent have mobile phones. That was a statistical data point that told me information matters more than access [to infrastructure]. Information is a key enabler – I don't believe that Maslow's hierarchy of needs was written with the understanding of the information age. I believe, food, water, basic healthcare, and then information before electricity or roads [in that order]. [Information] is higher priority than people give it the credit for. Not only because there is an organic bottom-up demand ... because of the impact of that is disproportionate ... These trips to Afghanistan, Iraq, Bangladesh ... [produced] very interesting internal reports ... [tens of thousands of our] employees read it, and have a large impact on the company [strategies]. Those data points told leadership and as well as the work force that there is a need to focus on these users.[47]

Although most social entrepreneurs we interviewed focused on serving the Indian market, the opportunity offered in India goes beyond its national boundary, and some had already expanded to Africa and parts of Asia. One social entrepreneur (S13) for example explored 11 countries, eventually focusing on four (Bhutan, East Timor, Cameroon, and Ethiopia) to provide technical consulting initially, with a plan to subsequently expand to offer products and other services.[48] Another social entrepreneur (S4) in medical devices specializes in developing a training and maintenance module for hospital workers, many of whom are low skilled, a condition shared by India and in many African countries. Their devices come with a platform that includes an online training module targeted for Africa and elsewhere.[49]

Finally, the bottom-up design facilitates reverse innovation, and a smoother geographical transfer of solutions from "emerging markets" of the Global South to "traditional markets" in the Global North. As another executive in a European MNE in electronics (M56) described, *"[d]esigning products from ground zero [can result in] a very good innovative solution to scale up for German or US markets."*[50]

---

[47] Interview, June 21, 2012.
[48] Interview, June 15, 2013.
[49] Interview, July 10, 2012.
[50] Interview, July 27, 2010.

"Reverse innovation" is predicated upon identifying the needs of Global North consumers by learning from the needs of Global South consumers. For example, given that Global South consumers are more adept at using mobile telephones with bandwidth constraints, an executive from an American MNE in ICTs (M1) described developing a better understanding of data purchase and consumption behavior to inform the future behavioral patterns of Global North consumers:

> *We have been studying and trying to understand the way in which people in India and Africa actually manage to deal with both minutes and bytes on the phones. Minutes are minutes and there is a very, very clear understanding of what that is, but bytes are actually really hard to understand. When you are downloading a web page, do you have any idea how many bytes you just downloaded? If you play a video do you have any idea how much that was? But yet you are getting charged, often more, for this kind of things, and not in an understandable way. And for an average European or North American, it doesn't matter – you will buy all-you-can-eat plan or the data you want – That's changing now. Suddenly folks in the developed world are paying attention to this notion. What does it mean to be living under a constrained bytes coming in? How do you understand that? How do you explore that? So it's been a **flip in the reflection**.*[51]

Seeing the relevance of consumer experiences in the Global South in the future in the Global North, the above-mentioned MNE has begun developing its knowledge base in the Global South.

> **We started by trying to explore what is happening in Africa and India. And it turns out that this is now having very huge relevance for people in developed economies** *that are now seeing a big clampdown on bandwidth available with mobile devices ... As long as you have got fiber, it's not been such a big problem. But physics tells you that there is only so much spectrum out there, you can do some fancy things with it, but it only goes so far ... One metaphor we use is – think of it as if you are roaming all the time. Suddenly you are paying attention to everything you download and why you download it and that has major repercussions to the things like advertising, bunch of things like that.*[52]

The "flip in the reflection" mentioned above is useful in the era of resource constraints, as we explore ways to alter how we produce and consume various resources.

---

[51]   Interview, May 28, 2012.
[52]   Ibid.

6.3 CONCLUSION

It is notable that India has emerged as a new location of innovation with social impacts with a significant involvement of the private sector. Many commercial enterprises large and small, foreign and domestic, are involved in developing products, services and business models that address social and material needs. This is partly explained by the challenges faced by the state (see Chapter 5), and partly explained by the challenges experienced by MNEs in penetrating the "glass floor." This chapter demonstrated how the transition to innovation with social impacts in the private sector is a growing necessity and central to strategies of corporations, rather than a luxury or a peripheral interest for the sake of image-building and branding. Corporations increasingly face competition from those who better address the needs of the poor, which in turn is creating interest, opportunities, and avenues for collaboration that cross the for-profit/non-profit boundaries. As the discussion in this chapter has shown, bottom-up design, combined with design for constraints, offers new arenas of innovation with strong social impact. The next chapter will provide detailed case studies of such design efforts that span sectors, domains and geographical scales.

7. Case studies from India

This chapter is devoted to case studies of social innovation observed in India. Fourteen case studies are organized into five key areas of social innovation: health (healthcare delivery and medical diagnostics), agriculture (small-scale farmers), rural development (inclusive development for rural populations), livelihoods in the informal sector, and renewable energy. The cases demonstrate how social innovation combines technological products and organizational processes. We focus on how various stakeholders conceptualize challenges, and how they develop approaches to best resolve bottlenecks, which are in part infrastructural, in part social practices. By providing training and improving accessibility, affordability and usability, solutions are increasingly designed to incorporate the goals of environmental or livelihood sustainability.

In many instances, social innovation is possible when different stakeholders, whether from the state, MNEs and corporations, NGOs or social entrepreneurs, find their own reasons for collaboration. Each brings prior experience from their domains with different technologies to conceptualize and innovate around a particular social challenge.

7.1 INNOVATING ON HEALTHCARE DELIVERY AND MEDICAL DIAGNOSTICS

India was ranked 112 among 191 countries by the WHO's World Health Indicators in 2000. Since then, the situation has not improved, as shown in Table 7.1. India's health system, at least in comparison with other BRICS countries, leaves much to be desired, especially when viewed against the backdrop of other health indicators (see Chapter 5, Table 5.2). Although India is the largest producer of pharmaceuticals in the Global South in volume terms (Horner, 2014), its reliance on imports for medical devices and diagnostics (Datta et al., 2013) increases healthcare costs. Access to diagnostics and testing in rural areas is plagued by long waiting times, low patient compliance, hidden costs, and degradation of samples. Of the three cases that follow, one illustrates innovative health-care delivery while the other two cases illustrate the development of diagnostics specifically to lower the barriers to healthcare access.

Table 7.1   Healthcare system indicators, BRICS countries

	Hospital beds (per 10,000 population, 2012)	Physicians	Nurses and mid-wives	Neo-natal mortality (per 1000 live deaths, 2013)
		(per 10,000 population, 2013)		
India	7	7.0	17.1	29.2
Brazil	23	18.9	76.0	8.4
China	38	14.9	16.6	7.7
Russia	17	n.a.	n.a.	5.3
South Africa	n.a.	7.8	51.1	14.8

Source: World Health Indicators, various years

7.1.1   Rural Healthcare Franchising with Local Social Networks

The problem of inadequate healthcare in India, especially in rural areas, is in part due to the physical isolation of many rural communities and the inadequate government service structure. While NGOs have augmented government services, their efforts are often difficult to scale and finan-cially unsustainable. Moreover, weak infrastructure and poor regulation lead to a dependence on private healthcare practitioners, many of whom are quacks – neither qualified nor certified to provide treatment. The absence of health insurance translates into high out-of-pocket costs which, in turn, leads to low adoption of preventive care that is more cost-effective in the long run.

To address this problem, the former manager of a family planning program in the state of Bihar launched an NGO (N26) in 2008 to provide better healthcare services to poor and vulnerable rural communities. The NGO began in the state of Uttar Pradesh with an 18-month pilot program, and found two structural issues: lack of rural clinics and trained healthcare professionals. After extensive discussions and experiments, the NGO designed a telemedicine program that relies on existing social and economic infrastructures, local market forces, and advances in communi-cation and medical technologies, to scale up and be cost-effective.

The telemedicine program provides health and family planning ser-vices with a tiered structure that networks private practitioners. Central to service provision are branded, Internet-based healthcare service franchises, which are linked to central medical facilities in urban areas staffed by qualified doctors. A rural healthcare provider (a franchisee) can initiate a service by giving a missed call[1] to the central facility, after which the call is returned. The rural provider acts as a facilitator between the doctor and the patient for the diagnosis while the doctor writes a prescription that is relayed telephonically. Networking existing rural healthcare providers, including the unqualified, ensures that the service is built on established trust, while the rural providers enhance their legitimacy through "branding." By incentivizing franchisees, the NGO offers an improved healthcare service. The services are subsidized for the most vulnerable populations, either by the government or by other donors. The Gates Foundation provides for patients with tuberculosis, diarrhea or pneumonia.

In addition to securing the space, franchisees purchase from the NGO a remote diagnostic tool comprising a computer or a laptop with Internet connection and a webcam. The diagnostic tool is designed to collect basic data such as blood pressure, heart rate, and pulse, and was developed by the NGO in collaboration with a Bangalore-based social enterprise. For areas where Internet connectivity is inadequate, the NGO developed a mobile phone application to substitute for the Internet connection. Currently, the system works on any tablet or smart phone, which also allows local providers to travel to remote hamlets if necessary. Another unique feature of this program is a network of reliable pathology laboratories that are connected to local pharmacies, so that patients get test results and their medicines in one location, instead of traveling long distances to the laboratory to collect their results. Most recently, the service added motorbike delivery of medicines to remote areas as last-mile provision.

Convinced that the experience could be duplicated elsewhere, the NGO expanded into Bihar in 2011 to reach 2 million rural residents. As of January 2014, the network included 600 health centers, 4,700 care providers, 35 clinics, 21 diagnostic centers, 10,000 pharmacies and 50 last-mile providers. In addition, 13 doctors in Delhi, 3 doctors in Patna and 18 doctors around the country participate in the program. The

---

[1] A missed call is a deliberately terminated call by the caller after one or two rings. It is widely used in South Asia and Africa to communicate a mutually agreed-upon message (such as will be late for a meeting, or arrived home safely) while avoiding call charges.

network is extending abroad; as of October 2014, a pilot project was in development in Kenya with a network of 18 facilities and 100 mobile providers.

7.1.2   From Thermoplastics to Silk Fabric Chips for Immunoassays

An engineer trained at an elite Indian institution, and armed with an advanced degree from a leading US university, co-founded a social enterprise to develop sophisticated and robust tests close to the point of diagnosis and treatment without compromising on the reliability offered by centralized laboratories. The objective is to simultaneously circumvent shipping-related costs, damages and delays of diagnostic tests, and ensure that doctors and patients have accurate and timely results. Making reliable diagnosis affordable would also help entrepreneurial local clinics to reduce costs and expand their client base.

The enterprise (S3) was established in 2009 when the founder returned to India after completing a Ph.D. on micro fluidics platforms to automate drug screening. He began developing a proprietary lab-on-chip platform to perform rapid immunoassays (protein tests) at low cost. The portable platform is an automated device that can be used by an untrained worker in a local clinic or a small laboratory. Once samples are loaded into plastic cartridges containing reagents, automated fluid handling systems located inside the reader complete the immunoassay and a sensitive fluorescence detection system provides the results.

The platform offers several advantages over existing approaches. First, micro-fluidic technologies require a smaller sample for diagnosis. Further, the automated reader takes care of dispensing and disposing as the waste is fully contained in a small disposable thermoplastic chip. Second, the technology allows for even sensitive assays to be completed much faster than central lab tests. Third, the scope of human error is eliminated as custom-built modules contain precisely loaded reagents, while an easy-to-use interface with a rugged touch screen permits repeated operator use and data entry. Fourth, a lithium-ion battery allows for 3 hours of uninterrupted usage of the device. Finally, the platform can be used for a wide range of assays that the enterprise is working on for point-of-care use, thus lowering the long-term costs of the platform. The enterprise has identified four clinical areas to work on: thyroid disorders, fertility, diabetes, and infectious diseases. To date, it has developed three product panels; a quantitative confirmatory test for the pregnancy hormone, a test for female fertility, and a test for thyroid disorders.

Despite the growing popularity of micro-fluidic lab-on-chips, the challenge of manufacturing functionally reliable chips that are robust enough to withstand extreme weather conditions, temperature and dust, is a problem in resource-constrained environments. As an alternative, the enterprise is working on a chip that incorporates woven silk fabric as a platform for diagnostic tests. The naturally hydrophilic property of fabric makes it a well-suited medium to manufacture biological sensors, and excellent local expertise and infrastructure already exists for silk, thanks to India's long tradition of silk production and weaving. During the development process, the enterprise worked extensively with silk weavers from the historic town of Kanchipuram, and quickly realized that silk can also have hydrophobic tendencies depending on how it is woven. The enterprise then manipulated the silk to create pathways through different weaving techniques and different yarn to attest to the presence or absence of particular protein molecules and diseases. Making a fabric chip starts with the selection of silk yarn. The yarn is coated with different reagents before it is dried and hand-woven into a complex fabric chip. Based on the weaving pattern, such as yarn twist frequency and the coverage and patterns formed, the chip is able to host different tests on a single surface. Strips of fabric are then cut out and packaged to create different biological testing devices.

The enterprise claims that a simple handloom can potentially create thousands of sensors at minimal cost. The costs reflect the weaving expertise in India and the manufacturing system of the textile industry. In addition, because weaving components are similar across the world, it permits a unified and scalable platform that can be transferred globally. The enterprise is supported by Grand Challenges Canada, and collaborates with various domestic and international firms and universities for clinical and scientific inputs.

7.1.3   Dry Reagents for Resource-constrained Supply Chains

A social enterprise (S1), identifying itself as a next generation biotechnology venture, was founded to develop affordable diagnostics. Although the founder was an Indian serial entrepreneur with a history of successful ventures in Silicon Valley, the new venture was located in India to design a complete ground-up solution, as the founder believed that "parachuted technologies" often miss out on the nuances of the locality. In this case, the constraint was the lack of an efficient temperature controlled supply chain.

Since reagents used in diagnosis are sensitive to temperature, their shipment and storage require controlled environments. Without cold-storage facilities, the integrity of reagents is likely to be compromised, making them less likely to provide accurate results, potentially leading to misdiagnosis. The absence of temperature-controlled facilities poses a challenge in resource-constrained environments both in terms of the cost and availability of reliable reagents.

Their initial goal was to make the product affordable through process optimization using locally available materials. For the enterprise, defining new products comes from insights provided by the sales force visiting hospitals and laboratories to observe and identify problem areas in workflow, distribution, and product usage. Upon discovering that the real costs came from the need for a cold chain storage infrastructure, they sought new forms of materials, and arrived at unique dry, temperature-stable reagents. Dry reagents allow testing in remote areas without compromising on either the quality or the integrity of the results. Moreover, they were able to reduce the price from USD 30 to USD 3. Success, however, was partially prevented by large medical device competitors offering a combination of reagents and instrumentation. To overcome this barrier, the enterprise decided to enter the instrumentation business and to own the entire solution.

In 2013, the enterprise was acquired by a research firm, which added two segments of the cell analysis market – HIV monitoring and clinical research. Dry reagents was an important part of the acquisition imperative, since the physical properties of the reagents make them useful not just in emerging markets, but also in advanced industrial countries.

7.2 RESOLVING INFORMATION ASYMMETRIES FOR SMALL-SCALE FARMERS

Although agriculture accounted for 47 percent of employment in India in 2012, its share of GDP was only 18 percent. This is, in part, due to small-scale operations. According to the Agriculture Census 2005–2006, the average size of an operational holding was only 1.23 hectares, with farms less than 2 hectares comprising 83 percent of all holdings and 41 percent of area (Planning Commission, 2013b, p. 20). Small farmers face inadequate market information, price volatility, and the lack of physical infrastructure and timely technical assistance. Agriculture in India is also subject to high post-harvest losses and weak farm-to-firm linkages. For instance, although India is the world's second largest producer of fruits and vegetables, only 6–7 percent is processed compared to 65 percent in the US and 23 percent in China (Planning Commission, 2013b, pp. 23–24). More generally, Aker (2011) points out that stagnating agricultural growth in poorer economies is because of the underutilization of improved technologies which, in turn, reflects information asymmetries. The three cases that follow illustrate efforts to overcome those asymmetries.

7.2.1   Video-based Content Creation and Distribution

An employee working on agricultural development at a US MNE quit in 2008 to found an NGO (N13) with a mission to integrate innovative technology and development efforts to improve well-being in rural areas. The NGO shares knowledge of agricultural practices, livelihoods, health, and nutrition in rural areas, in collaboration with various grassroots organizations. The channel for knowledge sharing is a participatory process of video production, video dissemination, and training. To ensure that the videos are accurate, current, topical, and of interest to users, a digital platform collects and analyzes data, in near real time, on the dissemination and adoption of content. Since it serves as a field data management tool, the platform is designed to work when Internet and electrical grid connectivity is neither steady nor continuous.

The NGO runs programs alongside grassroots-level partners to accommodate local needs and earn user trust. The NGO trains 4–5 member production teams within the partner organizations to shoot 8–10 minute videos using low-cost, durable equipment. A subject matter specialist at the district level (e.g. on poultry production) reviews and edits the post-production video. New videos are shown every two weeks to a group of no more than 20. A facilitator mediates a discussion, which serves both as a means of information dissemination and a feedback collection mechanism (e.g. why certain practices are not adopted).

The NGO initially took on the responsibility of identifying local needs. But the process was resource-intensive and took three years to scale to 100 villages. However, once the responsibility for needs identification was shifted to the local partners, the program scaled to 2,000 villages in two years. As a facilitator, the NGO draws on partnerships with research agencies, and corporations with relevant products, to introduce state-of-the-art practices to the community without any form of marketing. Overall, grassroots partners produce 80 percent of the videos and the videos are distributed by the NGO using a creative commons license, which serves to ensure quality.

By April 2015 the NGO was collaborating with over 20 partners. It had produced nearly 3,800 videos, and had reached over 650,000 (70 percent women) people across 7,650 villages in nine Indian states. Some 350,000 viewers have adopted one or more of the best practices in the videos. The NGO has also been approached to work in parts of Ethiopia, Afghanistan,

Ghana, Niger, and Tanzania, where the network of grassroots NGOs found in India is often absent. But the influence of this model has been much broader as it has also been replicated by various organizations that have no formal ties with this NGO.

The Government of India's Ministry of Rural Development, the UK's Department for International Development (DFID) and international private foundations such as the Gates and the Ford Foundations all support the NGO. The Gates Foundation provided an initial USD 3 million in 2009 and added another USD 10 million for 2012–2016 to scale the operations to 10,000 villages in India. To win the support of its donors, the NGO has demonstrated how video productions have proven to be more cost-effective than conventional practices of agricultural training and extension.

7.2.2 Text Messaging Service for Crop Prices

Not long after a Silicon Valley-based MNE (M27) made India the center of its Asia-Pacific product development initiatives, with Bangalore serving as the hub for its engineering, marketing, sales, and support operations in 2005, it became clear to the MNE that its core financial software products had little relevance in India. In scouting for a problem that acutely affected a large number of Indians, the MNE zeroed in on the opacity of agricultural markets.

In 2008, the MNE's emerging markets team visited 17 markets across rural Karnataka to examine the value chain and understand the role of every stakeholder within it. The team came to understand that farmers were often in debt or financial distress because perishable inventory either lay unsold or was sold at a suboptimal price, and 40 percent went to waste due to a weak supply chain. Not only was reliable price information scarce in volatile markets, but farmers also faced lower profits because of the presence of intermediaries. Thus, the MNE hoped to use technology to overcome information asymmetries.

After testing the best means of spreading information to farmers, (including a voice-based information system), the focus shifted to devices that were widely available to the farmers, namely low-end mobile phones. While the literacy levels among farmers seemed to challenge the prospect of providing information over SMSs, the MNE realized that illiterate farmers can memorize information patterns and they can read numbers. In addition, farmers often sought help from their children or their neighbors, to make sense of messages and information. Knowledge cultivated by the MNE resulted in the design of an interface where numbers conveyed relevant market information. Thus was developed a text messaging service to provide farmers with personalized and reliable price information.

The SMS platform was tested with a dozen farmers near Bangalore in keeping with a Community Driven Innovation philosophy of the MNE. The service was then scaled up to 1,000 farmers before the formal launch in October 2009 in the states of Andhra Pradesh and Gujarat where farmers' profiles best matched the service features. After learning that local tacit knowledge provided by on-the-ground partners is indispensable, the MNE collaborated with the Society for Elimination of Rural Poverty in Andhra Pradesh to facilitate multi-dimensional poverty alleviation by focusing on the livelihoods value chain and human development indicators.

The MNE trains on-the-ground partners who, in turn, generate word-of-mouth testimonials. Once a farmer registers through a toll-free number, an agent captures a user-profile, such as the crops planted by season, the number of acres farmed, and harvest dates. The farmer receives an SMS on the specified crops, and the various prices at which a list of buyers or market agents are willing to purchase the output. The information is disseminated many times a day after it is aggregated from various sources, including state-level Agricultural Product Market Committees and from contracted field staff. There was initial resistance to the service from intermediaries worried that their profits would vanish. But they were later brought in as partners and as users of the service. By contributing information that only they had on certain kinds of buyers, such as bulk buyers (e.g. hotel chains seeking certain produce), the intermediaries found that they could also boost their profitability.

Unlike other subscription-based SMS information models, the service is free for farmers, and the information is used to create user profiles, which can be easily updated. This generates valuable data and insights into farming practices, which the MNE sells to advertisers and other firms to generate revenues. This model has proven effective to attract farmers with diverse income profiles in multiple states and with various on-the-ground partners. By May 2013, about 1.5 million farmers across Andhra Pradesh, Gujarat, and Karnataka had signed up for the service, and another 8,000 were signing up for the service every month. The MNE estimates that enrolling for the service increases farmers' incomes on average by 20 percent. Interestingly, nearly 50 percent of farmers signing up grow cotton. Although cotton is not perishable, its price is subject to volatility. As a result, the MNE expects that up to 100 million cotton farmers worldwide could eventually enroll for the service. The MNE is also considering taking the service to other emerging markets.

7.2.3 Building Farmers' Capacities to Reach Markets

A Bangalore-based NGO (N7) was established in 1968 to help poor and socially marginalized farmers by strengthening their organizational capacity to access markets. The NGO works in collaboration with the government, multilateral agencies and the private sector, mostly in the drought-prone regions of the states of Karnataka, Tamil Nadu and Andhra Pradesh. It also supports projects in the states of Haryana, Assam, Meghalaya, Manipur, Jharkhand, Orissa, and Chattisgarh in addition to projects in other countries including Myanmar, Indonesia, East Timor, and Iran.

The NGO has long engaged with farmers in watershed management, improvement in soil quality, and water retention. In recent years, working with small dry land farmers in Karnataka, the NGO realized that while two-thirds grow *toor dal* (a type of lentils), which sold for INR 80/kilogram at a nearby small town market, the farmers' share hovered around INR 30. The price differential reflected how beholden the farmers were to moneylenders and middlemen for credit and other farm inputs such as seeds. High interest rates on loans left the farmers indebted.

To increase the farmers' share in the market price, the NGO collaborated with the National Commodity Exchange (NCX) in Mumbai which provided an electronic transaction platform that gave access to prevailing rates over mobile phones. Working with the state's Department of Agriculture, a Toor Board was established so that farmers could aggregate, sort, and clean their produce and have it assessed by the NCX. This also facilitated payments to farmers by banks. By 2012, the local producer society that the NGO initiated in Karnataka had 800 farmer participants. The NGO plans to add half a dozen societies by 2017.

A US MNE assisted in developing and maintaining the platform as a CSR initiative. The MNE sent two employees to Gulbarga in Karnataka for 4 weeks to examine the *toor dal* trade, such as the potential for value-added products and the benefits of a spot exchange. The MNE's employees were able to provide a perspective to connect production with markets that neither the NGO nor the farmers had. Although initially solicited by the NGO as a collaborator, the MNE now actively seeks opportunities to work together to gain knowledge about strengthening farming practices and institutions, such as carbon trading for small farmers.

7.3 PROMOTING INCLUSIVE DEVELOPMENT FOR RURAL POPULATIONS

As discussed in Section 5.1.3, the state's mandate for inclusive development involves healthcare, education, infrastructure, and various dimensions of rural livelihoods. What follows are three cases of innovation to promote inclusion in different ways: socio-political, financial, and economic opportunities.

7.3.1 Voice-enabled Mobile Phone Platform for Tribal Communities

Although mobile telephony has extensively penetrated India, the country remains underserved by many other forms of mass communication. Table 5.2 showed the limited access to the Internet; likewise, the penetration of older media, such as radio, also remains limited and controlled. For instance, in 2009, there were 374 radio broadcast stations in India (AM, FM and short wave) whereas Brazil already had 1,852 stations by 1999 (Central Intelligence Agency, 2013). The lack of access to any form of media or information channels is especially acute among an estimated 80 million belonging to India's tribal communities.[2] Radio is closely monitored by the government in many tribal areas of eastern India, which are hotbeds of radical left-wing groups (the Maoists) that have adopted violent means to challenge the state. Moreover, low wattage transmitters cannot reach beyond a radius of 10 to 15 kilometers, thereby leaving many communities without radio.

In order to provide these tribal communities with a means of communication that would circumvent government regulations and the technological limitations of radio transmission, an NGO established a Yahoo! Group in 2004. The group membership reached 2,500, but there were limits to further expansion in an area where the adult literacy rate is low and the Internet penetration rate is barely 7 percent. This led to the development of a voice-based platform, by combining the Internet with mobile phones. Anyone using a mobile phone can gain access and either listen to, or report stories, by making a missed call. The server registers the missed call, and returns the call with instructions on how to listen to

---

[2] India's tribal communities refer to various indigenous ethnic minority groups. The Constitution of India defines tribals as those who are scheduled in Article 342 by the President of India, that is, Scheduled Tribes (STs). STs accounted for 8.6 percent of the population and 90 percent live in rural areas, primarily in the central, eastern, and north-eastern states. STs are poorer and less educated on average (Ministry of Tribal Affairs, 2013).

or record messages. Recorded messages are vetted by trained journalists, fluent in the local dialect/language, and uploaded onto the server for others to listen in. The journalists ensure the accuracy of the messages to prevent the state from finding a pretext to silence the platform by accusing the NGO of "spreading propaganda" in a politically sensitive region. All materials are also uploaded onto the website for online users.

The current platform was born after a chance meeting between the founder and a graduate student from an elite US university at a mobile technologies conference in 2008. Since the student was already working on an audio wiki project, he drew on his university contacts to develop the first platform, using open-source software, a desktop computer, an Internet connection, and a telephony interface. The software was built at the university and is currently being maintained by several organizations including a US MNE. The outcome of the serendipitous meeting was an increase in reach from 7 percent to 70 percent of the population. They are now trying to integrate three technologies – the Internet, mobile phone, and short wave radio to allow an "audio Facebook" for the tribal communities, through which a message can be recorded, uploaded on a server and broadcast via radio.

The audio platform is accessible to all and fits the socio-political needs of the communities where strong oral narrative traditions exist. For example, the platform has been used to raise concerns over local government corruption, by users reporting names and phone numbers of officials accused of neglect, and officials being asked to publicly respond to these accusations. The platform was used to report incidences of malaria, which led the government to officially acknowledge the disease as a widespread problem in the region, instead of claiming zero incidence. The platform has also evolved into a cultural repository, whereby users record songs, poems, stories, and cooking recipes. Experiments are also underway to use the platform to listen to and vote for favorite songs.

Plans are also afoot to expand to other tribal languages to ensure greater community participation. Beyond India, operations have been established in Indonesia and Afghanistan with plans to expand into various African countries. The ultimate goal is to have "a free, independent, people-owned communication platform which people can afford." Financial support for the project, including the call costs, has been provided by the UN Democracy Fund, the MacArthur Foundation, the Hivos Foundation, the Gates Foundation, the International Center for Journalists, and other organizations.

7.3.2   ICT Employment Creation and Training in Rural Areas

As discussed in Section 5.1.3, MGNREGA was enacted primarily to address the limited employment options in rural India. While agricultural mechanization is reducing the demand for farm labor, the share of informal manufacturing enterprises in rural areas also declined from 76 percent to 71 percent between 1994–1995 and 2005–2006. Further, in the same period, the rural share of informal manufacturing employment declined too, from 71 percent to 66 percent (NCEUS, 2009, p. 257). Overall, the opportunities that exist in rural areas tend to be less productive; thus, while urban areas accounted for 31 percent of population according to the 2011 Census, the Central Statistical Organisation estimated that they contributed 62 percent of GDP in 2009–2010 (Planning Commission, 2013b, p. 318).

Although overall school enrollment increased in India after the Right to Education Act of 2009, it is not clear if the education necessarily gives students the skills for employment. For example, jobs in IT services, which have grown phenomenally in recent years, demands relatively high skills. In 2005, 64 percent of employment in ICT services was to be found within 50 kilometers of the seven largest metropolitan centers, and only 5 percent in rural areas (Vishwanath et al., 2013, p. 96).

Against this backdrop, an enterprise (S9) was launched in 2007 to establish BPO centers in rural areas to undertake tasks that are technically less demanding than writing software. The enterprise would also train locals for employment in the BPO centers and thereby contribute to local economic growth. Though headquartered in Chennai, operations – data entry, data validation and cleaning, digitization, data analytics, digital asset management, social media support, transcriptions, and testing – take place at three delivery centers in rural Tamil Nadu and Karnataka. The enterprise has developed multi-lingual text corpora, an Indian language translation service and vernacular language support for corporate IT applications and videos, and has processed GIS data for 50 countries.

The enterprise recruits rural youth from local colleges and educational institutions, computer training institutes, and local typewriting schools. The enterprise also coordinates with the local village administration, and offers on-the-job training. While the goal is to create economic opportunities which lead to upward mobility, BPOs in general suffer from annual employee attrition rates as high as 55 percent, adding considerably to the costs of recruiting, training and retention. This enterprise, however, has managed to hold its attrition rate to 8 percent.

The firm emerged from the Rural Technology and Business Incubator (RTBI) at the Indian Institute of Technology Madras, which offered office space for three years and start-up funding to support a small rural center with basic computer facilities. The RTBI also provided referrals, resulting in its first client, a US MNE, which was developing online platforms to allow user feedback in various Indian languages. With the growth of clients, both international and domestic, in areas such as IT and insurance, the enterprise upgraded its infrastructure, enhanced its training program, built additional rural centers, and currently covers 400 villages. By using the services of the enterprise, not only do clients benefit from paying around 40 percent of the cost of urban vendors, but they also gain insights into the social conditions in rural India.

7.3.3 "Bank-less" Banking for Rural Migrants

In 2011, only 35 percent of Indian adults had an account at a formal financial institution, whereas the figure for the other BRICS countries was 61 percent. Access to financial services is spatially uneven; 41 percent of urban residents and just 33 percent of rural residents had accounts in 2011 (Demirguc-Kunt et al., 2013). Approximately 40 percent of the branches of commercial banks in 2009 were in rural areas (Reserve Bank of India, 2010). Access to banks remains a challenge even in urban areas, especially for migrants. According to a survey by Gopinath et al. (2010, p. 10), of an estimated 100 million migrants in the cities, only 22 percent on average had access to banking services. The figure falls to 12 percent if migrants to Mumbai are excluded. Since migrants, especially in construction, move from site to site, accessing a branch and waiting for service can be time consuming and impacts their earnings. To send remittances home, many migrants prefer the service of informal couriers over banks or the post office network, despite the extra risk and cost involved.

A Reserve Bank of India report in 2005 recommended banks to widen their reach by involving microfinance institutions, NGOs and other civil society organizations as Business Correspondents, and offer financial services such as the collection of small deposits, the receipt and delivery of remittances, the disbursal of small value credit, and the sale of micro-insurance, mutual fund and pension products. In January 2008, the Ranga-rajan Committee's report on financial inclusion recommended that individuals also be permitted to act as Business Correspondents. The report encouraged the adoption of relevant technology to expand outreach by correspondents. The eventual goal was for banks to have a correspondent in every village in the country. In November 2009, the government permitted individuals, such as small groceries/pharmacy owners, public call office operators, agents of small savings schemes of the Government of India, and insurance companies, and designated functionaries of SHGs linked to banks, to become Business Correspondents.

The government's endorsement of Business Correspondents reaffirmed an observation of a founder of an NGO-turned-social enterprise (N6) providing value-added telecommunication services: when a migrant pays a small shopkeeper, not for a pre-paid card with minutes of talk time, but to send money home on his/her behalf as remittance, the shopkeeper is playing the role of a banking agent. Thus, in 2006, the founder set out to develop a network that extends bank-less financial transactions by using the existing retail, telecom, and banking infrastructure to serve the large number of migrants in Delhi from the states of Bihar and Jharkhand.

A migrant working in Delhi can go to any Customer Service Point (CSP) to open an account or transfer money into an account in his home state. The CSP is any local shop enrolled as a member of the social enterprise's network of franchisees and can register users. Transferring money involves the shopkeeper dialing the transaction for a given amount and the destination account number from his phone. Once the details are verified, an instant credit appears on the account along with a confirmation message to both the shopkeeper and the customer. The recipient uses a similar procedure to withdraw money. The enterprise and the CSP receive a commission on every transaction. The ability to promptly deposit and withdraw cash, remit funds and pay insurance premiums at the CSPs has led to rapid growth of the operations.

The enterprise encountered challenges in its third year, when the partner bank was merged and lost interest in continuing the service. But after a serendipitous visit by Bill Gates to a CSP in November 2008, the enterprise obtained a grant from the World Bank's Consultative Group to Assist the Poor (CGAP) that is jointly funded by the Gates Foundation. The grant allowed it to become a Business Correspondent for a public sector bank in 2009. With the success of a pilot, the enterprise also became a correspondent to a large private sector bank.

This service is based on the Micro Finance Open Source (Mifos) technology platform, which is widely used for financial inclusion programs since it was first adopted by the Grameen Foundation. The social enterprise reworked the platform for its use and also approached a US MNE to find simpler methods of authentication and verification. Initially, the platform was a closed system, and transactions were possible only between the account holders. But once the platform was connected to the core banking services in 2010, customers could make real-time transactions with banks' account holders and the number of transactions surged.

To ensure the reliability of CSPs, the social enterprise established qualification criteria that they must meet before joining the network. Once a background check and due diligence is completed, the CSP receives a dedicated phone, a manual, and training. A dedicated call center provides user support and generates feedback. The enterprise has also invested in analytics to detect sudden shifts and changes in the transaction patterns to monitor potentially fraudulent uses.

7.4 SUSTAINING LIVELIHOODS IN THE INFORMAL SECTOR

The availability of skills and infrastructure are essential to ensure better livelihood access for marginalized populations, but they are only the necessary conditions. The sufficient condition is the institutional means by which the supply of these essential factors is matched with demand for the valorization of skills. Informal employment suffers from limited skills, low wages, and a reliance on word-of-mouth for new opportunities. Similarly, informal businesses face constraints, especially when it comes to cash flows and access to credit. We now discuss three innovative efforts that explicitly bridge demand and supply gaps to facilitate livelihoods in the informal sector.

7.4.1 Training and Skill Certification for Construction Workers

Employment is as much a challenge in urban areas as it is in rural areas. In 2011–2012, an estimated 80 percent of employment in urban areas was in the informal sector and, as Table 7.2 shows, construction is one sector where urban informality is much in evidence. Further, the NCEUS (2009, p. 62) estimates that, in 2004–2005, 65 percent of males and 92 percent of females in construction had no more than primary level schooling, much higher than 56 percent (males) and 81 percent (females) for all sectors. Since a structured or conventional learning environment would unlikely be effective for them, an NGO (N1) was launched in 2006 to help marginalized and skills-deficient workers negotiate the labor market with a recognition that "the pedagogy needs to be different."

Table 7.2   Urban non-agricultural informal employment, India (percentage distribution by sector, 2011–2012)

Manufacturing	27.2
Construction	11.9
Trade (distributive services)	27.1
Street Vendors	*5.0*
Non-Trade Services	33.2
Transport	*9.1*
Waste Picking	*1.0*
Domestic Worker	*5.7*
Total	100.0

Source: Chen and Raveendran (2014, p. 10)

The NGO evolved into a social enterprise in 2011 to pursue an integrated model of economic mobility and social integration, to empower marginalized workers by creating an ecosystem built around training, employability, and employment. Training programs are designed to offer upskilling, assessment, and certification, to make workers employable. Pedagogical innovation in content creation includes "recognition of prior learning," which takes into account tacit knowledge of the worker's accumulated occupational experience, and uses it as a base-line for skills enhancement. It also incorporates diverse methodologies ranging from classroom and on-site training to e-learning portals.

To train adults with little formal schooling, time or patience, the enterprise consulted a US MNE for assistance. Drawing on research that demonstrated the effectiveness of learning-by-observing over learning by reading or from lectures, instructional videos and storytelling are used to train workers. These modules provide instruction on everything from new methodologies of building to cultural idioms of cleaning (see Section 6.2.1). Training is offered at counseling centers, schools, and multi-trade skill training livelihood centers. On-site "earn-and-learn" programs are designed to allow for the upgrading of skills without compromising work hours.

The enterprise works with private sector partners and governments. The government plays a key role, setting standards for curriculum and as a provider of contracts (through the Enterprise Skill Enhancement program). Employability of workers is also enhanced by incorporating productivity measures and occupational standards being piloted by the

National Vocational Education Quality Framework that identifies benchmarks for consistent individual performance for specific workplace functions. Employability is converted to employment by linking workers with potential employers one-on-one or through job fairs. The enterprise also maintains a database of its clients to track their movements and ensure their employability.

By 2013, more than 100,000 workers had been trained, and over 50 livelihood centers, 71 schools and 185 on-site training centers were established across 25 states in the country. Training was provided in skills ranging from bar-bending to welding not only in the domain of construction, but it had also expanded to the domains of engineering services, manufacturing, logistics, and wellness. In recognition of these efforts, the enterprise was named the "Most Sustainable Initiative" for 2014–2015 by the National Skill Development Corporation and it was chosen as the "Partner of the Year" by the Indian firm Godrej & Boyce in 2014.

Unlike most training providers, who are accountable to the firms that provide employment, this enterprise is accountable to the often undervalued informal workers, providing them with a sense of identity and limiting their exploitation. The database of workers' socio-economic profiles is used for their benefit, in helping them open bank accounts or register with industry specific welfare boards, such as the Construction and Other Workers Welfare Board, for insurance, health and maternity benefits, work tools, and housing loans. These services are designed to contribute to wage and quality of life improvements for the workers.

7.4.2 An Employment Portal for Informal Work

A third of urban informal employment in India is in various categories of non-trade services where employment is uncertain (see Table 7.2). Inspired by research which showed that job diversification is a route out of poverty, and that urban informal workers with strong social networks are more likely to succeed in creating job opportunities for themselves, an employee of an MNE quit his job to establish an enterprise (S11) that provides web and mobile platforms which aggregate and enlarge the information network in the marketplace for informal jobs. The enterprise connects employers with job seekers for positions such as office helpers, drivers, and cooks.

Originally, the idea was to develop a portal to strengthen the social networks among informal workers. The enterprise subsequently shifted its focus to an employment website to directly address the interests of both employers who seek to cut recruitment costs, and employees who seek to increase income and reduce commute time. The initial links the enterprise developed with NGOs and labor unions not only provided an in-depth understanding of local needs, but also generated enquiries and registrations of the first few hundred people.

After discovering that there were administrative and managerial limits to relying on other organizations, the enterprise began directly canvassing in lower-income localities and registering potential employees. They also started looking for potential employers – individuals and households, corporations and housekeeping services – by scouring local newspapers and websites for jobs ranging from domestic maids to security guards to data entry workers. Once the network reached 150,000 registrations, mobile phone and online registration were used extensively to further accelerate growth. The enterprise claims that those who have found jobs through its platform reported, on average, a salary increase of about 20 percent and a reduction in commute time by 14 minutes.

The revenue model is tiered and there are several free and paid models for both employees and employers. For employers, a basic model permits free postings of their positions and limited access to the database of job seekers. Employers have the option of paid services, which gives them full access to the details of the job seekers, pre-screening of applicants, and the promotion of the position using the web, mobile web, and SMS alerts. A recently introduced service permits employers to contract their employees out to the enterprise that will provide a no-cost replacement if a recommended employee leaves the job within two months. The workers have an option to sign up for job alerts, provided through agreements between the enterprise and all major telephone networks. As of April 2015, there were a million job alerts sent every month, 30,000 registered employers, and a net monthly addition of 20,000 job seekers.

The enterprise has expanded to many states in India, including Rajasthan, Bihar and Orissa, primarily through collaboration with NGOs. The plan ahead is to focus on building an ecosystem of employment services in India. Expanding overseas would require significant modifications to the service, as labor market conditions in the informal sector vary widely, along with differences in legal frameworks that govern occupations. In April 2015, the enterprise procured a minority investment of USD 10 million from a large global employment portal to expand telephony services and to develop mobile apps.

7.4.3 Enhancing the Cash Flows and Creditworthiness of Rural Informal Retailers

If accessing the formal financial network for those employed in the informal sector is difficult, it is also no less a challenge for India's many informal businesses. Informality is particularly prevalent in the retail sector; of the more than 14 million retail outlets in the country, only 8 percent are in the formal sector (KPMG, 2014). Barely 4 percent of the outlets are larger than 50 square meters, and most of them are mom-and-pop stores run by people with limited literacy, often in remote locations with limited infrastructure. It is these outlets which provide the crucial connection between the producers of various fast-moving consumer goods (FMCGs), a network of 80,000 wholesalers and 20,000 distributors, and the end-consumer. However, rural informal outlets face many challenges, including managing their cash flows and, by extension, their creditworthiness.

A European MNE (M43) in enterprise software and software-related services had been seeking to broaden its market beyond Fortune 1000 corporations, by taking advantage of the technological possibilities offered by cloud computing, mobile technologies, social media, big data, and the Internet of Things. The design of enterprise software used to be centered round the objective of enabling a corporation to profitably harness its internal functional capabilities with limited links to external organizations. However, the new technologies offer a means to bring together all stakeholders in entire industrial sectors, with electronic platforms or market places.

Since 2011, the MNE has been designing a cloud-based service connecting FMCG firms, distributors, wholesalers, all the way down to the informal retailer/grocer, along with other industry stakeholders including banks, telecommunications service providers, original equipment manufacturers (OEMs), and value-added service providers for real-time information exchange. For FMCG companies, the service provides retail sales data, which generates real-time market insights to be instantaneously reflected in production and advertising. For distributors, the service ensures timely deliveries, and digital payment allows efficient management of cash flows, purchasing and procurement. While these stakeholders access the service on a subscription basis, retailers are offered a POS device costing about USD 100. The device has a tablet-like screen, with a user interface that relies on icons rather than words, a keyboard and a printer. It allows retailers to manage their sales process, from billing and printing invoices to creating purchase orders for distributors. Most importantly, the software also allows the retailer to provide documentation for lines of credit, and banks can monitor and profile retailers to ascertain creditworthiness.

The system and device design are an outcome of visits to more than 250 retailers, 50 distributors and 100 FMCG companies across India. The MNE identified various personas and categories of users to iterate a prototype solution for users to integrate into their existing processes. Despite extensive research, during the pilot implementation the MNE discovered that small shopkeepers were reluctant to adopt the POS system. The reluctance reflected a desire to avoid paying the legally mandated value-added tax (VAT) on documented sales. Upon identifying this concern, the MNE modified the device, not to endorse tax-avoidance, but to give the shopkeeper discretion over the information available through the device.

The MNE owns just the software and the network, but it also designed the hardware to ensure that the device is modular, inexpensive, and easy to maintain and fix. At the time of the interviews, efforts were underway to redesign the POS device to serve as a micro-ATM which, with biometric verification, permits minimal deposits and withdrawals by the retailer, who will function as a remote banker. The MNE was also in discussion with the Unique Identification Authority of India to permit the transfer of benefits from the government through the micro-ATMs, using Aadhar identity number-linked bank accounts.[3] Although still experimental, the micro-ATM offers great potential in an ecosystem where shopkeepers are crucial sources of credit in small towns and rural areas. For the MNE, the success of the service in India would also see deployment in other countries, such as Brazil, Indonesia, or South Africa, where the retail sector has a similar structure.

7.5 INTRODUCING RENEWABLE ENERGY

Higher energy use is associated with well-being, but India's energy consumption is lower than what incomes would suggest (Khandker et al., 2010). The lower consumption is explained in part by uneven access to energy. In 2011, 93 percent of urban households and 55 percent of rural households had access to electricity (Government of India, 2013b). These numbers conceal the issue of unreliable supply, resulting in the per capita electricity consumption in rural areas reaching just a third of that in urban areas. Sources of energy also differ considerably between rural and

---

[3] India's biometric national identity card numbers.

urban areas. For instance, only 13 percent of rural households relied on modern fuels (Liquefied Petroleum Gas or kerosene) for cooking, whereas 82 percent relied on biomass (firewood, wood chips, or dung cakes) (Ramji et al., 2012). In the urban areas, the corresponding figures were 71 percent and 19 percent respectively. Biomass is typically burned in conventional stoves, which are not only an inefficient use of fuel but also a major source of indoor air pollution and a health hazard (Khandker et al., 2010). In rural areas, women and children collect fuel, taking time away from education and other productive pursuits. The following cases are innovative efforts to provide sources of alternative energy to improve the quality of life of users.

7.5.1 Solar Systems as a Catalyst for Social Change

An engineer trained at an elite Indian institution visited the Dominican Republic while attending a US graduate school. Struck by the use of solar lights in rural areas, he shifted the focus of his graduate research from rural electrification to decentralized solar systems. He began seeking ways to deliver a technologically effective energy solution that would simultaneously serve as a catalyst for social change. Upon graduating, he spent time in rural India and Sri Lanka to understand, more as an anthropologist than as an engineer, how people live without electricity, and concluded that the poor need collaborators rather than sympathy. He established a social enterprise (S22) in 1995 to (1) develop holistic energy delivery systems for the poor, not merely technologies, (2) install an after-sales service network to ensure maintenance and to build long-term relationships with users, and (3) develop consumer credit services to finance renewable energy users. The objective was also to disprove what he considered were myths: that the poor cannot afford or maintain sustainable technologies, and that sustainable technologies remain commercially undeliverable.

Using solar photovoltaic (PV) modules, the enterprise provides electricity for indoor and outdoor use (solar lanterns, home appliances, inverters, and water pumps). The enterprise also developed customized solutions, such as a portable system that could fit onto a cart, designed for users who are often evicted from their dwellings with little time to gather their belongings. Service centers provide assistance within 24 hours, and training is provided for users to trouble-shoot basic problems. Finally, the enterprise operates a service called "lights on lease," involving a local micro-entrepreneur operating solar charging stations and delivering charged batteries on hourly leases.

While the provision of energy can be a catalyst for socio-economic change, the founder is convinced that viewing the poor as a sales opportunity may neither improve their quality of life nor lead to their "inclusion." Instead, energy alternatives must encourage savings and asset creation among the poor. Further, the financial model must be flexible and accommodate the reality of irregular wages, and permit micro-payments. A vegetable vendor who cannot make a monthly payment is often able to make daily payments depending on the diurnal variation in her business.

The enterprise has formed financial relationships with banks as well as farmer cooperatives to develop credit structures that allow solar system purchase and credit-building. The enterprise typically acts as an inter-mediary, or a guarantor, for those who make some kind of down payment, and pay installments over a three- to five-year period. As banks find it difficult to collect micro-payments, the model provides opportun-ities for micro-entrepreneurs to collect payments when delivering leased batteries. Crucially, three major investors, who provide "patient" capital, finance the enterprise and are willing to accept a lower rate of return.

By late 2015, a decentralized, community-based distribution network of 46 energy service centers across six states reached remote com-munities, serving 300,000 users. Each center is assigned a territory for the marketing, sales, and installation, and is staffed by locals who perform frequent follow-up visits, provide word-of-mouth recommenda-tions and build trust-based relationships.

Working with external collaborators, including other NGOs as well as technical and financial providers, the founder set up an innovation lab specifically for underserved populations. He also established a foundation in 2010 as a public charitable trust that envisions a socially sustainable society by: (i) identifying the needs of underserved communities, and understanding the role of sustainability and energy in these communities; (ii) supporting and funding innovative and sustainable solutions, includ-ing pilots and prototypes, that positively impact well-being, education and livelihoods, and alleviate poverty; and (iii) sharing knowledge and building capacity to foster an ecosystem for technology, finance, entre-preneurship and policy. The foundation furthers its goals in India and beyond by encouraging and training local micro-entrepreneurs. It works closely with the enterprise to ensure that they share the common agenda of developing the alternative energy market.

7.5.2 Micro-franchises for Renewable Energy

A group of TSEs from the US and the UK established an enterprise (S18) to make "modern energy simple, affordable, and accessible for everyone." They noticed that, for those earning less than USD 10/month, energy is especially expensive, amounting to about 30 percent of income to cover lighting and the charging of mobile phones. Moreover, energy options for the poor – typically kerosene or candles – are often dangerous.

The enterprise's mission is to satisfy energy demand with "radical affordability," a concept characterized by three features: initial purchase price, the cost of ownership, and flexibility of expenditure. The concept combines social and economic missions; the former rests on the conviction that limited access to reliable energy affects not only the daily quality of life but also the ability to break the cycle of poverty in the long run, and the latter drew inspiration from observing an entrepreneur in rural Tanzania who used a solar PV panel to charge her customer's mobile phones. But combining these missions presented a challenge in India, partly because of the mistrust of energy providers (as a result of previous failures by both the state and corporate actors), and partly because of the diverse circumstances of BOP populations (some have irregular power access and even own refrigerators). The founders also realized that having a solar PV product and financing was insufficient, and a complete after-sales service model was also needed.

Thus, in 2010, the enterprise developed a small solar PV electricity generation system at a retail price of USD 400. When the founders realized that traditional lenders were unwilling to invest in or provide credit to small users, a financial model was developed to allow payments in installments. After a small down payment, energy is provided on a "pay-as-you-go" model, and each payment counts toward the total purchase price of a system that provides energy for at least ten years. The system was also designed to accommodate the financial model. A tamper-proof, system-integrated microcontroller and user interface regulates the function of the systems based on proof of payments by users who are otherwise not considered bankable. Similarly, a cloud-based revenue management software solution, accessible through SMS and over the Internet, permits payments using mobile phones, thereby reducing the transaction costs of micro-payment collection from a diverse user base.

What differentiates the system and its financial model is the fostering of village local entrepreneurs and technicians as micro-franchisees. The entrepreneurs act as evangelists and are usually chosen from the communities to build on existing relationships of trust. The entrepreneurs seek and collect applications which are then reviewed using a credit approval process developed by the enterprise and then verified with identification documents. Following approval, a certified solar technician trained by the enterprise installs the system in the user's home or place of work. The technicians are recruited and trained within the local areas, to provide local support to the communities and to generate employment.

Having tested the model in Karnataka, operations have expanded into eight districts in the state of Uttar Pradesh. In 2013, the enterprise decided to outsource production to two partners, one in Bangalore and another in China. By April 2015, the enterprise had 250 full time employees and nearly 350 village entrepreneurs servicing 9,000 customers. As a result, 120 metric tons of CO_2 emissions were saved and 100 megawatt of clean energy was produced. The enterprise received an Impact Award from the US Overseas Private Investment Corporation as a recognition of excellence in renewable energy.

In 2014, the enterprise raised USD 4 million internationally to expand its user base to 50,000, which is projected to reach one million in five years. The US office of the enterprise, and a multinational team of directors and advisors, allow access to international financial support from various private foundations, social finance, corporations and international organizations.

7.6 WHAT THE CASES TELL US

The case studies highlight the various roles stakeholders play in the constitution of the hybrid domain. Of the 14 cases of innovation, two are initiatives of MNEs, four of NGOs, and eight of social enterprises (including three TSEs). In two cases (7.3.3 and 7.4.1) the initiatives began as NGOs before becoming social enterprises, whereas in Case 7.5.1, an initiative that began as a social enterprise also launched an NGO (foundation) later to support its social mission. If social enterprises dominate our cases it shows that this is a preferred organizational means of combining social and economic goals. However, the shifting and combining of organizational forms also indicate that there is, at least as yet, no established organizational arrangements guaranteed to generate social innovation. It is noteworthy that the state has not taken the initiative in any of these innovations; indeed, if it had, perhaps social innovation in the hybrid domain would not be necessary. Yet, many of the innovations do involve the state in some capacity, especially as a provider of policy guidance (Case 7.4.3). Two MNE-led initiatives partner with the government at the national or the state levels, while also collaborating with NGOs or other private sector entities. Therefore, the state remains relevant for cross-domain collaboration.

Of the four NGO-led initiatives, three collaborate with MNEs, one with the government while another with a social enterprise. The work of the NGOs attracted funding from international foundations such as the Gates Foundation, the MacArthur Foundation and Hivos Foundation. All the NGOs operate across multiple Indian states, usually after starting off in one state. Three operate in other countries in either Africa or in Asia, and a couple of initiatives in medical diagnostics are likely to expand to other countries in the near future. Among the eight social enterprise led initiatives, there is one instance of a partnership with an MNE, one with an NGO, one with the government, in addition to which there are two instances of collaboration with either government-owned or -backed banks. There are also a couple of instances of collaboration with universities which, in one case, resulted in collaboration with an MNE. Three of the social enterprises had raised money from private investors overseas, while two raised money from foundations.

The range of stakeholders and the collaboration among them show the domain flexibility of the hybrid domain. Further, the ability of the stakeholders to combine resources, whether financial, organizational or technical, from different parts of the world, highlights scalar flexibility. In Chapters 8 and 9, we explore more evidence that supports these concepts.

8. Domain flexibility

This chapter and the next are devoted to features of the hybrid domain outlined in Chapter 3. In this chapter, we focus on domain flexibility, which refers to the blurring of boundaries between the public and private domains. We examine various hybrid activities that straddle the domains, and discuss how they evolved over time. We begin with the limits of CSR in producing desirable outcomes in terms of social impacts, then discuss the challenges of merging economic and social missions and achieving shared value creation. We then examine how learning through collaborating across the traditional boundaries of the public and private sectors facilitates social innovation. Finally, we explore why some NGOs are transforming themselves into social enterprises, and discuss the rise of hybrid organizations – those that combine, in one form or the other, for- and non-profit sub-entities in their organization.

8.1 FROM CSR TO SHARED VALUE CREATION

The 2004 Indian Ocean earthquake and tsunami, which left at least 7,000 people dead or missing, was a catalytic event for CSR initiatives in India. An estimated USD 200 million was donated by American MNEs alone, and launched an era in which MNEs began working with communities, the state, and civil society organizations. Good intentions do not necessarily translate into social impacts, however. Today there is widespread frustration expressed by both for-profit and non-profit sectors about the efficacy of CSR and the desire to generate greater impact through these activities.

8.1.1   The Limits of Goodwill

Both for-profit and non-profit organizations question the limited impact of CSR and how it can adversely affect the sustainability of social missions. An interviewee at an American MNE in ICTs (M18) provided the following insights.

Generally, most CSR projects **are one-off engagements because the pot of gold runs out**. *What inclusive growth does is to go beyond CSR and have something sustainable. That is why you need a sustainable business model in place ... which carries it forward.*[1]

The one-off nature of many CSR initiatives is compounded by the lack of necessary expertise among corporate employees, as they tend to move in and out of CSR sections through internal job rotation. A founder of NGO (N1) in education observed how job rotation prevents learning as follows:

They [corporations who sponsor CSRs] don't internalize [their previous failed experiences] to change their systems ... **if they don't internalize it, they will again do the same kind of grant which you've already [told them] doesn't work**.[2]

A social entrepreneur in energy (S22) has also seen how job rotation can lead to a badly designed CSR initiative, hindering opportunities for micro-entrepreneurship and adversely impacting livelihood sustainability.

One company came [to us] and said, "can you do 1,000 houses for us ... by March 31st, I have to show this [to my superiors], and the money has to [be spent] ... And I might not remain in this position." **They would have been happy doing 1,000 houses for free, [but] that would have destroyed the renewable energy market there** *... [They have] not thought about the sustainability.*[3]

Some corporations have learned from their previous experiences and are trying to address the issue of sustainable impacts. For example, an executive who works for the CSR section of an American MNE in ICTs (M39) made the following statement:

We don't believe in cutting checks ... because I don't believe [it] drives sustainability. *That is the biggest problem with CSR of the past ... give checks to an NGO and say – go do it. But then once [the project] is finished you'll have the NGO come back asking for more money – you're not building capacity to make it self-sustaining. At the end of the day, the company is going to go away, [and] the government cannot keep sustaining ... everything has to be self-sustaining.*[4]

---

[1] Interview, July 2, 2012.
[2] Interview, June 4, 2012.
[3] Interview, July 12, 2013.
[4] Interview, June 17, 2014.

CSR initiatives fail to deliver lasting impacts particularly when there is no "ownership" of solutions once the funding dries up. An executive in an American MNE in medical devices (M14) observed:

> *[CSR] is not sustainable in my view because it needs ownership. You could always take clean drinking water units and install them in a couple of places. It is great. The first month is great ... [but] who is going to maintain it? Who's got skin in the game?*[5]

Another representative from an American MNE in electronics (M11) offered a similar view.

> *CSR is less about a company's ability to provide funding, but a lot more to do with **the community's ability to integrate and develop ownership in order to sustain it**. Otherwise, it becomes a one-time one-off, ad-hoc help. It's a flip of a coin if it will succeed, and if it succeeds, it is a news item.*[6]

To date, neither CSR, nor NGOs, nor the state have been able to drive sustainable impacts. As a result, a series of experiments are underway, through business-CSR synergies that pursue shared value creation, collaboration, hybrid organizations and social entrepreneurship, to explore how best to sustain social missions.

8.1.2   Shared Value Creation: Opportunities and Challenges

Generating shared value by creating business-CSR synergies is being attempted in various ways. A representative at an American MNE (M39) in ICTs, who runs its CSR section, commented that "*[c]orporate sustainability is all about ... an intersection between what's good for business, and what's good for society ... that's the sweet spot.*"[7]

A social entrepreneur (S29) who works as a mediator and facilitates for-profit/non-profit partnerships observed that they encounter a spectrum of corporations that, on the one hand, aggressively seek synergy between their businesses and CSR initiatives and, on the other, seek to maintain a clear separation between them. She summarized the spectrum as follows:

> *I've worked with all kinds of companies ... [from] ones that are **purely philanthropic in their approach to avoid any kind of reputational risks**. An investment bank told us, "look we've got such a reputation bashing across the*

---

5   Interview, June 22, 2012.
6   Interview, June 14, 2012.
7   Interview, June 17, 2014.

*world that we [cannot be] seen to be taking advantage of even our CSR funds ... we're consciously choosing to take the purely philanthropic approach." At the other end of the spectrum companies are **looking at using CSR strategically for brand building purposes** to understand markets, to test their products, to engage with customers in the BOP.*[8]

Those who actively seek out synergy between their for-profit and non-profit activities do so to combine social and economic missions for dual sustainability. An executive working for an American MNE in ICTs (M12) described how CSR can serve as a pilot program and a laboratory to learn how things work on the ground and what the needs are, in meeting the deficiencies that arise from inadequate infrastructure.

*Some of the work that we are doing with remote education and remote healthcare started out as CSR ... We gave about 10 million dollars rebuilding four villages that got flooded a couple of years ago, then we applied the solution at a local hospital and in the local schools. That's where the intersection (between CSR and business) comes in, and it gives us great learning. **CSR is a lab in itself.***[9]

Similarly, a large European MNE (M35) in nutrition and chemicals stated that *"**CSR activities give us a platform to really understand the market** ... it helps you understand what it needs right now."*[10] Thus, in emerging economies, knowledge earned through CSR can be highly relevant to business interests, as social needs are the sources of latent demand that can inspire innovation.

However, corporations are aware of the challenges in creating shared value. For one, the links between business and CSR are often indirect at best. For another, as elaborated in Chapter 6, even revenue generation, let alone profiting, from the consumer segments that CSR-related activities engage with are unrealistic. According to an American MNE (M8) in energy, CSR could only serve as an ad-hoc source of knowledge and, while it may be useful in educating employees, it normally does not connect directly to R&D.

*The experience of going to tribal villages, looking at environmental sustainability ... it is very much part of our thought process in terms of – how do we come up with off-grid solutions which are as scaled down [in price] as possible. But **the internal communication** between CSR initiatives and*

---

[8]   Interview, July 1, 2014.
[9]   Interview, June 20, 2012.
[10] Interview, June 13, 2014.

*research **does not happen formally**. It is not like an everyday story that a CSR event becomes a product line.*[11]

A previously mentioned executive in an American MNE in ICTs (M39) also observed that *"[t]**here can never be a direct connection (between CSR and business)** ... from a business angle, CSR would not make any immediate sense, but (only) from a long-term perspective."*[12]

The same executive discussed how the current synergy between business and CSR largely lies in harnessing already existing intra-corporate resources, skills and expertise (in this case, ICT) for CSR activities, but not the other way around.

*Would I spend my CSR money on building toilets? It's probably better for some [other] organization in the health industry [to do that] ... Where I can get involved is ... **putting sensors to measure water levels and usage** to figure out where to put new toilets. I can offer something.*[13]

Some corporations opt to maintain a complete separation between CSR and for-profit activities, fearing reputational risk. An interviewee at a European MNE in pharmaceuticals (M38) claimed, *"You must remember that big pharma used to be seen ... or maybe, is still seen, next only to big tobacco."*[14] The strict separation was, in part, due to a potential conflict of interest, but also in part due to the challenges in developing synergy between the economic and social missions:

*We do not encourage, [nor] try to get any benefit from CSR. **It's 100% CSR and we stay away from getting anything back indirectly** ... There is basically no unintended benefit or any other conflict of interest. We absolutely don't feed anything we get from CSR into [our] products or anything like that, and not because it's illegal, but we don't get the information that is adequate for what we do [in business].*[15]

8.1.3   The Socially Sustainable Business Model (SSBM)

One outcome of CSR reform is a new business model called the social sustainable business model. The SSBM is characterized with longer time investment horizons and accepts lower profitability, thereby achieving social missions with built-in business sustainability. This model is also

---

11   Interview, June 12, 2012.
12   Interview, June 17, 2014.
13   Ibid.
14   Interview, June 12, 2013.
15   Interview, June 17, 2014.

distinctive from an ethical business model, which primarily focuses on an internal code of conduct and working conditions for employees.

A CEO of a pharmaceutical MNE with its own foundation became inspired after attending a lecture by Professor Prahalad. He urged his executives to consider options that are *"more sustainable from the business-end rather than from our philanthropy-end,"* according to an executive (M54). Recognizing the limits of charity in making impacts, the corporation began with an exploratory idea in 2006–2007 for accelerating access to medicine for the poor combined with some business growth in the mid to long term.

> *[The Chairman] encouraged and challenged some of our internal leaders to think whether we can really do it. Do we have the kind of internal capabilities and capacities? Do we have the internal will? … because that's more important than products and services, **to have leaders who can really think differently**, and really try and make a difference both for the organization and the society.*[16]

The same interviewee described SSBM as neither a traditional for-profit nor a non-profit model.

> *No, it wasn't charity for sure. We already give several millions of doses for poor people through international donor agencies or civil society [organizations]. It was not CSR, we are very sure. CSR means you give money and forget it. [But] it was not a [conventional] for-profit model. SSBM is … **built on strong foundations of values and ethics but, at the end of it, there was a tangible [business] delivery**.*[17]

The SSBM seeks the balance of three considerations: immediate social impact, business growth in the medium term, and future market potential.

> *The immediate [social] impact [is] … can you really help these poor people gain access to medicine and healthcare? [Another is] can you also deliver on division business growth in the medium term, and last, not the least, future market potential of growth opportunities; more than 50% of the global population will be in the middle-income group living in the developing countries. So, even from a corporate strategic growth point of view, **you cannot afford to miss the opportunity** as the market dynamics are evolving, thus setting your conditions to continue to be a lead sector player in pharmaceuticals.*[18]

---

[16] Ibid.
[17] Interview, July 22, 2013.
[18] Interview, July 16, 2013.

The model adopted by this corporation provides training to improve the skills and knowledge of physicians in rural India. Designing SSBM, however, is costly. As explained by the same executive, for most pharmaceutical firms, larger cities in India offer more than ample business opportunities, whereas cultivating customers in small towns or villages is difficult.

> **There's so much untapped [demand] even in the top and the middle of the pyramid.** *That usually becomes a bit of conflicting priorities. Organizations with limited resources probably would then try and maximize their returns on a shorter time frame, rather than doing something that takes you about 5 to 7 years to get your financial returns.*[19]

SSBM has been adopted by social entrepreneurs, and particularly among those who focus on service delivery. One social entrepreneur (S22) in the renewable energy sector discussed how his work achieves environmental, livelihood, and corporate sustainability. *"It is not about just selling and forgetting. This is a regular service industry to keep."*[20]

8.2 LEARNING THROUGH COLLABORATING

Our survey results suggest that collaboration is an important vehicle for learning "emerging market" contexts and needs. Among 158 respondents, a little over a third of the MNEs surveyed (35.4 percent) had worked with NGOs to conduct R&D. The majority has worked with one or two NGOs (77.8 percent), but two respondents claimed that they have worked with up to 12 NGOs. Larger R&D facilities tended to have more NGO partners.[21] Those MNEs that conducted R&D for BOP/MOP markets in the last two years are more likely to have collaborated with NGOs to conduct product/ service development.[22] MNEs that used NGOs as sources of knowledge for R&D were predominantly focused on the Indian market.[23] Four out of five (79.5 percent) MNEs that introduced BOP/MOP products outside India had

---

[19]   Ibid.

[20]   Interview, July 12, 2013.

[21]   Correlation coefficient = 0.546 (0.000).

[22] X^2 statistical test with $p = 0.004$. Conversely, those MNEs without interests in BOP/MOP markets were less likely to have collaborated with NGOs (X^2 statistical test with $p = 0.002$). Among those MNEs who responded that their partnerships are long term, three quarters had concrete plans to introduce BOP products in the next two years.

[23] X^2 statistical test with $p = 0.002$.

R&D collaboration with some kind of extra-firm partners,[24] and they preferred global NGOs over local NGOs.[25]

8.2.1 Varieties of Collaborative Arrangements

We categorize commonly observed collaborative arrangements between for-profit and non-profit social innovation stakeholders (see Table 8.1). The role of the NGO ranges from distribution and community access to market knowledge acquisition. In some cases, NGOs help identify local vendors/suppliers/service providers and distribution channels for foreign MNEs.

Table 8.1   Illustrative examples of collaboration in the hybrid domain

Objectives	Examples	Roles of stakeholders		
		MNE	*NGO*	*Others*
Distribution scale-up	Affordable medical devices	Global distribution, R&D	Training, maintenance	SE (R&D, local distribution)
Cross-sectoral synergy	Online education	Technological platforms	Service/content development	State (contracts)
Last-mile solutions	Financial services, telemedicine	Service architecture	Service architecture, training	Banks (credit), hospitals, SE (software)
Reputational synergy	Services for urban slum dwellers	Funder (CSR)	Financial/digital literacy	SE (micro-credit)
Rural empowerment	Improving agricultural productivity	Buyer, product development	Institution-building, training	Cooperatives
Catalytic	Renewable energy	Funder (CSR)	Buyer, funder (foundation)	SE (new business model)
Experimental	Logistics, training, affordable diagnostics	Research methods, R&D	Pilot studies, training	SE (R&D)
Cross-domain synergy	Digital certificates	Technological application, "know-how"	Problem identification, "know-who"	State (contracts)

Notes: SE = social enterprises; other key collaboration may also involve universities and research institutes

Source: Developed by authors based on qualitative research in India, 2012–2014

[24] X^2 statistical test with p = 0.003.
[25] X^2 statistical test with p = 0.048.

8.2.1.1   Collaborator selection

Both MNEs and NGOs are highly selective in developing collaboration, as they face considerable risks in protecting their reputations. A representative of an American MNE in distribution (M10) commented on the process and criteria of choosing an NGO as follows:

> *There are a couple of ways ... One, we do our own research, our team in the US as well as in India.* **The NGO has to be registered here for 5 years, with a certain number of clientele.** *And we should not be the only partner to ensure that the NGO is sustainable.*[26]

With 3.2 million NGOs in India, they vary from the large and established, to the miniscule with no track record. The same executive (M16) commented:

> *Of course there are clear guidelines [for partner selection]. We do not work with politically motivated NGOs or religious NGOs. We look at a whole lot of documentation before we engage with NGOs.* **Many NGOs are just mom-and-pop organizations,** *so we have to be very careful.*[27]

Another representative of an American MNE in ICTs (M1) shared a similar experience:

> **There are a lot of different NGOs out there.** *And many of them would suggest that they have the capability ... and it turns out that it's a guy and his cousin and they tell us they can do blah-blah and they have connections ... And then, you do a little digging and realize that they are clueless and don't have any of the things they say they do. So, you politely back out.*[28]

MNEs are not the only partners concerned with protecting their reputation. When asked about what leads to success, an executive from a European MNE in chemicals (M35) explained that NGOs are equally concerned about their reputations.

> *For partnership, to begin with ...* **it has to be a win-win situation** *... especially when you are working with NGOs or semi-government organizations,* **they also have to be very careful about their [own] reputations** *... and are very, very careful about what ultimately their farmers are going to be exposed to ... or whether they should be taking part in the trial. So it has to*

---

[26]   Interview, June 13, 2012.
[27]   Interview, June 28, 2012.
[28]   Interview, May 28, 2012.

be a win-win for both and ... is really very project specific. I really do not have one answer for that.[29]

Collaborator selection by MNEs rarely takes place with an open call for proposals.[30] As a representative of an American MNE in medical devices (M14) commented, *"if I go online today and put out a RFP, lots of NGOs will claim to have the right capacity."*[31] A representative of another MNE added, "in most cases, [NGOs] don't come to [MNEs]."[32] Instead, collaboration typically begins with MNEs conducting problem identification and, in the process, seeking a knowledgeable local partner. Some encounters are serendipitous, and occur by the virtue of overlapping interests. An executive from an American MNE in medical devices (M14) described their arrangement in which the NGO provides training and maintenance for the device produced by the MNE.

> *The way we met [our NGO partner] was in one of the conferences on rural health in the US two and half years back ... it's important to be present in all these places. And we happened to meet ... we happened to talk, found a lot of synergies ... then discussions kept going over a year and a half because it was something **completely new for us, and completely new for them** [to sign an MOU].*[33]

CSR relationships can serve as a basis for product/service development collaboration. An NGO in livelihood development (N22) described a collaboration with an MNE, which began as a CSR. The project initially began as a response to the 2004 tsunami, but evolved into a sustainable livelihood project that offered training for women on how to process and package raw cashews, as well as the basic skills, such as arithmetic, reading, and writing, to run their own businesses. Five years later, several groups have become self-sustaining, for whom the MNE functions as a buyer. The NGO (N22) described positive outcomes as follows:

> *That [project] has been a very good example of **innovation and [an experience] working with companies**. There was a lot learning, now we're trying to take it to other companies and scale it up.*[34]

---

29 Interview, June 13, 2014.
30 In our survey, about a fifth (21.3 percent) of the respondents reported that NGOs were identified through prior CSR relationships, for another fifth (21.3 percent) it was the outcome of a referral, while another fifth claimed that the relationship was initiated by the NGOs.
31 Interview, June 22, 2012.
32 Interview, June 12, 2013.
33 Interview, June 22, 2012.
34 Interview, June 18, 2014.

CSR may function as a useful testing ground for future collaboration. After getting to know a local NGO in education (N4) through CSR, an American MNE in ICTs (M12) began collaborating with the NGO for product/service development for distance education. An executive in the MNE emphasized previous collaboration and synergy with NGOs.

> *Credibility, trust and word-of-mouth – that's number one – if you have done work with them in the past, either independently, or in partnership or if you have heard good things. The second is **synergy between the two organizations**. Are they filling gaps you have in your portfolio and repertoire? Are you providing them access to a larger base of customers? Are you giving them the opportunity to scale? To me, that's probably the most important thing – synergy overrides everything else. And, of course, they check us out and we check them out – whether you have really done this thing before, or can we jointly make investments together and build this capability?*[35]

An executive in an American MNE in ICTs (M16) characterized the process of developing collaboration as relationship-building, instead of shorter-term, project-based alliances.

> *You need to see that the NGO is really interested in the same kind of thing. Both organizations have to be **on the same wavelength**. We need to understand each other before doing it ... Some NGOs start with one program, [then] want us to collaborate further. So it is an ongoing process. I think it is **relationship-building** ... not just doing something and getting out.*[36]

8.2.1.2   The division of labor
Perhaps the most straightforward and conventional for-profit/non-profit collaboration is a division of labor among stakeholders, with each contributing a distinct set of skills. A European MNE in chemicals (M35) described a partnership where an NGO completes the supply chain.

> *I wanted to see if we [MNE] could join hands with them [NGOs] ... and that worked very well for us. **We (MNE) brought in the products, ingredients, technical inputs, and some business-to-business networks, and the NGO knew the rest of the chain.** It was a very good combination. It was a great [experience] learning and understanding the end-consumers.*[37]

Another case demonstrates a division of labor among three partners; an American MNE (M19) in medical devices partnered with an NGO (N25)

---

[35]   Interview, June 20, 2012.
[36]   Interview, June 28, 2012.
[37]   Interview, June 13, 2014.

and a social entrepreneur (S19) to deliver a newly developed, affordable product. The rationale for this collaboration is described as a matter of scale. For the social entrepreneur (S19), the MNE functions as a global distributor for the product they developed. *"The partnership with [MNE] is a non-exclusive distribution partnership ... We sell products [to the MNE] at a certain price, and then they resell through their global sales force. That is the agreement."*[38]

The MNE (M19) interviewee described the relationship between the MNE and the NGO as follows:

> *The deal with our NGO partner works like this: **NGO can't scale [up the operations] by themselves** ... So they came to us and said: okay, you have got the engineering prowess, the manufacturing bandwidth, the "know how" to develop this and drive efficacy, so why don't you partner with us? We are working with them to scale it in terms of manufacturing, in terms of numbers, provide them the products at the right price point ... And **we can use their model of deploying the training, monitoring, and providing service on an ongoing basis** to all these primary healthcare centers in India.*[39]

This particular case, however, is notable as it was the MNE that had been approached by the NGO in search of technological solutions to the problem that the latter had identified. The NGO founder's (N25) perspective was similar to his MNE partner:

> *We are a tiny organization ... and they **have this massive global network** for manufacturing, distribution, sales, after-sale service. What we wanted was a partnership whereby they do the stuff they are good at – manufacturing and distribution – and we do the stuff that we're good at – training and program work. So, we saw an opportunity to scale up really quite dramatically ... What we should be doing is **looking for opportunities where we can reach transformative scale** by working with ... **either very large NGOs or government agencies or MNEs**. Those are the three options that are available [to small NGOs like us].*[40]

Moreover, this NGO initially approached the CSR section of the MNE. But the CSR section head saw a business potential and introduced the NGO to the R&D team. This example suggests how, in some instances, collaborative work can serve as a vehicle to generate dual-goal projects that fuse social and economic missions.

---

38   Interview, June 25, 2013.
39   Interview, July 5, 2012.
40   Interview, September 17, 2014.

*I met the head of the corporate foundation ... After I talked with her for a while about our initiative, she said that she felt like that was **more appropriate to be discussing this with the people on the commercial side.** She introduced me to the team and they were really ready to have a conversation with somebody like us.*[41]

8.2.1.3   Resolving information asymmetry

Our survey showed that, among those MNEs that collaborated with NGOs, 52.6 percent used NGOs as a source of knowledge for R&D projects. As Table 8.2 shows, the reasons offered included 1) NGOs have the best data, 2) NGOs know the MNE's needs based on previous collaboration; 3) only NGOs have the relevant data, and 4) working with NGOs improves corporate image. NGOs helped identify local commercial partners and innovation opportunities, and provided access to markets.

Table 8.2   Results of the questionnaire survey: MNE–NGO collaboration

Share of respondents (MNEs) who used NGOs as sources of knowledge	52.6%	
Reasons for collaborating with NGOs (multiple responses)	NGOs have the best quality data	30.2%
	NGOs know what we need, given previous collaboration	20.6%
	Only NGOs have the data needed	17.5%
	NGOs helped improve corporate image	17.5%
Outcomes of collaboration (multiple responses)	NGOs identified local vendors/ suppliers/service providers	31.4%
	NGOs provided access to markets	27.0%
	NGO identified opportunities for innovation	17.5%

The prevalence of information asymmetries in contemporary India is acknowledged by MNE and NGO. As the founder of an NGO in public health (N3) quipped, MNEs face challenges in accessing the knowledge necessary for social innovation.

---

[41]   Interview, September 14, 2014.

MNCs directly going to the community and trying to understand the needs is out of question. That's just not possible. That's when NGOs can play an important role.[42]

An executive at an MNE in ICTs (M1) corroborated the same point from his perspective.

*Sometimes, you might need a partner when you are entering a community. It's not easy to just walk into a slum and say, hey, tell me about your problems. The reason we often have NGOs or other partners, like hospitals or whatever, ... is that in our experience, **we are almost hopeless at having an actual impact**, of having a reasonable useful outcome, if you don't have somebody from the inside, or some kind of partner, that can carry it forward.*[43]

In this particular case, the MNE was seeking an avenue to access communities for deep context learning. For some MNEs, collaboration is an important means of inducing disruptive innovation. As an executive in a European MNE in electronics said:

*In order to think [about] disruption, not just [from a] technology point of view, we also **need to work out business models** – to penetrate these markets means working with the entire ecosystem, having partners – academic, non-profit organizations, NGO, micro finance, panchayat (local self-governing body).*[44]

Learning for social innovation through collaborating is a relatively new phenomenon. In particular, foreign MNEs were reluctant to work with NGOs, or local social entrepreneurs, for product development in the past. One social entrepreneur (S26) observed that collaboration was not only new but was also unthinkable until recently, even within the private sector.

* **Ten years ago, absolutely not** ... if I had gone to [an MNE] and said this [about a social innovation opportunity], it would be without any substantiation. There is no data, no information available for the business model, nothing about the devices ... Today fortunately, there has been enough learning and various funding, grants, various [CSR] initiatives ... today, there is more awareness.*[45]

---

42 Interview, June 15, 2012.
43 Interview, May 28, 2012.
44 Interview, July 27, 2010.
45 Interview, June 23, 2014.

An executive from an American MNE in ICTs (M39) observed the changes in perception across both for-profit and non-profit sectors:

> *The corporates see NGOs as predators, or people who just siphon off money, and NGOs look at corporates as the big bad people who are killing the environment or whatever. But I think that's changing ... we've been working with NGOs for the last 15 years ... maybe initially we had some problems, but after that actually ... **I have rarely seen a situation where the government or an NGO has turned me away.***[46]

A founder of an NGO in public health (N3) also reported recent changes; he has been approached by many MNEs in medical devices, ICTs and energy.

> *What I see [among] the MNCs, overall, there **is a thrust to contact NGOs and look at the problems of the poor. There is some awareness about it.** And it's a new thing ... [only in the] last 2 [or] 3 years. [But] it's happening ... which I think is a good step forward. So let us seize this opportunity and see how we can make them be concerned. I am open for that, instead of criticizing everything.*[47]

An executive in an American MNE in medical devices (M14) who collaborated with an NGO that conducts medical device maintenance and training observed that working with other organizations is indispensable in achieving social and economic missions.

> *You can't just say, I am going to develop a bunch of products, sell them and then see what happens. Our vision is to make a significant impact on infant mortality ... And it's impossible to take this path alone. **We need to have partnerships, because the equipment will go there and it won't get used** ... as I have seen, not just in India, in Vietnam, in Indonesia, in Thailand, in Ghana.*[48]

The founder of an NGO in public health (N3) used hand sanitizers as an example of potential synergy. Hand sanitizers are highly useful as a means of disinfection in the environment where water is scarce. But innovation in affordable hand sanitizers would require technical expertise that largely resides outside the NGO sector.

> *[MNEs] have such good marketing mechanisms ... can we reach out [to the communities] about healthy foods and health initiatives through them [in*

---

[46]   Interview, June 17, 2014.
[47]   Interview, June 15, 2012.
[48]   Interview, June 22, 2012.

*areas where] they would have vested interest? [For example,] soap companies did research on the importance of hand washing. They are promoting their own soaps, which is very good, at least better than nothing. But again, soap prices must come down, which is definitely possible. **Hand sanitizers are still very expensive and out of reach for the poor**. A lot of government schools have no running water, so sanitizers are the only way ... These are the issues which we will need to work out [with MNEs].*[49]

Our survey findings corroborate the importance of shared goals between MNEs, particularly foreign MNEs, and NGOs. A statistically significant difference was observed between foreign and domestic MNEs; foreign MNEs are more likely to involve extra-firm partners in R&D activities than domestic MNEs,[50] and they are also more likely to source knowledge from NGOs, foundations, and social enterprises,[51] as opposed to Indian MNEs who are more likely to name the Indian government as an important collaborator. Furthermore, more foreign MNEs cited "different goals and evaluation criteria for outcomes" as challenges in collaborating with NGOs. These findings suggest that MNEs, especially those new to the market, seek various strategies to compensate for their relative lack of familiarity and distribution channels in the Indian market, and face a greater knowledge gap, which translates into various collaboration challenges.

Social entrepreneurs also actively seek collaboration to compensate for their limited size and lack of internal resources. One social entrepreneur in the renewable energy sector (S18) emphasized the importance of collaborative work in making an impact.

*We – to be completely honest with you – had a few days of total meltdown – we could help five communities and spend the rest of our lives just working with them [on many things], or we can use our knowledge and specialization and help 100,000 communities, but only in one thing. Are we okay with that? It is a hard question, particularly when you are in these communities every day, like it is not easy to turn a blind eye to all the other things. After quite a lot of thinking we decided that [to focus on one thing] is probably the best use of our skills, but **work very closely with other NGOs that are servicing these communities. [Also] we do different things with quite a lot of corporates**, and have quite strong connections with academic institutions ... We are hoping to develop a research hub for access to energy in India as well. We*

---

[49]   Interview, June 15, 2012.
[50] X^2 statistical test with p = 0.013.
[51] X^2 statistical test with p = 0.026.

have just got some work done for a database with a grant from USAID and [a social enterprise] to develop a mobile phone app.[52]

This particular social enterprise was run by a TSE, who faced a knowledge gap locally; their strategy is to compensate for this deficiency by accessing knowledge and resources globally.

8.2.2   Collaborating with the State

Although the state may fail in delivering basic infrastructure (see Chapter 5), it still plays an important role in social innovation. State involvement is a prerequisite in social innovation in areas such as education, liveli-hoods, energy and health, in executing regulatory reform or offering large-scale contracts. As a representative of an American MNE (M18) commented, *"it's very fashionable to diss the government all the time, but actually if you approach the government and work with them in a very structured and partnership format, the government is really willing to work with you."*[53] The particular conditions of India also offer certain opportunities for MNEs to participate in social innovation. An executive in an American MNE in ICTs (M1) compared India and China:

> *The MNE relationship with the Chinese government is such that it's not easy to go out into the countryside and do development work … In India, nobody seems to care … In fact in India, it gets us kudos. The Indian government really likes [it] … And this is one of the ambassadorial things that we can do as a company;* **we are doing this work for the Indian common man and for the development of the country.** *And that buys us a certain amount of credibility or maybe little bit of goodwill from the government.*[54]

The same interviewee argued that government officials are fully aware of the difference between real deeds and the masquerading of good cor-porate citizenship, and that "kudos" will not be bestowed on the latter.

> *I mean, it's a rather mercenary way of framing it … but absolutely, I think most people in government also know the difference … the bullshit filter is there.*[55]

In some instances, NGOs serve as an intermediary between the state and the private sector. An MNE provided the example of developing an

---

[52]   Interview, June 25, 2013.
[53]   Interview, July 2, 2012.
[54]   Interview, May 28, 2012.
[55]   Ibid.

efficient and fail-proof system of digitizing, archiving and designing on-demand delivery of school examination certificates for students in a southern Indian state.[56] An NGO in education had identified a problem, and brought it to the attention of the MNE (M29). According to the representative:

> *It's really difficult for people in rural areas to obtain a copy [of these certificates]. And that's how the project essentially started. To me, it seemed like really a ridiculously simple problem. But, beyond that, [we had no knowledge of] what the nuances are, and that's when we found out how difficult [it is] ... Automating data collection [on the front end] is not difficult. But the [government] used to print out one set of certificates every year, these huge rolls of printouts, then they threw away the data, rebooting the system every year [and starting from] scratch ... And, there was concern that the data could have been corrupted ... what happens, suppose a person finds a mistake [in his certificate], then it becomes a newspaper article ... This was the problem that we* needed to solve. So *yes, sometimes **NGOs actually come with problem identification**.*[57]

The NGO identified the problem and brought it to the attention of the state, and sought a corporation that offered technical solutions. In addition, this particular NGO provided a high level contact in the government, which ensured that a credible opportunity existed for the MNE to work with the state.

> *NGOs brought in some of the knowledge of what exactly is happening on the ground. A lot of the data and knowledge were essentially, how to work with the government ... NGOs had the ear of the government and, almost always, it was a political connection. **Some had reasonably high, like ministry level contacts**. So they run [an idea] through the Under Secretary and the Secretary levels to get a sense ... if I (MNE) bring a solution, [will] the government be ready to fund? And that's when NGOs look out for [corporate] partners to see if there is somebody ready to take.*[58]

The NGO therefore provided know-how on how to work within the government, along with know-who, in the form of a high-ranking government contact. The MNE was not aware of the problem, and would have lacked the political access to get to the negotiating table with the

---

[56] These certificates are needed for admissions to colleges and for employment (especially government jobs).
[57] Interview, June 12, 2013.
[58] Ibid.

state. The MNE was responsible for the final negotiation, however. As the interviewee commented:

> *Once we were inside that room, with the Under Secretary, we were pretty much on our own. NGOs were really **useful in opening doors in the government**. But once they opened the door, you make your pitch and you do the hard work. And the NGO takes a percentage of the money that we bill the government.*[59]

In this particular case, the NGO acted as a business partner and an intermediary, while the MNE was sought as a collaborator who could develop technological solutions.

8.2.3 Challenges in Collaboration

Challenges in forging and maintaining cross-domain collaboration are many. First, MNEs and NGOs do not come with the same expectations over their respective roles and functions. Expectations are multifaceted, and go beyond success as measured by financials, the rate of adoption, or the delivery of goods and services by the initially agreed division of labor. They include, for example, expectations over effort dedicated to day-to-day operations and the time frame of development, implementation, and completion. A social entrepreneur (S29) who works as an intermediary in developing partnerships between for-profit and non-profit organizations had the following observation about the challenges faced by NGOs.

> *First, quite a few **NGOs have never dealt with companies** – this is the first time and they don't quite know how to go about it. Second, NGOs have traditionally worked with foundations and are now realizing, **companies are all about expectations** – companies expect NGOs to engage with employees, function in their area of operations, be more efficient and more transparent and send regular reports ... these are all impositions that NGOs will now have to start figuring out how to meet.*[60]

An executive in an American MNE in ICT (M1) was troubled by the tendency among some NGOs to confuse CSR with product development collaboration.

> *Basically, [NGOs] see us as **an engineering organization that can build some stuff and hopefully get it to them for free**. And then the idea of an*

---

[59] Ibid.
[60] Interview, July 1, 2014.

experiment that may not even work is a hard pill to swallow, if your organization is struggling to save peoples' lives … So it takes a fairly mature organization to understand the value in the first place.[61]

MNEs are comfortable in working with NGOs that are run by former corporate executives amidst a growing tendency of people with corporate backgrounds to make mid-career shifts to NGOs. The founder of an NGO (N5), a former corporate executive who is active in environmental conservation, made the following observation.

Invariably all the MNEs we work with say that they are comfortable with us for the sheer fact that I worked for many years at a MNE. I am able to understand how MNEs work [because] I've been on the other side of the table, so it is much easier for both sides, as compared to an NGO completely formed by people from the social work background … **Many NGOs emerging today that are founded by ex-MNE executives. MNEs will find it easier to deal with them.**[62]

NGOs claim that corporate expectations fail to take into account the challenges of program implementation and how field realities affect efficiency. According to the founder of the same NGO (N5):

A company will come up with the program structure and the **NGO would have to work on the ground and face reality.** *For example, in a slum project, a company would promise to commit X amount of money to give access to say 8,000 people. Well,* **the reality of any slum is that 30% migrate or are mobile,** *and there is constant influx and out flow … [which makes impacts difficult to track].*[63]

Another NGO founder in public health (N3) also observed that some MNEs suffer from unrealistic expectations over profitability.

[MNEs] write and contact … **probably thinking there are magical solutions, also profits, because of the volume in BOP** *… When they understand that it is a long process [and] it's not easy, there are no magical solutions, longer investments, and also they have to take risks … I think after initial efforts, [the BOP project] goes into cold storage … That's what I suspect … otherwise, they would have contacted [us] again and pushed it further … but this is a good thing at least, that they are thinking about it.*[64]

---

[61] Interview, May 28, 2012.
[62] Interview, July 2, 2012.
[63] Ibid.
[64] Ibid.

MNE counterparts also acknowledge that they must change their expectations to work successfully with NGOs. The executive from an American MNE in ICT (M1) offered:

> *And on our side, we have to compromise – what can we provide them with that are useful? Coming to an alignment and **getting expectations matched and still provide value from our side and from their side**, that's probably the hardest part. And I don't have a prescription for that.*[65]

A representative of an American MNE in ICTs (M38) with 15 years of experience in cross-domain collaboration characterized the challenges of collaboration as follows:

> ***I wouldn't call them tensions, but learning*** *… I wrote a business model on how you'll engage with the NGOs etcetera … don't expect reports to come in like this, they will work at their own pace, [or else] you would maybe want to fund your own programs etcetera.*[66]

The same executive (M38) emphasized the importance of merging expectations:

> *When we looked at which partnerships succeeded, and which failed, we figured out a very simple thing, irrespective of whether you even bankroll that NGO … First, **don't impose your ideas, your processes on another organization**. Yes, [as a company] we have to report back, and quarter on quarter, month on month, what we have and have not achieved, etcetera etcetera, but, less tensions if we agree up front how we are going to go about it. Secondly, it's important to have similar – you will never have the same – vision or goals. **I need to partner with an organization which has a similar ethos or objective in life**.*[67]

The divide over culture and practices between MNEs and NGOs is not the simple dichotomy often portrayed in the literature – of the efficient for-profit sector versus the inefficient non-profit sector. As the founder of an NGO (N25) commented:

> *I think there are plenty of NGOs that are small and incompetent and inefficient and slow to respond, and others that are ambitious and aggressive and move really fast … that's true in the private sector as well. **You could always have a mismatch in terms of the organizational culture** in addition to anything else that's going on with the personalities. We didn't have any*

---

65   Interview, May 28, 2012.
66   Interview, June 17, 2014.
67   Ibid.

*illusions about that, we were well aware of that working with MNEs and with universities. They're just **operating at a whole different timescale**. [As an NGO] we're used to moving really fast and delivering projects really quickly, so that didn't come as a surprise to us. That was never the big issue.*[68]

Second, the collaborators must co-own the projects. The previously quoted executive from an American MNE in ICTs (M1) elaborated on three aspects of a successful MNE–NGO collaboration; getting on the same page, dedicated efforts, and a buy-in.

*One of the things that is critical [for success] is **getting on the same page** [with the partner] … [it] is very important. The second piece is having a partner who is **dedicated to actually pushing the thing forward**. So, one of the things that often happens is that you get a partner who is very interested in you delivering them the product, but they really don't … they are all busy … they are massively overworked anyway and so it can be problematic to suggest that this is going to be more work on their part. And the really successful projects are the ones where the partners are bought in to the idea as well, and **willing to put their skin in the game**. And when that happens, then you really can get magical things happening.*[69]

Thus, while risk-taking may not be widely perceived as the strengths of NGOs, they increasingly face the risks of performance failure in collaboration, and the associated reputational and financial consequences. Corporations, by contrast, face a *modus operandi* completely different from what they are accustomed to, and must learn to cope with a new reality of cross-domain collaboration. The same executive (M1) observed that the crucial aspect of learning involves conceptualizing a mutually beneficial, yet implementable program for both the MNE and the NGO.

*You create a product with a particular target segment in mind, with our own good wisdom and experience of running programs for 13 to 14 years in the country. [And] we thought we knew our NGOs, we knew the rural areas … We tried to figure out why [some projects] don't work. [It wasn't the issue of] common goals and objective. Turns out, for some of the [stakeholders] … it **was not their priority area**. [Another reason is], there are issues with implementation models. Not everybody can take a program and run it in the way [we conceptualized]. They have to fit it into what they are currently doing. So, [the project changed] from my way to their way. **The humps that we had to cross, was [to go] from my way, to their way, to our way**.*[70]

---

[68] Interview, September 17, 2014.
[69] Interview, May 28, 2012.
[70] Ibid.

Learning through collaborating is therefore altering both MNEs and NGOs, and earning them invaluable experience in the emerging world of multi-stakeholder collaboration. This process is still very much in the initial stages, however. An American MNE in ICTs (M18) summarized the challenges and ambivalence about working with NGOs as follows:

> *Working with the NGOs, the jury is still out. I think **using NGOs as a means to do a proof of concept is okay**, but NGOs really are a one or two people kind of entity. If you had asked me the same question last year, I would have said – my vision is to create a federation of NGOs who will help me implement it all over the place. Now I am 180 degrees on the other side. NGOs aren't capable of providing a service for their own benefit, they lack professionalism and there are also significant tax implications ... And most NGOs are essentially do-gooders. Their heart is in the right place. They have the right ideas on how it can work in a specific environment, but they have no idea on how to scale.*[71]

The NGO sector remains divided on collaborating with the for-profit sector. Some NGOs acknowledge that MNE–NGO collaboration can potentially develop synergies that benefit the poor, while others remain ambivalent, and some are highly reluctant. The previously quoted founder of an NGO in public health (N3) offered the following observation and his position on the matter:

> *Good NGOs [are those that] understand the needs of the people at the grassroots level. We are all mostly activists, giving voice to the poor to meet their needs ... Of course, there are extreme left and right wing NGOs. [Some] left-wing NGOs would say **all MNEs are great exploiters**, [and they will have] nothing to do with them. I don't have that type of extreme position ... there are good MNCs also ... they have some concerns for the poor, so we work with them. There is nothing wrong [with that].*[72]

A representative of an NGO in livelihoods development (N22), who manages a number of corporate collaborations was cautiously optimistic:

> ***We have accepted that the private sector is a very important player if we want to achieve our goals and scale things up**. But that doesn't mean that we'll be compromising on our values or our programming framework. It is about getting the right match, the right kind of companies to partner with and we also believe there are many companies who will believe in what we believe*

---

[71] Interview, July 2, 2012.
[72] Interview, June 15, 2012.

in. So it's not that either they will have to compromise or we will have to compromise.[73]

Some NGOs find collaboration with for-profit organizations difficult, not necessarily because of their ideological aversion, but due to an unavoidable conflict of interest. For example, an NGO working on domestic workers' rights (N19) pointed out that, given their emphasis on rights-based issues, their missions are in conflict with for-profit entities.

> *So far, we have not had any continuous collaboration with any company. I had been on sexual harassment complaints committees of various companies, but that has not paved the way for them to do anything with us.* **We work on rights-based issues including rights of the workers, which brings about conflict of interest** *... and as long as it is rights-based issues, there are very few corporates that will come with us.*[74]

However, the same interviewee (N19) described her attempt to collaborate with an American MNE in ICTs (M1), which began after a chance meeting. When she expressed interest in introducing computer skills to the camp she ran for children in slums, the MNE offered to send volunteers to interact with the children and help with technology and skills issues.

> *I met [the corporate executive] through some ... I can't remember now how, but because* **I found him [to be] reasonably not controlling, and wanting to do research – which we also could benefit from, but [for which] we don't have the capacity, the people, or the money**. *So, I kind of placed this idea before him. It was also for their own research.*[75]

Opening the door for collaboration with the MNE gave the NGO a new perspective and the founder described the process as follows:

> *The intern started coming to work with us for about 2–3 months. He developed a very good design, mapping the slum. That whole process was new for us, and he was also very sensitive. I saw the women's faces and it was a new world for them. I said, very good, let them at least get the touch and the feel of these computers. Then I said –* **we have a lot to learn, so why not [proceed further] ... the idea slowly developed about user interface ... how technology can be made user friendly for domestic workers**. *We started as an experiment, matching maids with jobs.*[76]

---

73   Interview, June 18, 2014.
74   Interview, June 11, 2014.
75   Ibid.
76   Ibid.

This program, however, did not continue, partly because the proposed activity required a separate organization outside the expertise of both the MNE and the NGO involved. This and similar experiences with other MNEs frustrated the founder of this particular NGO. She attributes this frustration to the lack of immediate links between research and solutions.

> *We had a stream of research people who came ... mobile phone research, vocational skills research ... but again, **it turned out to be just research** ... Even when these researchers come from colleges, I often tell them that if it is going to go and sit in the cupboard and it is going to give you a PhD ... I'm sorry, because our women are giving you [their time], their contribution to you and if you are not going to act on it, then what is the use of research? So don't come and ask those questions ... but of course, they are all promises in the beginning that this research will help [in such and such ways] ... and I always dream in a small way, that these studies will have their impact [someday].*[77]

When there is a mismatch between the synergies sought by the MNEs and the needs of the NGOs, collaboration does not move forward. The founder of the NGO (N3) in public health described his experience of being approached by an American MNE in ICTs to develop a power-generating stationary bicycle for rural children. As much as the idea was well intended, the founder was convinced that it had little traction, as a bicycle that goes nowhere would not be readily adopted by the villagers even if it generated much needed electricity. The founder of another NGO (N24) in education described how some interests from the for-profit sector are at best divorced from, and at worst terribly incompatible with, the needs and interests of the people she serves.

> *IT companies think digital learning is going to transform education totally and pump our schools with a whole lot of digital aids and things, when the most important part of education in a school environment is relationship, bonding, understanding, values, character building. MNEs in food products want to pump all those food products to our children as a part of their promotional campaign. What happens after the promotion is over? I've been told – for example – we'll give you peanut butter. For a South Indian ... you can't have peanut butter with idly[78] and bread is much more expensive. **Definitely, we don't want to be guinea pigs.**[79]*

---

[77] Ibid.
[78] A savory Indian breakfast.
[79] Interview, June 23, 2014.

Thus, these sentiments suggest that mismatches between for-profit/non-profit interests generate fatigue and resentment among NGOs.

8.3 THE RISE OF HYBRID ORGANIZATIONS

New hybrid stakeholders are emerging in the hybrid domain. Hybrid organizations described in this section are unlike those in the literature in institutional economics. Albeit having the characteristics of neither "markets nor hierarchy" (e.g. subcontracting, firm networks, franchising, alliances), they nevertheless largely fall under the private domain (see Hodgson, 2002; Ménard, 2004). Alternatively, hybrid organizations in the past primarily referred to quasi-government organizations (e.g. state-run corporations, government contractors and public utility companies) (see Perry & Rainey, 1988). Today, however, emphasis is shifting to those organizations that combine social and economic missions, although no consensus exists on the definitions. Some view leveraged NGOs (see Section 3.3.3) as hybrid organizations, while others include social enterprises as a form of hybrid organization. For example, the Geneva-based Schwab Foundation for Social Entrepreneurship treats hybrid organizations as one category of social entrepreneurship. Such organizations constitute 44 percent of the Foundation's list of 260 social entrepreneurship organizations from around the world.[80]

Hybrid organizations described here are characterized by an organizational arrangement in which for-profit and non-profit entities co-exist to serve a social mission. In our interviews we observed various distinctive forms of hybrid organizations; some are *born-hybrid* organizations, while others are established sequentially. In some cases, a social entrepreneur may seek to establish a non-profit entity to access foundation grants and conduct product/service development while, in others, a non-profit organization may establish a for-profit technology

---

[80] According to the Foundation, hybrid non-profit ventures refer to non-profit entities established by entrepreneurs who seek cost-recovery through the sale of goods/services, or combine for-profit and non-profit entities to access funding from both public and philanthropic sectors. Other categories on the list are social business ventures (30 percent) – social enterprises in the for-profit sector which do not seek to maximize financial returns or prioritize wealth accumulation but, instead, reinvest profits in the enterprise to fund expansion of their social missions – and leveraged non-profit ventures (25 percent) – NGOs that actively partner with external stakeholders. Incidentally, 40 social entrepreneurs in India were included in the list.

firm to serve the techno-commercial needs of the organization and beyond. These hybrid organizations are increasingly acknowledged as new organizational models, and can diversify their revenues by accessing venture capital financing, impact investment, and foundation grants. Donor priorities and newly emerging social/impact investing are likely to be a factor driving organizational hybridity observed among social entrepreneurs.

8.3.1 Transitions from NGOs to Social Enterprises

Although not strictly hybrid organizations, we encountered a trend toward conversion from non-profit to for-profit entities (e.g. from an NGO to a social enterprise) in India. The reasons behind such conversions are many, including the need to generate sustainable revenues, and the increased expectations of greater financial viability. NGOs in India, as elsewhere, are increasingly being challenged on two fronts, economic accountability and social legitimacy.

> *[Now] we are a private limited company ... because we just found it too tiring to be a NGO. **I had to again and again prove my credentials** [with companies I deal with].*[81]

A backdrop to this statement is provided by the preference of an American MNE in ICTs (M18) to work with social entrepreneurs rather than with NGOs.

> *[Instead of trying to work with an NGO], the best way is to look for social entrepreneurs who want to run this as a business. **And that is something you can understand**, you pay them license fees. Money is what keeps them alive, so they deliver the service.*[82]

The social enterprise model appears to combine NGOs' existing social missions with an opportunity to build market credibility. According to the same NGO-turned social entrepreneur, NGOs lack credibility in the market, especially when dealing with corporations. In her experience, corporations did not lend their ears when she was operating an NGO but, as soon as she converted her organization to a social enterprise, she became an important client and customer. She saw more advantage in operating as a social enterprise while maintaining the same clientele and the social mission.

---

[81] Interview, June 8, 2012.
[82] Interview, July 2, 2012.

*[It is better to] be taken seriously in the market ... Now if I go back to [vendor x] today and say, I want [your service] to be in this form [to serve my client better], they listen to me, because I [too] am a paying client. As I said, it's not a huge difference between our activity [before and after the conversion]. **It's just a perception.** [But now] there is a listening capacity [in our business partners].*[83]

As NGOs expand their scope of activities from advocacy to implementation, including delivery of products and services, their engagement with businesses inevitably increases. However, it is important to note that social entrepreneurs do struggle, as the juxtaposition of their dual missions poses challenges in the field. A social entrepreneur in renewable energy (S22) described it as follows:

*I personally don't want to be in a branch manager's position, because I'd be hammered on profitability and on the mission ... **One day, you tell me mission, and then one day you tell me profits** ... [But] If you sacrifice on the mission, will you [generate] more revenues? It is actually not the case. The guys who are able, are able to increase revenues, reach the mission and are profitable.*[84]

As described in Section 8.1.3, the social sustainability business model is compatible for social enterprises that seek to achieve dual missions. Social entrepreneurship can potentially combine scalability with sustainability, in a manner that charity or NGOs cannot. As one social entrepreneur in the medical device field claimed:

*[U]nless somebody ... **makes a profit out of it, it would be uninteresting for them to run it continuously, on a scale.** You may run certain numbers, maybe five or ten, 15, 100 ... but it won't scale if it does not take care of the financial interests of the people who are implementing at the ground level.*[85]

The definition of social enterprises, however, remains elusive. For example, two medical device manufacturers with comparable product line-ups were adamant in claiming that their corporate identity was purely commercial for one and purely social for another. Others believe that it is a matter of priority, as well as a matter of degree. As one social entrepreneur (S26) quipped, *"we are for-profit, but not for profiteering."*[86] A social entrepreneur in renewable energy (S22) perhaps provided the

---

[83]   Interview, June 8, 2012.
[84]   Interview, July 12, 2013.
[85]   Interview, June 23, 2014.
[86]   Ibid.

best insight into the distinction between social and commercial enterprises, despite the blurred boundaries between them, by arguing it was one of prioritizing stakeholders over shareholders.

> *What were the criteria [for the social enterprise]? ...* **For me, the stakeholders are number one.** *Is it actually providing value to the stakeholder? My shareholders are the last. But they will benefit, only when it goes from the [poor, rural customers] ... [to] the technicians, my manager of the local office, then our regional manager, the manager, the management, so everybody ... is on the same page. Only if the [customer] is happy, then everything else is right.*[87]

To this entrepreneur, the distinction between social and commercial entrepreneurship is particularly clear when considering how they approach India's government mandated "inclusive development" differently.

> *For us, inclusiveness is ...* **making underserved ...** *from unserved to served* **in many ways, multiple ways** *... Our definition of inclusiveness involves a sustainable, holistic, intervention. Is this a market intervention? No, it is a holistic intervention for people [who need to be served].*[88]

While some NGOs are averse to for-profit activities (see Section 8.2.3), many social entrepreneurs argue that market discipline can reinforce, rather than dilute, their social missions. One interviewee (N1) claimed that better efficiency meant improved effectiveness in delivering the social missions.

> *[Today]* **we are accountable to our clientele.** *My clientele pays me. I don't do anything [for] free ... [but the service we provide] is highly subsidized ... [as a client] if you expect a delivery of service, I can't be playing around.*[89]

Finally, agility, or the ability to capture opportunities and reach out to stakeholders in a timely manner, is another potential advantage of social entrepreneurship. An entrepreneur (S17) in the business of disseminating health and nutrition information, that was otherwise unavailable in India, describes the different priorities and timelines of NGOs.

> *[NGOs and foundations] just don't move as fast as we do ...* **We are a start-up, we have an opportunity to capture, we have a fixed timeline to do**

---

[87]   Interview, July 12, 2013.
[88]   Ibid.
[89]   Interview, June 8, 2012.

it, we've got limited resources, but we've got to capture that opportunity ...
I sometimes get exasperated ... I show the data to NGOs and foundations
with budgets for maternal health and HIV education, and say "Look, two
years ago, [our clientele] was 30 people a day. It's 30 people a minute." ...
Then I'm like, "Great, if you guys are ready too, we will shoot on Thursday.
We'll get working on the scripts," and they're like, "Whoa, we've got to go to
a Committee and the Committee's got to release something, and then we've
got to do a review process."[90]

In sum, sustainability, promoting self-reliance, and agility are three
features that distinguish social entrepreneurship from charity, CSR and
NGOs. In addition, the complexity of achieving the dual economic-and-
social-mission is leading to the growth of "hybrid" organizations.

8.3.2   NGOs Established by Social Enterprises

A social enterprise (S22) established a foundation after 15 years in
business in renewable energy (see Section 7.5.1). The objective of the
foundation is to use the revenues generated to benefit the clientele, by
supporting activities on problem identification.

Why should we have a foundation? ... We were building an ecosystem,
experimenting [on the solutions] ... [but] we are also being very selfish ...
the money that is generated [by the clients] should be used for them ... And
everybody [organizations] was coming to us with a solution, and we were
trying to fit the problem to the solution, without realizing what the problem
*was ... so we said, **can the foundation be a collector of problems**? We have*
partners with solutions ... technology, finance, market linkage partners ...
[The foundation] supports these efforts through grants, using the hard equity
of the people.[91]

Another example is a micro-credit corporation, which established an
NGO to help women and children in urban slums (N18). The for-profit
entity has been in operation for two decades, whereas the non-profit
entity was established a decade later by the wife and a US-educated
daughter of the CEO. The microfinance company provides small loans to
poor working women in 24 states with 2.5 million beneficiaries. Whereas
the company operates 450 branches and has 4,700 employees with a
ground staff of around 3,500, the NGO is far smaller, with 70 dedicated
staff, and provides healthcare, education, and livelihood support. The
NGO strengthens the financial and health backbone of the microfinance

---

[90]   Interview, June 21, 2013.
[91]   Interview, July 12, 2013.

beneficiaries by using the branches and field staff of the company to offer complimentary services such as financial literacy, scholarships, renewable energy and specialty healthcare (e.g. eye care, dental care) programs. According to them, the *"for-profit can gain and the non-profit can work with them to help them with their business and also help those customers grow."*[92] The NGO works to solidify the reputation of the for-profit entity.

> *[The for-profit arm] is really getting the benefit of the reputation of caring for their customers. We as an NGO don't really care. We just want to help people, we don't gain anything from them thinking great about us.*[93]

Simultaneously, a corporation with a good reputation can also offer reputational capital to a civil society organization. Resource sharing between the for-profit and non-profit entities further contributes to the effectiveness of the non-profit entity. According to the founder of the same NGO (N18):

> *If you talk to any other NGOs, I can guarantee you **the biggest issue is mobilization** [identifying participants] ... they have to build a reputation [to gain acceptance by the community] and that is a struggle ... Mobilization is not our issue because the microfinance staff pick and get those women to come ... which most NGOs don't have the money to do, and are wasting most of the funds.*[94]

Therefore, contrary to a widely held assumption, it is not always civil society organizations that contribute to the legitimacy and acceptance for corporations; the reverse is also possible. When reputations are mutually reinforcing, synergy develops between for-profit and non-profit activities. Taking the case of their renewable energy program run by the above-mentioned NGO, the interviewee emphasized:

> *There's a tremendous synergy between what you do inside the foundation and then having outside companies give you things like solar lamps, you're killing multiple birds with one stone. You're [nurturing] the [micro-credit funded] entrepreneurs, giving them opportunities, and your knowledge of where entrepreneurial talents are in the community ... [can be] used as a channel to distribute new technologies.*[95]

---

92 Interview, June 11, 2014.
93 Ibid.
94 Ibid.
95 Ibid.

Thus, although economic and social missions are often viewed to reside at opposite ends of the spectrum, there is a greater recognition for complementarity and overlaps that can be exploited on the ground.

8.3.3 The Robin Hood Model

A commercial enterprise in the Global North has established a social enterprise (S4) in the Global South, adopting the so-called "Robin Hood model," which was popularized by the Grameen Bank Eye Care program. The program was designed as a tiered pricing model based on the client's educational level by getting them to choose eye charts in symbols, a native language, and English. Two physicians, who returned to India in 1999, after training and working in US hospitals, founded a hybrid organization with a geographically-tiered pricing model providing teleradiology services for hospitals. This enterprise uses the revenues generated by providing teleradiology services for US hospitals to provide the same services at a far lower rate to Indian hospitals.[96] Thus, revenues generated by services provided in the Global North largely subsidize services for the underserved in the Global South.

> *We charge the U.S., we charge Singapore. We don't charge poor hospitals, and poor patients in India. In order to have this model work, we need to own the technology* ... *We look at it as a social cause* ... *not as CSR so much as it's our responsibility. We have a solution for the needs of India. We must therefore use it optimally. Perhaps we are also blessed, we don't need to make profits from India* ... *For us, we look at [India] more just as* ... *what good can we do, and we can make it sustainable and slightly profitable* ... *5% profitable, it's great.*[97]

The goal of the organization is to deliver a higher standard of diagnosis and care to patients in rural/semi-rural and underserved areas in Asia. Using the same technology platform used for their US clients, the organization established relationships with rural hospitals to provide radiology and other services. Being physicians themselves, the founders paid attention to the format of the reports generated by the system, and rigorously tested their service within the medical community. To overcome reluctance among doctors to move away from familiar software systems, they constantly adapted the platform to suit local constraints and contexts. Recently, the organization has established rural telemedicine and training centers in collaboration with healthcare providers in the

---

[96] Interview, July 12, 2012.
[97] Interview, July 10, 2012.

Indian states of Karnataka and Madhya Pradesh, as a first step toward a national network.

8.3.4   Corporations Established by NGOs

Some social enterprises are established by existing NGOs that seek to generate revenues to sustain their social missions. This model appears to be particularly suitable for organizations operating in the affordable medical device field, where IP ownership is involved for potential revenue generation while ensuring access to grants from private foundations through having some kind of non-profit status. An NGO (N25) in Bangalore established a for-profit entity that generates revenues by licensing the IP owned by the NGO. The NGO in turn uses the revenue for training, monitoring and evaluation activities. The founder's rationale was three-fold: operational independence that shortens response time, operational sustainability and, finally, IP ownership that feeds into the other two.

> *If we had really good medical devices, we could sell them directly rather than trying to convince donors to pay for them. It offered a way to get these devices into places where they were needed,* **without having to wait for somebody to write a check** *... [And] we wanted this company to be really focused on efficiency and cost effectiveness and cover all their own costs. We didn't want to create something which is going to be a liability, my Board of Directors would never agree to that anyway. So it had to be* **a separate stand-alone entity. We own all the IP** *... at some point in the future, we would benefit financially through a small revenue stream that comes from the sales of equipment.*[98]

Another example comes from a newly emerging area of CSR consulting. A venture fund financed by an entrepreneur in ICTs in India established a non-profit organization, within which a for-profit consulting section was developed to advise corporations on their CSR activities. This type of consulting capacity is expected to grow with the newly enacted law on mandatory CSR (see Section 3.3.2). The need for effective collaboration exists for both for-profit and non-profit organizations, as companies must seek partners to implement projects to comply with the new law, whereas NGOs seek new resources to sustain their social objectives. The head of the consulting firm (S29) described the gap in networks between the for-profit and non-profit sector as follows:

---

[98]   Interview, September 17, 2014.

*We did fairly extensive research and found out that a large number of NGOs on the ground, and a large number of companies and individuals, are very keen to engage with the social sector, but don't have the ability to do it on their own ... **companies don't have the networks, the expertise, the patience or the ability to really reach out to social organizations and form long-term relationships.** So, we were set up to facilitate the partnerships between those who have resources and those that need the most.*[99]

These intermediaries bridge otherwise vastly different objectives and expectations between for-profit and non-profit organizations, and help design programs, enhance NGO capability, and offer tools for assessment.

*It's very difficult to find NGOs that can meet the expectations within a certain time frame, within certain budgets. We essentially bridge the NGO's capability or [help] build it up, for example, by providing them with **survey tools for community need assessment, and using the tablet to improve data collection and accuracy.***[100]

Therefore, these emerging intermediaries are functioning as a catalyst in forging cross-domain collaboration.

8.3.5 Joint NGO–Corporate Set-up and Collaborative Polygon

The joint NGO–corporate organization, one that truly has parallel operational features, is by no means common, but they do exist, and are an intriguing phenomenon of intra-organizational hybridity. An example of a hybrid organization is a foundation established with a specific purpose of operating a social enterprise in solar energy (S18). In their words:

*[T]he way that we are set up, we are **an Australian charity that wholly owns a for-profit Indian entity. [And] we are incorporated in India as a for-profit business.** All of the profits – the few that we will make – will be re-entered as dividends into the charity, and the charity can only re-enter those as investment in the organization. It fits the laws here in India, but also fits the laws in Australia.*[101]

Another example is a group of nested organizations that alternate between the for-profit and the non-profit sector. A social enterprise (S13)

---

[99] Interview, July 1, 2014.
[100] Ibid.
[101] Interview, June 25, 2013.

evolved into a collaborative polygon, a network of 13 entities. The organization originated with micro-credit operations and subsequently branched out to related services to villages, such as financial services (remittances, insurance, and savings), business development (local value-addition, cost reduction, productivity enhancement, alternative market growth, and local institution-building). Some are run as for-profit social enterprises and some are run as non-profit organizations.

> We call ourselves *a Triad Strategy* ... *[and partnerships] have been one of our strengths, what we call a collaborative polygon. It can be multiple partners in each of our work, especially in business development services as well as in institutional development.*[102]

Business development in many sectors, in reality, goes hand in hand with social development which, in turn, is linked to the need to facilitate income generation, education and training, and local institution-building. As such, social and economic missions are fused at their roots, and organizations that became specialized in one mission in the past are increasingly tracing their tracks back to cover the other mission.

8.4 CONCLUSION

This chapter demonstrates various forms of organizational transitions and blended missions that are enriching the hybrid domain. First, although clear distinctions exist between business and CSR initiatives, a measured blurring of the two activities was also observed. Second, some MNEs emphatically keep business and CSR activities separate and independent, claiming that it is important that their business objectives don't influence charitable activities. However, others are exploring synergies between business and CSR, and seeking ways to fuse knowledge that used to reside in different sections of a corporation. Third, various partnerships exist that cross for-profit and non-profit boundaries in the ways social innovation, organizational division of labor, and financing are coordinated. Evolution of organizations is also observed; CSR is increasingly being leveraged, the business model is changing, some NGOs are being converted to social enterprises, and various hybrid organizations are emerging. Fourth, social enterprises are key stakeholders of social

---

[102]   Interview, June 15, 2013.

innovation in the hybrid domain, as they combine economic sustainability (through revenue-generating activities) with social mission sustainability, in a manner that prioritizes stakeholders over shareholders. Finally, hybrid organizations are emerging in various combinations to balance social and economic missions within organizations. They include transitional (from NGOs to social enterprises), R&D/IP-driven, geographically tiered (e.g. the Robin Hood model), and networked forms, and organized to overcome both public- and private-sector constraints in delivering merit goods.

9. Scalar flexibility

In this chapter, we turn to scalar flexibility of the hybrid domain, and demonstrate how stakeholders for social innovation cross scalar boundaries in the hybrid domain. Scalar flexibility refers to the way stakeholders combine local solutions with global actions, and bridge scales by marrying territorially based knowledge and resources with transnational access to technology and financing for social innovation. In this section, we discuss the transnational features of social enterprises in India, and the underlying motivations behind TSE, before concluding with the financing of transnational ventures.

9.1 GLOBALIZING SOCIAL ENTERPRISES

India has drawn globally-minded and globally-mobile entrepreneurs in general, but increasingly it is attracting those who seek social impacts that go beyond economic gains. TSEs are part of the hybrid domain in contemporary India in sectors where social and economic values intersect, such as health, renewable energy, and education. They are emerging as important stakeholders in social innovation in the Global South. With their capacity to identify transnational social opportunities, TSEs are seeking to scale up and transnationalize their operational and organizational capacities.

Various transnational features are prominent in social entrepreneurship in India. The overwhelming majority (87 percent) of social entrepreneurs we interviewed fell into one of the following three groups with transnational ties.[1] Nearly three-tenths of the social entrepreneurs we interviewed belonged to a growing group of non-Indians from the Global North relocating to India seeking social entrepreneurship opportunities. Most had few connections to India prior to arrival. Some had worked in the Indian subsidiaries of foreign MNEs for a few years before launching

---

[1] The remaining 13 percent of the social enterprises involved no transnational founders. Our discussion of local social entrepreneurship is kept at a minimum, although their role is not insignificant.

their enterprise, while others had come directly out of universities in the US, or the UK. The second group was smaller than the first group (about one-fifth of the interviewees) and consisted of those who were second- and third-generation overseas Indians,[2] who relocated to India primarily to seek opportunities in social development. Although second- and third-generation overseas Indians have family ties and cultural exposure that the first group lacks, they are effectively outsiders in India. The following quote from one such social entrepreneur is typical of this group:

I was born and raised in the US. **I came to India in a very real way, as a blank slate** *... [Besides] I never really worked in development, I had no idea what it was. I just came with an intention. So, I really had to learn on the fly and observe.*[3]

The third group was returnee Indian founders (about two-fifths) who, unlike previous generations that stayed back in the Global North after advanced education, opted to return home to launch businesses and do so with strong social missions.

The three groups have in common their experience in attending elite institutions in the Global North and belong to the same cadre of professionals who otherwise become commercial technology (argonaut) entrepreneurs,[4] academics, or executives in MNEs, rather than those in the traditional development sector, such as NGOs or the state. TSEs come with considerable understanding of technology, and simultaneously share the social missions with the development sector. However, given their backgrounds, the solutions they develop and the technologies deployed in these solutions are distinctive and reflect their particular knowledge base. One social entrepreneur in telemedicine radically changed the emphasis of technology use, from sophisticated diagnosis to primary care, by drawing on her transnational experience.

There are lot of benefits of cross-cultural exchanges *... having trained and worked in the U.S., I felt the Indian medical system was very hospital based. Everyone was investing in hospitals and bigger hospitals ... but 90% of medical conditions don't need a hospital. Your skin lesion, your little eye problem, your diarrhea, asthma, your broken bone ... I am a super specialist*

---

[2] We chose not to use the term non-resident Indians (NRIs) as it generally refers to any person of Indian origin living outside India. Our focus involves non-Indians and Indians living in India with transnational links.

[3] Interview, July 20, 2013.

[4] See Saxenian (2006) for the definition of argonauts.

actually, but increasingly, I feel in India we are just missing the boat on primary care, and telemedicine is ideally suited for it. A lot of the tele-medicine programs in India didn't take off because they were in hospitals [where doctors are attending emergencies and operations] ... It was a great marriage for telemedicine – understating technology, and after working in the Indian system and having seen the US system where physician primary care is so important.[5]

TSEs play a catalytic role in devising solutions that combine globally sourced technologies with social opportunities in the Global South. They combine "insider" advantage of on-the-ground field knowledge, with an "outsider" advantage of identification of technological and business solutions.

9.2 THE ROLE OF UNIVERSITIES IN THE GLOBAL NORTH

Elite institutions in the Global North play a significant role in inspiring the new generations of TSEs. For example, MIT nurtures research interests of faculty with various initiatives. The Tata Center for Tech-nology and Design trains entrepreneurs and engineers to invent solutions for resource-constrained communities in India and the Global South. In addition, the Deshpande Center, established in 2002 by Gururaj Desh-pande, an argonaut entrepreneur, offers grants to increase the impact of MIT technologies in the marketplace. The Media Lab hosts an "imaging café" that brings together academics, entrepreneurs, and venture capital-ists interested in optical technologies. Such initiatives expose faculty and students to a combination of technological and entrepreneurial chal-lenges. Thus, for instance, in the areas of health engineering and informatics, a handful of faculty members developed a mobile phone-based open-source platform for medical data. One American entrepreneur in medical diagnostics (S8) who was previously pursuing a Ph.D. in computer science at MIT described his experience as follows:

*[In the] third year [of] my PhD ... [I was] looking around and trying things. I ended up ... just helping out with ... an Android app ... it was like a volunteer research group. It wasn't anyone's full time research, but on your free time, people would meet ... graduate students, **mostly from Harvard and MIT** in computer science, MBA students, doctors in the community, designers*

---

[5]　Interview, July 10, 2012.

... We were about 20 people, it wasn't that big ... And the whole idea was to bring healthcare to low resource areas ... with mobile phones.[6]

Harvard Business School (HBS) predated MIT in developing an initiative for social enterprises in 1993, as a stream within its MBA program and as a specialized executive education program. Since 2000, HBS and Kennedy School of Government co-sponsor an annual student-run Social Enterprise Conference that draws over 1,000 participants. Stanford University launched Stanford Biodesign program, which has become a model in teaching the process that combines technological and medical knowledge with entrepreneurship. Since its inception in the early 2000s, it has added international partnerships with Mexico, India, and Singapore. The program for India began in 2007, thanks to the friendship between a Dean at Stanford University and a minister in the Government of India. Every year, it has brought a handful of Indian nationals to the US for a six-month stay at Stanford, followed by a six to 18 month residency in India. While the US program includes NRIs, the Indian nationals are mostly trained and specialized in a single discipline, and are intimately familiar with on-the-ground issues. The program is designed to broaden the scope of their expertise, while fellows across programs learn from each other in social settings.[7]

Subsequently, there was a marked expansion of graduate programs that link engineering, medicine, and entrepreneurship beyond the elite institutions in the past decade. In 2003, the Stanford Biodesign program initiated the Biomedical Engineering Innovation, Design, and Entrepreneurship Alliance (BME-IDEA), a network of universities with interests in hosting programs for biomedical engineering design and entrepreneurship. Today, BME-IDEA includes 103 programs in major institutions in North America, along with 29 programs in Europe and Oceania. A book co-authored by Stanford faculty entitled *Biodesign: The Process of Innovating Medical Technologies,* was published in 2010 by Cambridge University Press and has become a foundation module for these programs.

At this particular juncture, it is predominantly elite US institutions that serve as seedbeds of TSE, providing inspiration, legitimation, and sponsorship.[8] An NGO founder (N25) who launched a transnational social enterprise observed:

---

6   Interview, June 6, 2013.
7   Interview, October 15, 2014.
8   There is a conspicuous absence of similar programs in other parts of the world. Although our interviews indicated that local elite universities in India play

*The message that's getting out there is … if you are a graduate of a business school, you don't have to go work for a consulting firm or go work in Wall Street, you can start your own business and **be financially successful and also change the world**. That's really compelling to a lot of idealistic young people who want to make money but don't want to go work for some evil corporation.*[9]

The TSE we interviewed relied on faculty mentorship, particularly in initial stages, in developing social networks in India. One entrepreneur (S8) described his advisor's role and influence as follows:

*… **you get a mentor assigned in Harvard Business School**. [The faculty] was basically like a co-founder [for us] very early on … helps us a lot with things … to get his friends or … It's hard to do a start-up … we never ran a company before … so someone has to vouch for you, that's really import-ant.*[10]

Another transnational social entrepreneur (S24) also shared with us a similar experience:

*me coming from an academic background … from academic institutions … there was a lot of support from Stanford and from Berkeley … my Ph.D. advisor … a collaborator and a co-founder of [social enterprise]. **None of this would have happened without him and without Berkeley support** … absolutely I mean none of this … without the opportunities to be in positions to learn [from] what other people provided me, there was no way I would have been able to do what I did.*[11]

The entrepreneur described how he was introduced to his mentor's father-in-law, who ran an NGO in India. The mentor introduced him as a student with some interesting ideas, and eventually the NGO became a partner organization once he founded the social enterprise.

We pitched our ideas to them, and they were generally open in giving us a shot … we made the most of that opportunity.[12]

Another social entrepreneur in logistics (S23) was supported by MIT's Deshpande Centre, which provided the initial seed grant to conduct a

---

a limited role in explicitly educating social entrepreneurs, they more typically facilitate start-ups by operating incubator facilities.

9   Interview, September 17, 2014.
10 Interview, June 6, 2013.
11 Interview, July 20, 2013.
12 Ibid.

feasibility study, links to MIT faculty to jointly analyze data, and contacts to crucial local partners in India. According to the entrepreneur:

> *Even though I was gung-ho about just hitting the ground running … **a discipline was forced onto us by people [with] more experience** … The professor and his graduate student at MIT looked at the data, and they were able to see a huge impact. They used some very simple examples that we can make up to 33%–35% impact on [the adopters'] bottom line … which was like amazing. That's big. That could get them into another economic class almost. That drove the creation of our organization.*[13]

Thus, his entrepreneurial hunches were validated and supported by rigorous data analysis performed by the professor. A final observation on the role of faculty mentors is that, while the nationality and ethnic backgrounds of TSEs themselves varied, their faculty mentors invariably involved at least one non-resident or second- and third-generation Indians. Clearly, these faculty members provided the most useful support on the ground, as they come equipped not only with knowledge of the society, but often offer crucial social networks otherwise unavailable to the TSE.

9.3 LOOKING FOR IMPACTS, PRACTICE-ORIENTED RESEARCH

Why would a young person from an elite institution in the Global North turn to social entrepreneurship in the Global South? An entrepreneur (S37) who quit a promising career as a NASA engineer to launch an enterprise for water monitoring systems in Africa and in India told us how his experience as an intern at *Engineers without Borders* during college shaped his interest. He described the generation of Millennials as follows:

> *We're after one thing, impacts, social impacts, and big impacts. I guess one thing I can think of with respect to our generation is that, **we are too impatient to wait for a couple of decades**, work in the bureaucracy, and move up the ranks before we see impacts. And we are maybe somewhat arrogant but really believe in our ability to make an impact. And you can make a much bigger impact in these areas where people's needs are acute.*[14]

---

[13] Interview, July 15, 2013.
[14] Interview, July 19, 2015.

Another TSE from the US (S8) described his rationale as the strong desire for societal impact winning over the excitement of conducting research and pursuing an academic career.

> *We were doing cutting edge medical research ... I was working on these really high-end medical imaging devices, on the algorithms ... brain imaging and all sorts of things. The problem, though, is that ... I mean a few of us realized that ... [only] a few countries would actually have one [of those devices]. For **most of the rest of the world ... there is no way to really make an impact**.*[15]

A similar sentiment was echoed by another entrepreneur (S16), a second-generation Indian who grew up in the San Francisco Bay Area. He too once considered a career in academia. He also identified with a path defined by technological start-ups, such as *"the Google's and the Microsoft's and the Facebook's of the world."*[16] Yet, he was more interested in using his technical expertise not for commercial but for social causes.

> *[with] these companies in Silicon Valley ... I can really put to use my technology skills. While those are great opportunities from a technology development standpoint ... cutting edge technology work ... it ultimately wasn't clear to me that those ... technologies that I'd be working on would reach unreached people today. And I think, on a very personal level, I felt that I wanted my work to be something that reached beyond just the easiest market or the most lucrative market. I wanted to serve underserved communities, in some way ... so, **I have a technology background and I wanted to reach underserved people**, and that really narrows the focus down quickly to what you can work on.*[17]

Instead of rejecting academia, however, this entrepreneur viewed the academic environment as a breeding ground for new ideas and as a place to explore how the unmet social needs can be met with new technologies. For him, social entrepreneurship is an extension of research outcomes, and a vehicle to put new ideas into practice.

> *the reason I considered academia was because it was a place where you could actually ask those questions ... **how I can contribute in the best possible way toward the needs of underserved communities** ... [and] take a step back and ask those questions before you jump in and create a start-up ...*

---

[15] Interview, June 6, 2013.
[16] Interview, July 20, 2013.
[17] Ibid.

We were doing a research intervention that we felt was adding a lot of value. And users felt there was a lot of value, and very organically we saw a need ... a market need, so to speak, a commercial, a technology transfer story that made sense ... where we could provide a service that was actually of value to the community we're trying to serve.[18]

For this TSE and for others, the seed ideas came out of research projects. One social entrepreneur in the renewable energy sector (S18) described how the enterprise grew out of her master's thesis at the London School of Economics. The thesis examined the willingness of urban slum dwellers to pay for energy, and she is continuing with a Ph.D. while running the enterprise. Her observation below also suggests a combination of academic interests and the desire to make broader social impacts through entrepreneurship.

I was doing this academic research on people's willingness to pay for access to energy solutions for urban slum communities starting in the northern region of Bangalore ... There is a huge amount of research about willingness to pay for a lot of different goods and services, but there has never been a study on access to energy in India, in the developing world. And I found that despite all of their other needs, access to electricity had a very high value for them. When the research project was finished, we realized there was this huge demand that nobody was servicing, and the very real willingness to pay. Then **we had to decide whether or not we are actually going to do this, or if it was just going to be a research project basically** *... I flew back to London and that night – on 1 July, India had a major power outage. That was a sign for us to come back and to actually do something.*[19]

TSEs are motivated by challenges inherent in the Global South, and capitalize on transnational access to technical knowledge, social networks, and financing. Social entrepreneurship is also an outcome of a combination of motivations – altruistic, social, and personal – and the necessary conviction to lead others in the organization. Another entrepreneur (S17), a second-generation Indian and a former Peace Corp volunteer who attended Harvard Business School says it well:

Why do individuals pick certain directions ... you'll hear good stories. Particular incidents where I was traveling to the small town, I saw this, and that inspired me to do this. I'm not saying there is no truth to it. But I'll also point out that there are many people who had these experiences, yet only a few actually choose to start organizations. **It's not the stories themselves that compel them, there is something more than stories.** *I have a very selfish*

---

[18] Ibid.
[19] Interview, June 25, 2013.

reason for doing what we are doing here ... I tell people that this is my way
of pre-empting my midlife crisis ... **I would look back and regret not having**
done this. *[Then] you look at the combination of secondary data and look at*
primary research and look at what you are enthused by. What is it that you
find exciting, worthwhile spending the next few years of your life doing? And
if you don't find that compelling enough, you will unlikely be able to inspire
other people to find it compelling ... [as an entrepreneur] ... you have to
really believe ... data is good but ultimately there has to be a conviction.
Data will help you with that conviction.[20]

The above quote demonstrates that exposure to social issues in the Global
South is not a sufficient condition for TSE. Instead, it must also be
combined with a desire to launch a new organization. The question,
however, is whether the organization must be a for-profit entity, or if
the same social mission can be achieved by launching a non-profit
organization.

9.4   ACCESSING TRANSNATIONAL FINANCING

Both commercial and social entrepreneurs rely on social networks to
access resources, and this is particularly important for financing during
the initial phases. For immigrant entrepreneurs, financing may largely
come from a single country in the Global North (i.e. immigrant destination), and, at least initially, markets may also be primarily located in
their place of residence in the Global North. TSEs also use transnational
networks as resources and access financing predominantly (although not
exclusively) in the Global North. Yet they differ in their market orientation, which is located in the Global South. This introduces a twist to
their financing strategies.

Academic institutions offer institutional ties to social networks in
India. Tata Trusts fund MIT's Tata Center and provide links to another
Tata Center at IIT Bombay. The benefactor of MIT's Deshpande Center
brings together a significant social network too. He is not only an alumna
of IIT Madras, but is also related by marriage to N. R. Narayana Murthy,
the principal co-founder of Infosys, which is among India's largest
software service firms. Particularly for early stage entrepreneurs, social
networks are critical in providing access to financing.

A challenge for TSE in India is raising risk capital. They must
convince either a local investor whose familiarity with their business
model and cultural norms may be limited, or convince an investor abroad

---

[20]   Ibid.

whose familiarity with social issues in India is limited. One TSE (S16) describes the access to transnational financing as a culturally nuanced process, where start-ups seek to satisfy the implicit norms and business expectations held by investors.

> *I think, in India investors are new to … new technology start-ups and so, they have a different view of what an organization like ours can and should be … and my vision is much more influenced by America because I'm American. And so, it's easier for me to talk about our vision and where we want to be in 5 years with an American investor compared to an Indian investor. I would say that that's what I get out of having US connections.*[21]

Another entrepreneur (S11) put it, *"it is easier to get money abroad, absolutely,"*[22] in part because of the above-mentioned cultural norms and, in part, because dollars go a long way in India. Similar statements were made by other interviewees. At least two-thirds of those interviewed said that the initial capital was raised in the Global North (primarily in the United States). Sources of funding varied and, as in commercial entrepreneurship, family, friends, and relatives residing in the Global North provided initial capital. Those who had access to venture capital were a small minority. Other sources included foundation grants and international aid.

The TSEs' backgrounds and credentials give them the capacity to write proposals for grants available in the Global North. The US government established the Social Innovation Fund in 2009, administered by the Corporation for National and Community Service, a federal agency which has provided more than half a billion dollars in federal grants and non-federal matching funds since then. The Canadian government funds Grand Challenges Canada, and combines resources with the Gates Foundation to promote innovation in global health for low- and middle-income countries by offering grants to organizations including social enterprises. These initiatives provided crucial seed grants to some TSEs we interviewed, and particularly for those in the fields of medical devices and diagnostics. For one TSE (S8), half the firm's financing came from grants, and the other half from:

> *seed investments from these doctors at Massachusetts General Hospital in Boston. So, that's our main investors, angel investors … a group of doctors that decided to get together and they believed in our idea.*[23]

---

[21] Interview, July 20, 2013.
[22] Interview, July 12, 2013.
[23] Interview, June 6, 2013.

For another entrepreneur (S20), it was his peer networks through his alma mater that provided access to financing. His Berkeley connection was essential to reach a Silicon Valley investor, especially after failing to raise capital in India.

> *I tried to raise money in India. I really tried and couldn't ... So, I finally got a lead investor in Silicon Valley ... I mean this guy really puts his money where the mouth is. **I am lucky that I have the connection in the US** ... again it is the Berkeley network.*[24]

However, there are drawbacks in relying on foreign capital to fund social entrepreneurship in India. One entrepreneur (S16) describes it as follows:

> *Now, the disadvantage is that **an American investor is only going to invest in things that they know, and they don't know India** and they don't know Indian start-ups.*[25]

This insight raises some concerns for the future of social entrepreneurship in the Global South. Financial instruments developed in the Global North are influencing the choice of business models among organizations with social missions in the Global South. TSE in this context serves as a vehicle that bridges financial trends in the Global North and the social mission in the Global South. Trends in the Global North influence conversions to for-profits in India. The clearest case came from one interviewee (S24), who described why he abandoned the idea of launching an NGO.

> *[We tried] for 3 months until we realized that no one will give us any money and we actually met this guy, a famous social entrepreneur and an author of a book called The End of Charity, where he basically talks about how we can scale up and how NGOs can have bigger impacts as for-profits. So he gave us some money actually ... that was the best decision we ever made ... because, without that money, we wouldn't have been able to get to the point that we've gotten to.*[26]

The growth of social finance may be a double-edged sword, however. One social entrepreneur (S16) expressed his concerns as follows:

> *I know many social entrepreneurs ... [who] because of ... **social investors putting all of this pressure ... to think about it as a business** ... think about*

---

[24] Interview, June 28, 2013.
[25] Interview, July 20, 2013.
[26] Ibid.

being a business person, and the social mission of organizations are being diluted, if not lost. I'm actually skeptical of somebody who calls himself a social entrepreneur, because often ... they've been brainwashed by investors to think of their company as ... a cold-blooded for-profit business in order to be recognized as something legitimate ... and in that process, have really disillusioned themselves about why they got into it in the first place.[27]

In sum, TSEs are experimenting with diverse technological applications, organizational structures, and/or marketing and financing models for social missions. In the process they are not only defining and executing development objectives, but are critical in engaging and mediating between global development goals and local social needs.

9.5 CONCLUSION

In this chapter we explored the rise of TSEs, particularly those who originate from the Global North and migrate to India to fulfill social and economic objectives. The transnational orientation of social entrepreneurship can be analyzed at various and multiple levels. Entrepreneurial motivations and inspirations are comprised of two parts. One involves entrepreneurial role models and knowledge of organizational innovation. They also differ from commercial entrepreneurs in terms of motivations, strategies for financing, and the business models they believe to be viable given the combination of social and economic missions. The second is that TSE must possess sufficient knowledge of the Global North and the South, in order to effectively navigate between social investors from the Global North with little knowledge of social problems in the Global South, and investors from the Global South unfamiliar with the start-up cultures of the Global North. The geographical mismatch between the source of financing and the source of problems may in part be leading to the growth of hybrid organizations.

TSEs play a significant role in catalyzing social innovation, bridging technology and global finance (venture capital and foundations) with unmet local needs. Beyond the agility that comes with smaller size and a niche-market orientation, social entrepreneurs actively take advantage of their transnational insights for product/service development and design. TSEs are subject to complex institutional and organizational hybridities and must develop expertise that enables them to operate in multiple environments. They "bricoleur," by mixing and matching transnational

---

[27]   Interview, June 15, 2013.

contexts with opportunities, through transnational access to resources, including talent, financing, and social capital.

We demonstrated why India attracts TSEs, who take part in the world's laboratory for social innovation. TSEs combine resources across domains and multiple scales to produce and deliver social innovation. They are inspired by the needs of the poor in the Global South, are networked among themselves as well as with global sources of finance, and are often supported by communities and mentors in elite institutions in the Global North, especially the US.

10. Conclusions

What is the hybrid domain? The swelling of the middle that lies between the public and the private domains is a culmination of various institutional experiments and quests for social solutions. The hybrid domain is neither the public nor the private domain. The hybrid domain is not an independent third, fourth, or fifth domain, separated from states and markets. Rather it is an arena where actors from the public and the private sectors, and civil society collaborate and become stakeholders in social innovation. From large MNEs to local start-ups, from state bureaucracies to NGOs, from well-established foundations and newly emerging sources of social finance, to newly formed hybrid organizations and networks, multiple and sometimes overlapping combinations of stakeholders are involved in overcoming outstanding social challenges. Not only are such challenges plentiful in contemporary India, but also in many other contexts, rich and poor.

The hybrid domain is conceptually unique in many respects. For one, unlike Ostrom's "polycentric governance," it does not presuppose cohesive norms among actors, nor territorial boundaries for the public (more likely merit) goods being produced. It is comprised of diverse actors from different sectors, with different priorities, norms and cultures, and many have transnational links to technological, social, and financial resources. For another, unlike network governance and Jessop's heterarchy, which refers to the relativization of power within and across organizations and stakeholders, the hybrid domain is without predetermined power relations. For example, in a heterarchy, although the state becomes one among many nodes, it assumes the role of meta governance. In the hybrid domain, power is only specific to each project of social innovation, and even then it can shift between its inception and completion. As a result, the state is neither reduced to a node, nor privileged as in a traditional hierarchy. Finally, unlike "bricolage," the hybrid domain is far from being an improvised assemblage of *en vogue* actors. Instead, the hybrid domain has emerged with strong intentions and responses to the failures of the market and the state to deliver social outcomes that are simultaneously relevant and sustainable.

The hybrid domain is an experimental ground in which diverse stakeholders have *only* one mission in common, which is to find a solution to a social project that encounters bottlenecks of innovation, implementation, and adoption. Stakeholders come together because they are unable to identify and develop solutions on their own, whether driven by exclusively non-profit or for-profit motives, or by adopting strictly global or grassroots paradigms. While most theories of collaboration require developing cohesion by way of shared norms and common agendas, the hybrid domain draws strengths from heterogeneous stakeholders from various geographies to converge with a common desire for social change. These stakeholders possess knowledge that is complementary, but seldom overlapping. The hybrid domain is where solution-centered alliances of various stakeholders seek new solutions. The dialog is difficult and collaboration challenging, often crossing national and cultural boundaries. But this difficult dialog is more representative of the contemporary world and its future. Theorizing for collaboration assuming homogeneity is no longer useful in the globalized world. We need to begin theorizing for collaboration in circumstances characterized by heterogeneity.

Domain flexibility is a result of rescaled public interests, and the rise of civil society organizations as legitimate and credible representatives of the public interest. It is also an outcome of an increasing recognition of the rise of global merit goods and rescaled spillovers of externalities, the shifting role of the state, and the changing nature of private sector organizations. As private sector organizations more consciously incorporate stakeholder interests and not just shareholder interests, they begin to transform, however gradually, the dominant forms of capitalism.

Stakeholders in the hybrid domain have the interest and the willingness to go beyond their conventional knowledge to identify sustainable solutions for social missions. It is notable that there exists an implicit consensus that drives these efforts, and an acknowledgment that the hybrid domain exists out of necessity for experiments that bridge disciplinary, ideological, and sectoral divides. One consensus we observed is that social objectives in the Global South are no longer met effectively by the conventional division of labor between the state, CSR initiatives by MNEs, and NGOs. This suggests a systemic failure of public/private goods provision, with the risk of repeating the failures by reinforcing the conceptual dichotomy between states and markets. Rather, we have proposed to take a different approach, by first acknowledging that the conceptual boundaries developed between for-profit and non-profit entities are artificial, and that such distinction is increasingly being blurred by various hybrid models. Empirical evidence prompts us to reconceptualize the functional roles of corporations, the state, and NGOs in delivering social value in emerging economies. If these stakeholders expand beyond their traditional boundaries, and overlap in their functions in multiple ways, what implications would this have for our understanding of development, industrialization, and livelihoods today and in the future?

Social innovation can be framed as concerted efforts by multiple stakeholders seeking to achieve social impacts. As such, development should also be understood as an outcome of successful social innovation, and not only as an outcome of *either* state *or* market development. Organizational configuration for social innovation can take multiple forms, ranging from corporate-led to state-led, but each involving many stakeholders across domains and sectors. Just as important are hybrid entities, and regulations should be considered to encourage them. Collective efforts toward accountability, monitoring, and ensuring that social objectives are appropriately set and met will continue to be necessary, since mistrust, confrontation, and antagonism have seldom produced outcomes sought by societies. Seen in this light, industrialization and entrepreneurship are not efforts driven exclusively by either individuals or by the private sector, nor are they simply a case of the state being co-opted by private interests. Rather, it is a collaboration with a goal of co-producing social impacts in which all stakeholders are involved and, where not just one or the other, are accountable. Social innovation in the hybrid domain contributes to institutional thickness, prompting societal capacity and economic sustainability on the ground.

The hybrid domain is comprised of chaotic, dynamic, heterogeneous, experimental and bottom-up processes to solve a problem. The most notable aspects of the hybrid domain is how it transforms both states and markets. The hybrid domain is neither a result of state failure nor of market failure, but the combination of both – a double failure. In some ways, the combined extension of the three sectors culminates as the hybrid domain. On the one hand, in circumstances in which a highly interventionist state (i.e. the developmental state) is not feasible, and a regulatory state is the only option, the hybrid domain is particularly relevant to the challenge of providing basic infrastructure and sustaining livelihoods. On the other hand, the active experimenting we observe today, in and around the hybrid domain, suggests that capitalism is changing, that relevant knowledge and forms of learning are evolving, and strategies for collaboration are multiplying. The simultaneous emergence of various stakeholders is particularly striking, as they strive to straddle the public/private domains, and fuse economic and social missions. Thus, by revising the scope of Polanyi's double movement to a triple movement, the hybrid domain is comprised of not bilateral, but multilateral stakeholder collaboration.

The hybrid domain will likely grow, even if it is unlikely to be the dominant domain. States and markets will exist for the foreseeable future as long as they continue to perform certain functions well, such as the distribution and efficient allocation of resources. But they will likely exist in altered forms, partly influenced by, and partly due to, competition from the stakeholders and solutions of the hybrid domain. It is important to recognize its emergence and its growth, for the hybrid domain is a fertile seedbed for social innovation, from which catalytic, systemic solutions may emerge. Hybrid logics and collaboration among unlikely partners and stakeholders who do not think alike, will increasingly find social acceptance.

The states versus markets paradigm in the social sciences needs to consider this new area of the hybrid domain. The public–private sector distinction is not likely to disappear completely in the near future but, in our view, the social sciences will be better served if we recognize and conceptualize the rise of the hybrid domain, with its multiple trends from different directions in search of solutions. To incorporate the hybrid domain more explicitly in institutional analysis, we must devise a method of dealing with hybridity.

We are not alone in advocating a solution-based paradigm to further the scope of governance. On the one hand, we may speculate that the combination of the "double failure" is frustrating an ever increasing number of people, thereby generating interests/incentives for a growing share of the population to find a solution to the great state–market divide that has developed in our consciousness. On the other hand, skepticism, cynicism, and mistrust can abound, leading to an outright dismissal of an emerging trend. We do not situate the hybrid domain as exclusively an outcome of neoliberalism, nor do we consider the hybrid domain a compromised socialism of sorts. Rather, it is an emerging trend to fuse economic and social missions by blending market logics and social welfare. Such blending is indeed possible, and should be experimented more, not discouraged as a result of ideological schisms and skepticism.

To date, as myriad phenomena that lie at the heart of the hybrid domain have been analyzed separately, it suffers from a lack of conceptual acknowledgment and, thus, insufficient theorization. As a result, activities within the hybrid domain are often dismissed as mere anecdotal evidence of marginal (instead of dominant), patchwork (instead of concerted) efforts by isolated actors. Moreover, without a formalized and well-established method of evaluation, the "success rates" of social innovation projects have been called into question. While these are legitimate concerns, we contend that dismissing or disregarding of the hybrid domain is a vicious cycle that pushes us back to the old states versus markets ideological battle. While more successful cases would undoubtedly validate and serve to legitimize the hybrid domain, we believe that active instances of experimentation are important in finding solutions and furthering the debate. This is akin to recognizing the importance of entrepreneurship even though nine out of ten businesses ultimately fail. But there are phenomenally successful ones that can generate disruptive innovation, altering organizations and institutions with beneficial socio-economic impacts.

We have avoided suggesting that the hybrid domain is new. The hybrid domain of the previous era may well encompass various establishments that produce positive social externalities, such as mass media (e.g. newspapers), research institutes, and educational facilities (e.g. universities). However, we contend that what is notable is the simultaneous, if not the collective, movement toward it. Also striking is its heterogeneity and transnationality. Stakeholders in the hybrid domain are diverse in their orientation and primary goals, and operate under different rationales, logics, and speed. Territorially, the hybrid domain stretches beyond the boundaries of nation states. The hybrid domain is made possible by crossing scales and, as such, involves both transnational and local processes. While much of the debate over scale in geography has been ontological, the hybrid domain is an empirical manifestation of the relativization of scale. The cross-scalar hybridity is a key underpinning of the hybrid domain, shaped strongly by the emergence of ICTs.

Finally, just as with states and markets, the hybrid domain also evolves, and its outcomes will be shaped by collective action and desires. In addition to the rise of TSE, we may observe new forms of hybrid stakeholders once we have a conceptual framework of the hybrid domain to identify them as such.

Appendix

Table A.1   List of interviewees

		Interview Date	Industry	Organizational Status	Position
S	1	01/06/2012	Health	For-profit	Director, Product Development
S	2	20/06/2012	ICT	For-profit	Chief Executive Officer
S	3	03/07/2012	Health	For-profit	CEO and Co-Founder
S	4	10/07/2012	Health	Hybrid	Chief Dreamer
S	5	10/07/2012	Health	For-profit	Chairman and CEO
S	6	16/07/2012	Health	For-profit	President and CTO
S	7	24/07/2012	Health	For-profit	Unknown
S	8	06/06/2013	Health	For-profit	Co-Founder
S	9	11/06/2013	Employment	For-profit	Unknown
S	10	11/06/2013	Finance	Hybrid	Co-Founder
S	11	12/06/2013	Employment	For-profit	Founder
S	12	14/06/2013	Health	For-profit	Director
S	13	15/06/2013	Finance	For-profit	Managing Director
S	14	17/06/2013	Communications	For-profit	Co-Founder
S	15	18/06/2013	Health	For-profit	Country Director, India
S	16	20/06/2013	Communications	For-profit	Co-Founder, CFO
S	17	21/06/2013	Communications	For-profit	Founder and CEO
S	18	25/06/2013	Energy	Hybrid	Co-Founder and Director
S	19	25/06/2013	Health	Hybrid	Co-Founder, President, Products
S	20	28/06/2013	Environment	For-profit	Co-Founder and CEO
S	21	03/07/2013	Energy	For-profit	Co-Founder and Vice President, Product
S	22	12/07/2013	Energy	Hybrid	Managing Director
S	23	15/07/2013	Transport	For-profit	Co-Founder and CEO
S	24	20/07/2013	Communications	For-profit	Co-Founder and CEO
S	25	20/06/2014	Health	For-profit	President and CEO
S	26	23/06/2014	Health	For-profit	CEO

		Interview Date	Industry	Organizational Status	Position
S	27	30/06/2014	Health	For-profit	Founder and CEO
S	28	01/07/2014	Communications	For-profit	Assistant Manager (Marketing)
S	29	01/07/2014	Consulting	For-profit	Founder and Joint Managing Director
S	30	02/07/2014	Health	For-profit	Founder and CEO
S	31	03/07/2014	Health	For-profit	Director
S	32	04/10/2014	Health	For-profit	CEO
S	33	07/10/2014	Education/ Training	For-profit/ University	Entrepreneur/Educator
S	34	15/10/2014	Education/ Training	University	Director
S	35	17/12/2014	Livelihoods	Non-profit	Founder
N	1	04/06/2012	Education/ Training	For-profit	Chief Executive Officer
N	2	04/06/2012	Education/ Training	Non-profit	Managing Director
N	3	15/06/2012	Health	Non-profit	Founder and Honorary Secretary
N	4	18/06/2012	Education/ Training	Non-profit	Founder and Managing Trustee
N	5	02/07/2012	Environment	Non-profit	Managing Trustee
N	6	23/07/2012	Finance	Non-profit	Vice President, Design
N	7	17/09/2012	Livelihoods	Non-profit	Executive Director
N	8	18/09/2012	Health	Non-profit	Technical Director
N	9	07/06/2013	Communications	Non-profit	Co-Founder
N	10	13/06/2013	Finance	Non-profit	Head, Mobile and NFC payment
N	11	17/06/2013	Health	Non-profit	Programme Director
N	12	18/06/2013	Livelihoods	Non-profit	Programme Director
N	13	19/06/2013	Agriculture	Non-profit	CEO
N	14	19/06/2013	Education/ Training	Non-profit	Educational Director
N	15	20/06/2013	Finance	Non-profit	CEO
N	16	23/07/2013	Finance	Non-profit	Senior Strategic Advisor, R&D Initiative – India
N	17	23/07/2013	Finance	Non-profit	Senior Programs Officer
N	18	11/06/2014	Livelihoods	Hybrid	CEO
N	19	11/06/2014	Education/ Training	Non-profit	Founder
N	20	16/06/2014	Health	Non-profit	Country Director

		Interview Date	Industry	Organizational Status	Position
N	21	18/06/2014	Finance	Non-profit	Representative
N	22	18/06/2014	Livelihoods	Non-profit	Manager, Strategic Partnerships and Alliances
N	23	19/06/2014	Health	Hybrid	President/Country Director
N	24	23/06/2014	Education/ Training	Non-profit	Founder and CEO
N	25	17/09/2014	Health	Non-profit	CEO
N	26	03/10/2014	Health	Hybrid	Vice President
N	27	08/12/2014	Health	Non-profit	Medical Officer
M	1	28/05/2012	ICT	For-profit	Research Manager, Technology for Emerging Markets
M	2	04/06/2012	ICT	For-profit	Director
M	3	07/06/2012	Finance	For-profit	Director, Projects
M	4	07/06/2012	ICT	For-profit	Senior Manager, Corporate Communications
M	5	07/06/2012	ICT	For-profit	Head, Corporate Affairs, India and Asia Pacific
M	6	11/06/2012	ICT/Medical Devices	For-profit	Senior Vice President and Head (also interviewed July 27, 2010)
M	7	12/06/2012	ICT	For-profit	Director
M	8	12/06/2012	Energy	For-profit	Consulting Engineer, IEO Materials
M	9	13/06/2012	ICT/Medical Devices	For-profit	Senior Director
M	10	13/06/2012	Retail	For-profit	Group Manager, Talent Acquisition
M	11	14/06/2012	ICT/Medical Devices	For-profit	Technology Leader
M	12	20/06/2012	ICT	For-profit	Vice President, Information Technology and Chief Information Officer, Globalization
M	13	21/06/2012	ICT	For-profit	Country Head, India Products
M	14	22/06/2012	Medical Devices	For-profit	General Manager, Maternal–Infant Care

References

Acs, Z. J. (2013). *Why philanthropy matters: How the wealthy give, and what it means for our economic well-being.* Princeton, NJ: Princeton University Press.

Adler, P. S. (2001). Market, hierarchy, and trust: The knowledge economy and the future of capitalism. *Organization Science, 12*(2), 215–234.

Agrawal, A., & Gibson, C. C. (1999). Enchantment and disenchantment: The role of community in natural resource conservation. *World Development, 27*(4), 629–649.

Ahluwalia, I. J. (1985). *Industrial growth in India: Stagnation since the mid-sixties.* New York: Oxford University Press.

Ahluwalia, I. J. (1996). India's opening up to trade and investment. In C. Oman (Ed.), *Policy reform in India.* Paris: OECD.

Aker, J. C. (2011). Dial "A" for agriculture: A review of information and communication technologies for agricultural extension in developing countries. *Agricultural Economics, 42*(6), 631–647.

Almeida, P., & Phene, A. (2004). Subsidiaries and knowledge creation: The influence of the MNC and host country on innovation. *Strategic Management Journal, 25*(8/9), 847.

Altenburg, T., & Lundvall, B.-Å. (2009). Building inclusive innovation systems in developing countries: Challenges for IS research. In B.-Å. Lundvall, K. J. Joseph, C. Chaminade, & J. Vang (Eds), *Handbook of innovation systems and developing countries: Building domestic capabilities in a global setting* (pp. 33–56). Cheltenham, UK and Northampton, MA, USA: Edward Elgar Publishing.

Alvarez, S. A., & Barney, J. B. (2014). Entrepreneurial opportunities and poverty alleviation. *Entrepreneurship Theory and Practice, 38*(1), 159–184. doi:10.1111/etap.12078

Amsden, A. H. (2001). *The rise of the rest: Challenges to the west from late-industrializing economies.* Oxford: Oxford University Press.

Aoyama, Y. (2007). Oligopoly and the structural paradox of retail TNCs: An assessment of Carrefour and Wal-Mart in Japan. *Journal of Economic Geography, 7*(4), 471–490. doi:10.1093/jeg/lbm014

Aoyama, Y., & Parthasarathy, B. (2012). Research and development facilities of multinational enterprises in India. *Eurasian Geography and Economics, 53*(6), 713–730.

Aoyama, Y., & Schwarz, G. (2006). The myth of Wal-Martization: Retail globalization and local competition in Japan and Germany. In S. Brunn (Ed.), *Wal-Mart world* (pp. 275–291). New York: Routledge.

Argenti, P. (2004). Collaborating with activists: How Starbucks works with NGOs. *California Management Review*, *47*(1), 91–116.

Arora, A., Arunachalam, V. S., Asundi, J., & Fernandes, R. (2001). The Indian software services industry. *Research Policy*, *30*(8), 1267–1287.

Arrow, K. J. (1962). The economic implications of learning by doing. *Review of Economic Studies*, *29*(3), 155–173.

Arrow, K. J. (1970). Political and economic evaluation of social effects and externalities. In J. Margolis (Ed.), *The analysis of public output* (pp. 1–30). UMI.

Asheim, B., Coenen, L., & Vang, J. (2007). Face-to-face, buzz, and knowledge bases: Sociospatial implications for learning, innovation, and innovation policy. *Environment and Planning C: Government and Policy*, *25*(5), 655–670.

Audretsch, D. B., & Feldman, M. P. (1996). Innovative clusters and the industry life cycle. *Review of Industrial Organization*, *11*(2), 253–273.

Austin, J. E. (2010). From organization to organization: On creating value. *Journal of Business Ethics*, *94*, 13–15. doi:10.2307/29789681

Austin, J. E., & Seitanidi, M. M. (2012). Collaborative value creation: A review of partnering between nonprofits and businesses: Part I. Value creation spectrum and collaboration stages. *Nonprofit and Voluntary Sector Quarterly*, *41*(5), 726–758. doi:10.1177/0899764012450777

Austin, J. E., Stevenson, H., & Wei-Skillern, J. (2006). Social and commercial entrepreneurship: Same, different, or both? *Entrepreneurship Theory and Practice*, *30*(1), 1–22. doi:10.1111/j.1540-6520.2006.00107.x

Bacq, S., & Janssen, F. (2011). The multiple faces of social entrepreneurship: A review of definitional issues based on geographical and thematic criteria. *Entrepreneurship & Regional Development*, *23*(5–6), 373–403. doi:10.1080/08985626.2011.577242

Baker, T., & Nelson, R. E. (2005). Creating something from nothing: Resource construction through entrepreneurial bricolage. *Administrative Science Quarterly*, *50*(3), 329–366.

Banerjee, A., Banerjee, A. V., & Duflo, E. (2011). *Poor economics: A radical rethinking of the way to fight global poverty*. New York, NY: PublicAffairs.

Barker, J. L., Barclay, P., & Reeve, H. K. (2012). Within-group competition reduces cooperation and payoffs in human groups. *Behavioral Ecology*, *23*(4), 735–741. doi:10.1093/beheco/ars020

Barney, J. (1991). Firm resources and sustained competitive advantage. *Journal of Management*, *17*(1), 99–120.

Battilana, J., Lee, M., Walker, J., & Dorsey, C. (2012). In search of the hybrid ideal. *Stanford Social Innovation Review, 10*(3), 50–55.

Bergstrom, T., Blume, L., & Varian, H. (1986). On the private provision of public goods. *Journal of Public Economics, 29*, 25–49.

Bhachu, P. (2003). *Dangerous designs: Asian women fashion the diaspora economies.* London and New York: Routledge.

Bishop, M., & Green, M. (2008). *Philanthrocapitalism: How the rich can save the world.* New York, NY: Bloomsbury Press.

Bodansky, D. (2012). What's in a concept? Global public goods, international law, and legitimacy. *European Journal of International Law, 23*(3), 651–668. doi:10.1093/ejil/chs035

Boddewyn, J., & Doh, J. (2011). Global strategy and the collaboration of MNEs, NGOs and the government for the provisioning of collective goods in emerging markets. *Global Strategy Journal, 1*, 345–361. doi:10.1111/j.2042-5805.2011.00026.x

Bonini, S., Greeney, J., & Mendonca, L. (2007). Assessing the impact of societal issues: A McKinsey Global Survey. *The McKinsey Quarterly,* 1–9.

Boschma, R. (2005). Proximity and innovation: A critical assessment. *Regional Studies, 39*(1), 61–74. doi:10.1080/0034340052000320887

Bovaird, T. (2004). Public–private partnerships: From contested concepts to prevalent practice. *International Review of Administrative Sciences, 70*(2), 199–215.

Brown, J. S., & Duguid, P. (1991). Organizational learning and communities-of-practice: Toward a unified view of working, learning, and innovation. *Organization Science, 2*(1), 40–57.

Bruni, L., & Zamagni, S. (2007). *Civil economy: Efficiency, equity, public happiness* (Vol. 2). Oxford: Peter Lang.

Bruyn, S. T. (2000). *A civil economy: Transforming the marketplace in the twenty-first century.* Ann Arbor, MI: University of Michigan Press.

Burchell, J., & Cook, J. (2013). Sleeping with the enemy? Strategic transformations in business–NGO relationships through stakeholder dialogue. *Journal of Business Ethics, 113*(3), 505–518.

Burns, T. E., & Stalker, G. M. (1961). The management of innovation. *University of Illinois at Urbana-Champaign's Academy for Entrepreneurial Leadership Historical Research Reference in Entrepreneurship.*

Campbell, S. (1998). Social entrepreneurship: How to develop new social-purpose business ventures. *Health Care Strategic Management, 16*(5), 17.

Cantwell, J., & Piscitello, L. (2005). Recent location of foreign-owned research and development activities by large multinational corporations in the European regions: The role of spillovers and externalities. *Regional Studies, 39*(1), 1–16.

Carment, D. (2003). Assessing state failure: Implications for theory and policy. *Third World Quarterly, 24*(3), 407–427. doi:10.1080/0143659032000084384

Carson, S. J., Madhok, A., Varman, R., & John, G. (2003). Information processing moderators of the effectiveness of trust-based governance in interfirm R&D collaboration. *Organization Science, 14*(1), 45–56.

Cartwright, N., & Hardie, J. (2012). *Evidence-based policy: A practical guide to doing it better.* New York, NY: Oxford University Press.

Castells, M. (2000). *The rise of the network society. The information age: Economy, society and culture, Volume I.* 2nd edition. Oxford: Blackwell.

Castells, M. (2002). Preface. In P. B. Evans (Ed.), *Livable cities? Urban struggles for livelihood and sustainability* (pp. ix–xi). Oakland, CA: University of California Press.

Castells, M. (2005). Global governance and global politics. *PS: Political Science & Politics, 38*(01), 9–16. doi:10.1017.S1049096505055678

Castells, M. (2008). The new public sphere: Global civil society, communication networks, and global governance. *Annals of the American Academy of Political and Social Science, 616*(1), 78–93.

CECP, The Conference Board. (2015). *Giving in Numbers: 10th Anniversary 2015 Edition,* at http://cecp.co/measurement/benchmarking-reports/giving-in-numbers.html (accessed June 23, 2011).

Central Intelligence Agency (CIA). (2013). The World Factbook 2013–14. *Central Intelligence Agency,* at https://www.cia.gov/library/publications/the-world-factbook/index.html (accessed January 6, 2016).

Central Statistical Office (CSO). (2012). *Final Report on Non-Profit Institutions in India: A Profile and Satellite Accounts in the Framework of System of National Accounts.* Ministry of Statistics and Programme Implementation, Government of India.

Chakravarty, S. (1987). *Development planning: The Indian experience.* Oxford: Clarendon Press.

Chaminade, C., & Vang, J. (2008). Globalisation of knowledge production and regional innovation policy: Supporting specialized hubs in the Bangalore software industry. *Research Policy, 37*(10), 1684–1696. doi:http://dx.doi.org/10.1016/j.respol.2008.08.014

Charity Aid Foundation. (2006). *International comparisons of charitable giving.* Kent: Charity Aid Foundation.

Charity Aid Foundation. (2014). *World Giving Index 2014 report,* at https://www.cafonline.org/docs/default-source/about-us-publications/caf_wgi2014_report_1555awebfinal.pdf (accessed July 5, 2015).

Chell, E., Nicolopoulou, K., & Karataş-Özkan, M. (2010). Social entrepreneurship and enterprise: International and innovation perspectives. *Entrepreneurship & Regional Development*, *22*(6), 485–493. doi: 10.1080/08985626.2010.488396

Chen, M. A., & Raveendran, G. (2014). *Urban Employment in India: Recent Trends and Patterns*. WEIGO Working Paper No. 7, at http://wiego.org/sites/wiego.org/files/publications/files/Chen-Urban-Employment-India-WIEGO-WP7.pdf (accessed January 15, 2016).

Chen, Y.-C. (2008). Why do multinational corporations locate their advanced R&D centres in Beijing? *Journal of Development Studies*, *44*(5), 622–644.

Chenier, J. A., & Prince, M. J. (1990). *Aid for small business exporting firms: The role of governments and information networks*. IRPP.

Chesbrough, H. (2003). *Open innovation: The new imperative for creating and profiting from technology*. Boston, MA: Harvard Business School Press.

Chesbrough, H. (2004). Managing open innovation. *Research-Technology Management*, *47*, 23–26.

Chesbrough, H., & Crowther, A. K. (2006). Beyond high tech: Early adopters of open innovation in other industries. *R&D Management*, *36*(3), 229–236.

Choguill, M. B. G. (1996). A ladder of community participation for underdeveloped countries. *Habitat International*, *20*(3), 431–444.

Chonko, L. B., Tanner, J. J. F., & Smith, E. R. (1991). Selling and sales management in action: The sales force's role in international marketing research and marketing information systems. *Journal of Personal Selling & Sales Management*, *11*(1), 69–80.

Christensen, C. M., & Bower, J. L. (1996). Customer power, strategic investment, and the failure of leading firms. *Strategic Management Journal*, *17*(3), 197–218.

Chrysostome, E., & Lin, X. (2010). Immigrant entrepreneurship: Scrutinizing a promising type of business venture. *Thunderbird International Business Review*, *52*(2), 77–82.

Churchman, C. W. (1967). Guest editorial: Wicked problems. *Management Science*, *14*(4), B-141–142.

Cleaver, F. (2002). Reinventing institutions: Bricolage and the social embeddedness of natural resource management. *European Journal of Development Research*, *14*(2), 11–30. doi:10.1080/714000425

Cornish, S. L. (1995). "Marketing matters": The function of markets and marketing in the growth of firms and industries. *Progress in Human Geography*, *19*(3), 317–337.

Cornish, S. L. (1997). Strategies for the acquisition of market intelligence and implications for the transferability of information inputs. *Annals of the Association of American Geographers, 87*(3), 451–470.

Cornwall, A. (2004). Spaces for transformation? Reflections on issues of power and difference in participation in development. In S. Hickey & G. Mohan (Eds), *Participation: from tyranny to transformation* (pp. 75–91). London: Zed Books.

Crets, S., & Celer, J. (2013). The interdependence of CSR and social innovation. In T. Osburg & R. Schmidpeter (Eds), *Social innovation, CSR, sustainability, ethics & governance* (pp. 77–87). New York: Springer.

Dahan, N. M., Doh, J. P., Oetzel, J., & Yaziji, M. (2010a). Corporate-NGO collaboration: Co-creating new business models for developing markets. *Long Range Planning, 43*(2), 326–342.

Dahan, N. M., Doh, J. P., Oetzel, J., & Yaziji, M. (2010b). Innovative MNE/NGO partnerships. *Long Range Planning, 43*(2–3), 326–342. doi:10.1016/j.lrp.2009.11.003

Datta, P., Mukhopadhyay, I., & Selvaraj, S. (2013). Medical devices manufacturing industry in India: Market structure, import intensity, and regulatory mechanisms. ISID-PHFI Collaborative Research Programme Working Paper Series 02.

Davidson, K. (2009). Ethical concerns at the bottom of the pyramid: Where CSR meets BOP. *Journal of International Business Ethics, 2*(1).

Deaton, A. (2010). Instruments, randomization, and learning about development. *Journal of Economic Literature, 48*(2), 424–455.

Dees, J. G. (1998a). Enterprising nonprofits. *Harvard Business Review, 76*, 54–69.

Dees, J. G. (1998b). The meaning of social entrepreneurship. *Comments and suggestions contributed from the Social Entrepreneurship Funders Working Group,* 6pp.

Dees, J. G., & Anderson, B. B. (2006). Framing a theory of social entrepreneurship: Building on two schools of practice and thought. *Research on Social Entrepreneurship: Understanding and Contributing to an Emerging Field, 1*(3), 39–66.

Defourny, J., & Nyssens, M. (2013). Social innovation, social economy and social enterprise: What can the European debate tell us. In F. Moulaert, D. MacCallum, M. Abid, & A. Hamdouch (Eds), *The international handbook on social innovation* (pp. 40–52). Cheltenham, UK and Northampton, MA, USA: Edward Elgar Publishing.

Demirguc-Kunt, A., Klapper, L., & Randall, D. (2013). *The Global Findex Database: Financial inclusion in India*, at http://www.worldbank.org/content/dam/Worldbank/Research/GlobalFindex/PDF/old%20pdfs/N8india6pg3.pdf (accessed January 16, 2016).

Department of Scientific & Industrial Research, Government of India. (2014). *Directory of Recognized In-House R&D Units*, at http://www.dsir.gov.in/direct/14_rdidir.pdf (accessed December 29, 2015).

Desa, G. (2012). Resource mobilization in international social entrepreneurship: Bricolage as a mechanism of institutional transformation. *Entrepreneurship Theory and Practice, 36*(4), 727–751.

Di Domenico, M., Haugh, H., & Tracey, P. (2010). Social bricolage: Theorizing social value creation in social enterprises. *Entrepreneurship Theory and Practice, 34*(4), 681–703. doi:10.1111/j.1540-6520.2010.00370.x

Dixit, A. (2009). Governance institutions and economic activity. *American Economic Review, 99*(1), 3–24.

Doh, J. P., & Guay, T. R. (2006). Corporate social responsibility, public policy, and NGO activism in Europe and the United States: An institutional-stakeholder perspective. *Journal of Management Studies, 43*(1), 47–73.

Donner, J. (2008). Research approaches to mobile use in the developing world: A review of the literature. *The Information Society, 24*(3), 140–159.

Drache, D. (2001). *The market or the public domain: Redrawing the line* (Vol. 9). London and New York: Routledge.

Dreze, J., & Sen, A. (1999). *India: Economic development and social opportunity*. New York: Oxford University Press.

Drucker, P. F. (1987). Social innovation—Management's new dimension. *Long Range Planning, 20*(6), 29–34. doi:http://dx.doi.org/10.1016/0024-6301(87)90129-4

Dunn, D., & Yamashita, K. (2003). Microcapitalism and the megacorporation. *Harvard Business Review, 81*(8), 46–54, 139.

Dutta, S., Lanvin, B., & Wunsch-Vincent, S. (2015). *Global Innovation Index 2015: Effective innovation policies for development*, at https://www.globalinnovationindex.org/userfiles/file/reportpdf/GII-2015-v5.pdf (accessed January 23, 2016).

Edwards, M., Bishop, M., & Green, M. (2014). Who gains, who loses: Distributional impacts of the new frontiers of philanthropy. In L. M. Salamon (Ed.), *New frontiers of philanthropy* (pp. 539–561). Oxford: Oxford University Press.

Elkington, J. (1997). *Cannibals with forks: The triple bottom line of 21st century business:*. Oxford: Capstone.

Esposito, R. T. (2013). The social enterprise revolution in corporate law: A primer on emerging corporate entities in Europe and the United States and the case for the benefit corporation. *William & Mary Business Law Review, 4*(2).

Evans, P. B. (1995). *Embedded autonomy: States and industrial transformation.* Cambridge and New York: Cambridge University Press.

Evans, P. B. (1996). Government action, social capital and development: Reviewing the evidence on synergy. *World Development, 24*(6), 1119–1132.

Farnsworth, K., & Holden, C. (2006). The business-social policy nexus: Corporate power and corporate inputs into social policy. *Journal of Social Policy, 35*(3), 473–494. doi:10.1017/S0047279406009883.

Farrell, D., Laboissiére, M., Pascal, R., de Segundo, C., Rosenfeld, J., Stürze, S., & Umezawa, F. (2005). *The emerging global labor market.* McKinsey Global Institute.

Fawcett, S. B., Paine-Andrews, A., Francisco, V. T., Schultz, J. A., Richter, K. P., Lewis, R. K., Fisher, J. L. et al. (1995). Using empowerment theory in collaborative partnerships for community health and development. *American Journal of Community Psychology, 23*(5), 677–697.

Feldman, M. P. (2000). Where science comes to life: University bioscience, commercial spin-offs, and regional economic development. *Journal of Comparative Policy Analysis: Research and Practice, 2*(3), 345–361.

Feldman, M. P., & Massard, N. (Eds). (2002). *Institutions and systems in the geography of innovation.* Boston, MA: Kluwer Academic Publishers.

Ferroni, M. A., & Mody, A. (2002). *International public goods: Incentives, measurement, and financing.* Washington, DC: World Bank Publications.

Findlay, M. C., III, & Whitmore, G. A. (1974). Beyond shareholder wealth maximization. *Financial Management, 3*(4), 25–35. doi:10.2307/3664927

Fletcher, K., & Wheeler, C. (1989). Market intelligence for international markets. *Marketing Intelligence & Planning, 7*(5/6), 30–34.

Foster, C., & Heeks, R. (2013). Conceptualising inclusive innovation: Modifying systems of innovation frameworks to understand diffusion of new technology to low-income consumers. *European Journal of Development Research, 25*(3), 333–355.

Foucault, M. (1991). Governmentality. The Foucault effect. In G. Burchell, C. Gordon, & P. Miller (Eds), *The Foucault effect: Studies in governmentality.* Chicago: University of Chicago Press.

Franke, N., & Piller, F. (2004). Value creation by toolkits for user innovation and design: The case of the watch market. *Journal of Product Innovation Management, 21*(6), 401–415.

Fraser, E. D. G., Dougill, A. J., Mabee, W. E., Reed, M., & McAlpine, P. (2006). Bottom up and top down: Analysis of participatory processes for sustainability indicator identification as a pathway to community empowerment and sustainable environmental management. *Journal of Environmental Management*, *78*(2), 114–127.

Freeman, C. (1995). The "national system of innovation" in historical perspective. *Cambridge Journal of Economics*, *19*(1), 5–24.

Freeman, C., & Perez, C. (1988). *Structural crises of adjustment, business cycles and investment behaviour*. London: Pinter.

Freeman, R. E. (1984). *Strategic management: A stakeholder approach*. Boston, MA: Pitman.

Friedmann, J. (1987). *Planning in the public domain: From knowledge to action*. Princeton, NJ: Princeton University Press.

Fromhold-Eisebith, M. (2002). Regional cycles of learning: Foreign multinationals as agents of technological upgrading in less developed countries. *Environment and Planning A*, *34*(12), 2155–2174.

Frost, T. S. (2001). The geographic sources of foreign subsidiaries' innovations. *Strategic Management Journal*, *22*(2), 101–123.

Gaffney, R. J. (2012). Hype and hostility for hybrid companies: A fourth sector case study. *Journal of Business, Entrepreneurship & the Law*, *5*(2), 329–343.

Gambetta, D. (Ed.) (1988). *Trust: Making and breaking of cooperative relations*. New York: Basil Blackwell.

Garud, R., & Karnøe, P. (2003). Bricolage versus breakthrough: Distributed and embedded agency in technology entrepreneurship. *Research Policy*, *32*(2), 277–300.

Gates, B. (2008). Making capitalism more creative. *Time Magazine*, *31*.

Gereffi, G., Garcia-Johnson, R., & Sasser, E. (2001). The NGO-industrial complex. *Foreign Policy*, *125*(4), 56–65.

Gertler, M. S. (1995). "Being there": Proximity, organization, and culture in the development and adoption of advanced manufacturing technologies. *Economic Geography*, 1–26.

Gertler, M. S. (2003). Tacit knowledge and the economic geography of context, or the undefinable tacitness of being (there). *Journal of Economic Geography*, *3*(1), 75–99. doi:10.1093/jeg/3.1.75

Gerybadze, A., & Reger, G. (1999). Globalization of R&D: Recent changes in the management of innovation in transnational corporations. *Research Policy*, *28*(2), 251–274.

Giddens, A. (1998). *The third way: The renewal of social democracy*. London: Polity Press.

Global Impact Investing Network. (2015). The landscape for impact investing in South Asia: Understanding the current status, trends, opportunities, and challenges in Bangladesh, India Myanmar, Nepal, Pakistan, and Sri Lanka, at https://thegiin.org/assets/documents/pub/South%20Asia%20Landscape%20Study%202015/Pakistan_GIIN_southasia.pdf (accessed December 29, 2015).

Godfrey, J. (2015). Why have 9,000 Indian NGOs been deregistered? *Nonprofit Quarterly*, May 4.

Godoe, H. (2000). Innovation regimes, R&D and radical innovations in telecommunications. *Research Policy*, *29*(9), 1033–1046.

Goldberg, D. E. (2013). *The design of innovation: Lessons from and for competent genetic algorithms* (Vol. 7). Berlin: Springer Science & Business Media.

Gomez, G. M., & Helmsing, A. H. J. (2010). Social entrepreneurship: A convergence on NGOs and the market economy? *NGO Management* (pp. 391–402). London: Earthscan.

Gopinath, S., Oliver, J., Tannirkulam, A., Bhattacharya, S., & Kulkarni, R. (2010). *Putting money in motion—How much do migrants pay for domestic transfers*, at http://ifmrlead.org/wp-content/uploads/2015/OWC/42_Putting_Money_in_Motion.pdf (accessed July 12, 2015).

Government of India. (2013a). The Companies Act, 2013, 2015 C.F.R.

Government of India. (2013b). *Statistical Yearbook 2013: State-wise percentage of distribution of rural and urban households having electricity*, at https://data.gov.in/catalog/state-wise-percentage-distribution-rural-and-urban-households-having-electricity (accessed July 13, 2015).

Govindarajan, V., & Trimble, C. (2012). *Reverse innovation: Create far from home, win everywhere*. Cambridge, MA: Harvard Business School Press.

Grabher, G., Ibert, O., & Floher, S. (2008). The neglected king: The customer in the new knowledge ecology of innovation. *Economic Geography*, *84*(3), 253–280.

Guha, R. (2007). *India after Gandhi: The history of the world's largest democracy*. London: Pan Macmillan.

Gupta, D., Goldar, B., Bora, S., Gill, H., & Anuradha, K. (1995). *Ancillarisation and subcontracting in Indian industry*. New Delhi: Government of India.

Håkansson, H. (1989). *Corporate technological behaviour (Routledge Revivals): Co-operation and networks*. London: Routledge.

Hall, P. A., & Soskice, D. (Eds.). (2001). *Varieties of capitalism*. New York: Oxford University Press.

Hammond, A. L., Kramer, W. J., Katz, R. S., Tran, J. T., & Walker, C. (2007). *The next 4 billion: Market size and business strategy at the base of the pyramid*. Washington, DC: World Resources Institute International Finance Corporation.

Hanson, K., Gilson, L., Goodman, C., Mills, A., Smith, R., Feachem, R., Kinlaw, H. et al. (2008). Is private health care the answer to the health problems of the world's poor? *PLoS Med*, 5(11), e233.

Harris, N. (1986). *The end of the Third World: Newly industrializing countries and the decline of an ideology*. London: IB Tauris.

Harris, N. (2005). Towards new theories of regional and urban development. *Economic and Political Weekly*, 669–674.

Hartley, J. (2004). The "value chain of meaning"and the new economy. *International Journal of Cultural Studies*, 7(1), 129–141.

Haufler, V. (2001). *A public role for the private sector: Industry self-regulation in a global economy*. Washington, DC: Carnegie Endowment for International Peace.

Heeks, R. (1996). *India's software industry: State policy, liberalisation and industrial development*. New Delhi: SAGE.

Heeks, R. (Ed.) (1999). *Reinventing government in the information age: International practice in IT-enabled public sector reform*. Abingdon: Routledge.

Heitzman, J. (2004). *Network city: Planning the information society in Bangalore*. New York: Oxford University Press.

Hershberg, E., Nabeshima, K., & Yusuf, S. (2007). Opening the ivory tower to business: University–industry linkages and the development of knowledge-intensive clusters in Asian cities. *World Development*, 35(6), 931–940.

Hess, D., Rogovsky, N., & Dunfee, T. W. (2002). The next wave of corporate community involvement: Corporate social initiatives. *California Management Review*, 44(2), 110–125.

Hirschman, A. O. (1982). *Shifting involvements: Private interest and public action*. Princeton, NJ: Princeton University Press.

Hitt, M. A., Li, H., & Worthington, W. J. (2005). Emerging markets as learning laboratories: Learning behaviors of local firms and foreign entrants in different institutional contexts. *Management and Organization Review*, 1(3), 353–380.

Hodgson, G. M. (2002). The legal nature of the firm and the myth of the firm-market hybrid. *International Journal of the Economics of Business*, 9(1), 37–60.

Horner, R. (2014). The impact of patents on innovation, technology transfer and health: A pre-and post-TRIPs analysis of India's pharmaceutical industry. *New Political Economy*, 19(3), 384–406.

Humphreys, S., Fitzgerald, B. F., Banks, J. A., & Suzor, N. P. (2005). Fan based production for computer games: User led innovation, the "drift of value" and the negotiation of intellectual property rights. *Media*

International Australia Incorporating Culture and Policy: Quarterly Journal of Media Research and Resources, (114), 16–29.

Ioannides, S., & Minoglou, I. P. (2005). Diaspora entrepreneurship between history and theory. In Y. Cassis & I. P. Minoglou (Eds), *Entrepreneurship in theory and history* (pp. 163–189). London: Palgrave Macmillan.

Israel, B. A., Checkoway, B., Schulz, A., & Zimmerman, M. (1994). Health education and community empowerment: Conceptualizing and measuring perceptions of individual, organizational, and community control. *Health Education & Behavior*, *21*(2), 149–170.

Jenkins, R. (2010). NGOs and Indian politics. In N. G. Jayal & P. B. Mehta (Eds), *The Oxford companion to politics in India* (pp. 409–426). Oxford: Oxford University Press.

Jensen, M. C. (1988). Takeovers: Their causes and consequences. *Journal of Economic Perspectives*, 21–48.

Jeppesen, L. B. (2005). User toolkits for innovation: Consumers support each other. *Journal of Product Innovation Management*, *22*(4), 347–362.

Jessop, B. (1998). The rise of governance and the risks of failure: The case of economic development. *International Social Science Journal*, *50*(155), 29–45. doi:10.1111/1468-2451.00107

Johnson, C. (1982). *MITI and the Japanese miracle: The growth of industrial policy: 1925–1975*. Stanford, CA: Stanford University Press.

Joshi, V., & Little, I. M. D. (1994). *India: Macroeconomics and political economy, 1964–1991*. Washington, DC: World Bank Publications.

Kanter, R. M. (1999). From spare change to real change: The social sector as beta site for business innovation. *Havard Business Review*, *77*(3), 122–132.

Kaplan, R. S., & Grossman, A. S. (2010). The emerging capital market for nonprofits. *Harvard Business Review*, *88*(10), 110–118.

Karlan, D. S., & Appel, J. (2011). *More than good intentions: How a new economics is helping to solve global poverty*. New York: Dutton.

Karmani, A. (2007). The mirage of marketing to the bottom of the pyramid. *California Management Review*, *49*(4), 91–111.

Kaul, I. (2012). Global public goods: Explaining their underprovision. *Journal of International Economic Law*, *15*(3), 729–750.

Kaul, I., Conceição, P., Le Goulven, K., & Mendoza, R. U. (2003). Why do global public goods matter today? In I. Kaul, P. Conceição, K. Le Goulven, & R. U. Mendoza, (Eds), *Providing global public goods: managing globalization* (pp. 2–20). United Nations Development Programme.

Kaul, I., Grunberg, I., & Stern, M. A. (Eds). (1999). *Global public goods: International cooperation in the 21st century.* New York: Oxford University Press.

Keefer, P. (2009). The SAGE handbook of comparative politics. In T. Landman & N. Robinson (Eds), *The SAGE handbook of comparative politics* (pp. 439–462). London: SAGE Publications.

Khandker, S. R., Barnes, D. F., & Samad, H. A. (2010). *Energy poverty in rural and urban India: Are the energy poor also income poor?* Washington, DC: The World Bank.

Khanna, T. (2014). Contextual intelligence. *Harvard Business Review, 92*(9), 58–68.

Kindleberger, C. P. (1981). Dominance and leadership in the international economy: Exploitation, public goods, and free rides. *International Studies Quarterly, 25*(2), 242–254. doi:10.2307/2600355

Kitching, G. (2010). *Seeking social justice through globalization: Escaping a nationalist perspective.* Philadelphia, PA: Penn State Press.

Kloosterman, R., van der Leun, J., & Rath, J. (1999). Mixed embeddedness: (In)formal economic activities and immigrant businesses in the Netherlands. *International Journal of Urban and Regional Research, 23*(2), 252–266. doi:10.1111/1468-2427.00194

Kohli, A. (2006). Politics of economic growth in India, 1980–2005: Part II: The 1990s and beyond. *Economic and Political Weekly, 41*(14), 1361–1370.

Kohn, L. B., & Bruysten, S. (2016). Mobilizing commercial investment for social good: The social success note. In E. A. Thomas (Ed.), *Broken pumps and promises: Incentivizing impact in environmental health* (pp. 231–238). Heidelberg, New York, Dordrecht, London: Springer.

Kolk, A., & van Tulder, R. (2006). Poverty alleviation as business strategy? Evaluating commitments of frontrunner multinational corporations. *World Development, 34*(5), 789–801. doi:http://dx.doi.org/10.1016/j.worlddev.2005.10.005

Korten, D. C. (1980). Community organization and rural development: A learning process approach. *Public Administration Review, 40*(5), 480–511. doi:10.2307/3110204

Kottak, C. P. (1985). When people don't come first: Some sociological lessons from completed projects. In M. M. Cernia (Ed.), *Putting people first: Sociological variables in rural development* (pp. 325–356). New York: Published for the World Bank by Oxford University Press..

KPMG. (2014). *Indian retail: The next growth story*, at https://www.kpmg.com/IN/en/IssuesAndInsights/ArticlesPublications/Documents/BBG-Retail.pdf (accessed July 13, 2015).

Krasner, S. D. (Ed.) (1985). *International regimes.* Ithaca and London: Cornell University Press.

Kuemmerle, W. (1997). Building effective R&D capabilities abroad. *Harvard Business Review*, *75*, 61–72.

Kuemmerle, W. (1999a). The drivers of foreign direct investment into research and development: An empirical investigation. *Journal of International Business Studies*, 1–24.

Kuemmerle, W. (1999b). Foreign direct investment in industrial research in the pharmaceutical and electronics industries—results from a survey of multinational firms. *Research Policy*, *28*(2), 179–193.

Kumar, S., & Corbridge, S. (2002). Programmed to fail? Development projects and the politics of participation. *Journal of Development Studies*, *39*(2), 73–103.

Kyle, D. (1999). The Otavalo trade diaspora: Social capital and transnational entrepreneurship. *Ethnic and Racial Studies*, *22*(2), 422–446. doi:10.1080/014198799329549

Lakha, S. (1990). Growth of computer software industry in India. *Economic and Political Weekly*, 49–56.

Lall, R., & Rastogi, A. (2007). *The political economy of infrastructure development in post-independence India*, at https://www.idfc.com/pdf/publications/the_political_economy_of_infrastructure_development_in_post_independence_india.pdf (accessed December 29, 2015).

Lall, S. (1992). Technological capabilities and industrialization. *World Development*, *20*(2), 165–186.

Laverack, G., & Wallerstein, N. (2001). Measuring community empowerment: A fresh look at organizational domains. *Health Promotion International*, *16*(2), 179–185.

Lawson, C., & Lorenz, E. (1999). Collective learning, tacit knowledge and regional innovative capacity. *Regional Studies*, *33*(4), 305–317.

Leadbeater, C. (1997). *The rise of the social entrepreneur*. London: Demos.

Leadbeater, C. (2000). *Living on thin air: The new economy*. London: Penguin.

Leslie, D., & Rantisi, N. M. (2006). Governing the design economy in Montreal, Canada. *Urban Affairs Review*, *41*(3), 309–337.

Lévi-Strauss, C. (1962). *The savage mind*. Chicago: University of Chicago Press.

Light, I., Bhachu, P., & Karageorgis, S. (1993). Migration networks and immigrant entrepreneurship. In *Immigration and entrepreneurship: Culture, capital, and ethnic networks* (pp. 25–50). New Brunswick, London: Transaction.

Lindblom, C. E. (1977). *Politics and markets: The world's political economic systems*. New York: Basic Books.

Liu, J., Chaminade, C., & Asheim, B. (2013). The geography and structure of global innovation networks: A knowledge base perspective. *European Planning Studies*, *21*(9), 1456–1473.

London, T., & Hart, S. L. (2004). Reinventing strategies for emerging markets: Beyond the transnational model. *Journal of International Business Studies*, *35*(5), 350–370.

Lundvall, B.-Å. (1988). Innovation as an interactive process from user producer interaction to the national system of innovation. In G. Dosi, C. Freeman, R. Nelson, G. Silverberg, & L. Soete (Eds), *Technical change and economic theory* (pp. 349–369). London: Pinter.

Lundvall, B.-Å. (1992). *National systems of innovation: Towards a theory of innovation and interactive learning*. London: Pinter.

Lundvall, B.-Å., Joseph, K., Chaminade, C., & Vang, J. (2011). *Handbook of innovation systems and developing countries: Building domestic capabilities in a global setting*. Cheltenham, UK and Northampton, MA, USA: Edward Elgar Publishing.

Malecki, E. J. (1987). The R&D location decision of the firm and "creative" regions–a survey. *Technovation*, *6*(3), 205–222.

Malena, C. (1995). *Working with NGOs: A practical guide to operational collaboration between the World Bank and nongovernmental organizations*. Washington, DC: The World Bank.

Mansuri, G., & Rao, V. (2004). Community-based and -driven development: A critical review. *The World Bank Research Observer*, *19*(1), 1–39.

Marano, V., & Tashman, P. (2012). MNE/NGO partnerships and the legitimacy of the firm. *International Business Review*, *21*(6), 1122–1130. doi:http://dx.doi.org/10.1016/j.ibusrev.2011.12.005

Martin, R. L., & Osberg, S. (2007). Social entrepreneurship: The case for definition. *Stanford Social Innovation Review*, Spring.

Martin, S., & Scott, J. T. (2000). The nature of innovation market failure and the design of public support for private innovation. *Research Policy*, *29*(4), 437–447.

Maskus, K. E., & Reichman, J. H. (2004). The globalization of private knowledge goods and the privatization of global public goods. *Journal of International Economic Law*, *7*(2), 279–320.

McMillan, S. (2013). An end in sight for extreme poverty: Scaling up BRAC's graduation model for the ultra-poor, at http://tup.brac.net/images/BRAC_Briefing_Document_on_TUP.pdf (accessed January 31, 2016).

McMullen, J. S. (2011). Delineating the domain of development entrepreneurship: A market-based approach to facilitating inclusive economic growth. *Entrepreneurship Theory and Practice*, *35*(1), 185–193.

McWilliams, A., & Siegel, D. (2001). Corporate social responsibility: A theory of the firm perspective. *Academy of Management Review, 26*(1), 117–127.

Ménard, C. (2004). The economics of hybrid organizations. *Journal of Institutional and Theoretical Economics, 160*(3), 345–376. doi: 10.1628/0932456041960605

Michelini, L. (2012). *Social innovation and new business models: Creating shared value in low-income markets.* New York: Springer.

Miles, I. (2000). Services innovation: Coming of age in the knowledge-based economy. *International Journal of Innovation Management, 4*(4), 371–389.

Millar, C. C., Choi, C. J., & Chen, S. (2004). Global strategic partnerships between MNEs and NGOs: Drivers of change and ethical issues. *Business and Society Review, 109*(4), 395–414.

Ministry of Tribal Affairs. (2013). *Statistical profile of scheduled tribes in India 2013.* Government of India.

Mittelman, J. H. (2011). *Contesting global order: Development, global governance, and globalization.* Taylor & Francis Online.

Mittelman, J. H. (2013). Global bricolage: Emerging market powers and polycentric governance. *Third World Quarterly, 34*(1), 23–37.

Mohan, A. K. (2014). *From hierarchy to heterarchy in the information age: The state and the municipal reforms programme in Karnataka, India.* (Unpublished Ph.D. Dissertation), International Institute of Information Technology, Bangalore.

Mohan, R., & Aggarwal, V. (1990). Commands and controls: Planning for Indian industrial development, 1951–1990. *Journal of Comparative Economics, 14*(4), 681–712.

Mohin, T. (2012). The top 10 trends in CSR for 2012. *Forbes.*

Montagu, D. (2002). Franchising of health services in low-income countries. *Health Policy and Planning, 17*(2), 121–130.

Moon, J., Crane, A., & Matten, D. (2011). Corporations and citizenship in new institutions of global governance. In C. Crouch & C. McLean (Eds), *The responsible corporation in a global economy.* Oxford Scholarship Online.

Moore, J. F. (1993). Predators and prey: A new ecology of competition. *Harvard Business Review,* 75–86.

Moulaert, F., & Nussbaumer, J. (2005). The social region beyond the territorial dynamics of the learning economy. *European Urban and Regional Studies, 12*(1), 45–64.

Moulaert, F., MacCallum, D., & Hillier, J. (2013). Social innovation: Intuition, precept, concept, theory and practice. In F. Moulaert, D. MacCallum, A. Mehmood, & A. Hamdouch (Eds), *The international handbook on social innovation* (pp. 13–24). Cheltenham, UK and Northampton, MA, USA: Edward Elgar Publishing.

Murphy, P., & Coombes, S. (2009). A model of social entrepreneurial discovery. *Journal of Business Ethics, 87*(3), 325–336. doi:10.1007/s10551-008-9921-y.

Murray, J. (2012). Choose your own master: Social enterprise, certifications and benefit corporation statutes. *American University Business Law Review*, June 15, 2.

NCEUS (National Commission of Enterprises in the Unorganised Sector) (2009) The challenge of employment in India: An informal economy perspective.

Neale, M. R., & Corkindale, D. R. (1998). Co-developing products: Involving customers earlier and more deeply. *Long Range Planning, 31*(3), 418–425.

Nonaka, I. (1994). A dynamic theory of organizational knowledge creation. *Organization Science, 5*, 14–37.

Nordhaus, W. D. (1994). *Managing the global commons: The economics of climate change*. Cambridge, MA: MIT Press.

NSTMIS (National Science and Technology Management Information System) Division (2015). *Directory of R&D Institutions 2015*. Department of Science and Technology, Government of India.

OECD. (2003). Philanthropic foundations and development co-operation. *DAC Journal, 4*(3).

OECD. (2008). Recent trends in the internationalisation of R&D in the enterprise sector: Special session on globalisation. *Working Party on Statistics, Committee on Industry, Innovation and Entrepreneurship, Directorate for Science, Technology and Industry*. Paris: OECD.

OECD. (2015). *Social impact investment: Building the evidence base*. Paris: OECD.

Olson, M. (1965). *The logic of collective action: Public goods and the theory of groups, revised edition*. Cambridge: Harvard University Press.

Ostrom, E. (1996). Crossing the great divide: Coproduction, synergy, and development. *World Development, 24*(6), 1073–1087.

Ostrom, E. (1999). Revisiting the commons: Local lessons, global challenges. *Science, 284*(5412), 278–282. doi:10.1126/science.284.5412.278

Ostrom, E. (2000). Collective action and the evolution of social norms. *Journal of Economic Perspectives, 14*(3), 137–158.

Ostrom, E. (2010a). Beyond markets and states: Polycentric governance of complex economic systems. *American Economic Review*, 641–672.

Ostrom, E. (2010b). Organizational economics: Applications to metropolitan governance. *Journal of Institutional Economics, 6*(1), 109. doi:10.1017/s1744137409990208

Ostrom, E. (2012). Nested externalities and polycentric institutions: Must we wait for global solutions to climate change before taking actions at other scales? *Economic Theory*, *49*(2), 353–369.

Ostrom, V., & Ostrom, E. (1999). *Public goods and public choices*. Paper presented at the Polycentricity and local public economies. Readings from the workshop in political theory and policy analysis.

Ottaway, M. (2001). Corporatism goes global: International organizations, nongovernmental organization networks, and transnational business. *Global Governance*, *7*(2), 265–292.

Oxley, J. E., & Sampson, R. C. (2004). The scope and governance of international R&D alliances. *Strategic Management Journal*, *25*, 723–749.

Parthasarathy, B. (2000). *Globalization and agglomeration in newly industrializing countries: The state and the information technology industry in Bangalore, India*. (Unpublished Ph.D. Dissertation), University of California, Berkeley.

Parthasarathy, B. (2004). India's Silicon Valley or Silicon Valley's India? Socially embedding the computer software industry in Bangalore. *International Journal of Urban and Regional Research*, *28*(3), 664–685.

Parthasarathy, B. (2010). The computer software industry as a vehicle of late industrialization: Lessons from the Indian case. *Journal of the Asia Pacific Economy*, *15*(3), 247–270. doi:10.1080/13547860.2010.494902

Parthasarathy, B., & Aoyama, Y. (2006). From software services to R&D services: Local entrepreneurship in the software industry in Bangalore, India. *Environment and Planning A*, *38*(7), 1269–1285.

Parthasarathy, B., & Ranganathan, V. (2010). *The national innovation system in India and its globalization*. Paper presented at the 8th Globelics Conference International Conference, Kuala Lumpur, Malaysia.

Patra, R., Pal, J., Nedevschi, S., Plauche, M., & Pawar, U. S. (2009). The case of the occasionally cheap computer: Low-cost devices and classrooms in the developing regions. *Information Technologies & International Development*, *5*(1), 49–64.

Paul, S. (1995). Community participation in development projects: The World Bank experience. *The World Bank Discussion Papers No. 6*. Washington, DC: The World Bank.

Penrose, E. T. (1959). *The theory of the growth of the firm*. Oxford: Oxford University Press.

Perry, J. L., & Rainey, H. G. (1988). The public–private distinction in organization theory: A critique and research strategy. *Academy of Management Review*, *13*(2), 182–201.

Pitroda, S. (1993). Development, democracy, and the village telephone. *Harvard Business Review, 71*(6), 66–68.

Planning Commission. (2008). *Eleventh Five Year Plan (2007–2012): Inclusive Growth.* Government of India.

Planning Commission. (2013a). *Twelfth Five Year Plan (2012–2017): Faster, More Inclusive and Sustainable Growth.* Volume I. Government of India.

Planning Commission. (2013b). *Twelfth Five Year Plan (2012–2017): Economic Sectors.* Volume 2. Government of India.

Platteau, J.-P., & Gaspart, F. (2003). The risk of resource misappropriation in community-driven development. *World Development, 31*(10), 1687–1703.

Polanyi, K. (1944). *The great transformation: The political and economic origins of our time.* Boston, MA: Beacon Press.

Porter, M. (1990). *The competitive advantage of nations.* New York: The Free Press.

Porter, M., & Kramer, M. R. (2006). Strategy & society: The link between competitive advantage and corporate social responsibility. *Harvard Business Review,* 1–14.

Porter, M. E., & Sakakibara, M. (2004). Competition in Japan. *Journal of Economic Perspectives,* 27–50.

Powell, W. (1990). Neither market nor hierarchy. *Research in Organizational Behavior, 12,* 295–336.

Prahalad, C. K. (2002). Strategies for the bottom of the economic pyramid: India as a source of innovation. *Reflections: The SOL Journal, 3*(4), 6–17.

Prahalad, C. K. (2006). *The fortune at the bottom of the pyramid.* India: Pearson Education.

Prahalad, C. K. (2009). *The fortune at the bottom of the pyramid, revised and updated 5th anniversary edition: Eradicating poverty through profits.* Upper Saddle River, NJ: FT Press.

Prahalad, C. K., & Hammond, A. (2002). Serving the world's poor, profitably. *Harvard Business Review, 80*(9), 48–59.

PricewaterhouseCoopers. (2011). Millennials at work: Reshaping the workplace. Press release, at https://www.pwc.com/m1/en/services/consulting/documents/millennials-at-work.pdf (accessed July 11, 2015).

PricewaterhouseCoopers. (2015). *Millennials at work: Reshaping the workplace,* at http://www.pwc.com/gx/en/managing-tomorrows-people/future-of-work/millennials-survey.jhtml (accessed July 11, 2015).

Quan, X., & Chesbrough, H. (2010). Hierarchical segmentation of R&D process and intellectual property protection: Evidence from multinational R&D laboratories in China. *Engineering Management, IEEE Transactions on Engineering Management, 57*(1), 9–21.

Radjou, N., Prabhu, J., & Ahuja, S. (2012). *Jugaad innovation: Think frugal, be flexible, generate breakthrough growth.* San Francisco, CA: John Wiley & Sons.

Ramdorai, A., & Herstatt, C. (2015). *Frugal innovation in healthcare: How targetting low-income markets leads to disruptive innovation.* Switzerland: Springer.

Rangan, H. (1996). From Chipko to Uttaranchal. *Liberation ecologies: Environment, development, social movements*, 205–226.

Rangan, H. (2007). "Development" in question. In K. Cox, M. Low, & J. Robinson (Eds), *The SAGE handbook of political geography.* London: SAGE.

Ray, P. K., & Ray, S. (2010). Resource-constrained innovation for emerging economies: The case of the Indian telecommunications industry. *IEEE Transactions on Engineering Management, 57*(1), 144–156.

Reddy, P. (1997). New trends in globalization of corporate R&D and implications for innovation capability in host countries: A survey from India. *World Development, 25*(11), 1821–1837.

Reich, R. (2008). Supercapitalism. The transformation of business, democracy and everyday life. *Society and Business Review, 3*(3), 256–258.

Reserve Bank of India. (2010). *Branch banking statistics*, at https://www.rbi.org.in/Scripts/AnnualPublications.aspx?head=Branch+Banking+Statistics (accessed January 6, 2016).

Rifkin, J. (2010). *The emphatic civilization: The race to global consciousness in a world in crisis.* New York: Tarcher.

Riggs, W., & von Hippel, E. (1994). Incentives to innovate and the sources of innovation: The case of scientific instruments. *Research Policy, 23*(4), 459–469.

Rioux, M., & Zubrow, E. (2001). Social disability and the public good. In D. Drache (Ed.), *The market or the public domain? Global governance and the asymmetry of power* (pp. 148–173). London and New York: Routledge.

Rittel, H. W., & Webber, M. M. (1973). Planning problems are wicked problems. In N. Cross (Ed.), *Developments in design methodology.* New York: John Wiley & Sons.

Roberts, S. M., Jones III, J. P., & Fröhling, O. (2005). NGOs and the globalization of managerialism: A research framework. *World Development, 33*(11), 1845–1864.

Rodin, J., & Brandenburg, M. (2014). *The power of impact investing: Putting markets to work for profit and global good.* Wharton Digital Press.

Rodrik, D. (1997). *Has globalization gone too far?* Washington, DC: Institute of International Economics.

Rondinelli, D. A., & London, T. (2003). How corporations and environmental groups cooperate: Assessing cross-sector alliances and collaborations. *Academy of Management Executive, 17*(1), 61–76.

Ruggie, J. G. (2004). *Reconstituting the global public domain: Issues, actors, practices.* Faculty Research Working Paper Series. John F. Kennedy School of Government. Harvard University.

Sabeti, H. (2011). The for-benefit enterprise. *Harvard Business Review, 89*(11), 98–104.

Salamon, L. M. (2014). *New frontiers of philanthropy: A guide to the new tools and actors reshaping global philanthropy and social investing.* New York: Oxford University Press.

Samuelson, P. A. (1954). The pure theory of public expenditure. *Review of Economics and Statistics, 36*(4), 387–389. doi:10.2307/1925895

Sandler, T. (1997). *Global challenges: An approach to environmental, political, and economic problems.* Cambridge, MA: Cambridge University Press.

Sandler, T. (1998). Global and regional public goods: A prognosis for collective action. *Fiscal Studies, 19*(3), 221–247.

Santiso, C. (2001). Good governance and aid effectiveness: The World Bank and conditionality. *Georgetown Public Policy Review, 7*(1), 1–22.

Sassen, S. (2006). *Territory, authority, rights: From medieval to global assemblages*: Princeton, NJ and Oxford: Princeton University Press.

Saxenian, A. (1999). *Silicon Valley's new immigrant entrepreneurs* (Vol. 32). San Francisco: Public Policy Institute of California.

Saxenian, A. (2006). *The new argonauts: Regional advantage in a global economy.* Cambridge, MA: Harvard University Press.

Schelling, T. (1978). *Micromotives and macrobehavior.* Toronto, Canada: George J. McLeod Ltd.

Schlüter, A., Then, V., & Walkenhorst, P. (2001). *Foundations in Europe.* Washington, DC: Brookings Institution Press.

Schoenberger, E. (2015). *Nature, choice and social power.* London and New York: Routledge.

Scholte, J. A. (2004). Civil society and democratically accountable global governance. *Government and Opposition, 39*(2), 211–233.

Scholte, J. A. (2011). *Building global democracy? Civil society and accountable global governance.* Cambridge: Cambridge University Press.

Schuler, D., & Namioka, A. (1993). *Participatory design: Principles and practices.* Oxon, UK: CRC Press.

Schwittay, A. (2011). The marketization of poverty. *Current Anthropology, 52*(S3).

Scott, A. J. (2002). Regional push: Towards a geography of development and growth in low- and middle-income countries. *Third World Quarterly, 23*(1), 137–161.

Sending, O. J., & Neumann, I. B. (2006). Governance to governmentality: Analyzing NGOs, states, and power. *International Studies Quarterly, 50*(3), 651–672. doi:10.2307/4092797

Serapio, M. G., & Dalton, D. H. (1999). Globalization of industrial R&D: An examination of foreign direct investments in R&D in the United States. *Research Policy, 28*(2–3), 303–316.

Sharir, M., & Lerner, M. (2006). Gauging the success of social ventures initiated by individual social entrepreneurs. *Journal of World Business, 41*(1), 6–20.

Sharma, A., Srivastava, H., & Belokar, R. (2011). Case study analysis through the implementation of value engineering. *International Journal of Engineering Science and Technology, 3*, 2204–2213.

Shaw, E., & Carter, S. (2007). Social entrepreneurship: Theoretical antecedents and empirical analysis of entrepreneurial processes and outcomes. *Journal of Small Business and Enterprise Development, 14*(3), 418–434.

Sheppard, E., & Leitner, H. (2010). Quo vadis neoliberalism? The remaking of global capitalist governance after the Washington Consensus. *Geoforum, 41*(2), 185–194.

Simms, S. V., & Robinson, J. (2009). Activist or entrepreneur? An identity-based model of social entrepreneurship. In J. Robinson, J. Mair, & K. Hockerts (Eds), *International Perspectives on Social Entrepreneurship*, 9–26. Taylor & Francis Online.

Slaughter, A.-M. (2004). *A new world order*. Princeton, NJ: Princeton University Press.

Smillie, I. (1995). *The alms bazaar: Altruism under fire—non-profit organizations and international development*. London: IT Publications.

Sommerrock, D. K., & Sommerrock, K. (2010). *Social entrepreneurship business models: Incentive strategies to catalyze public goods provision*. Basingstoke, UK: Palgrave Macmillan.

Sonne, L. (2012). Innovative initiatives supporting inclusive innovation in India: Social business incubation and micro venture capital. *Technological Forecasting and Social Change, 79*(4), 638–647.

Sonnemans, J., Schram, A., & Offerman, T. (1998). Public good provision and public bad prevention: The effect of framing. *Journal of Economic Behavior & Organization, 34*(1), 143–161.

Spero, J. E. (2014). *Charity and philanthropy: In Russia, China, India and Brazil*, at http://foundationcenter.org/gainknowledge/research/pdf/philanthropy_bric.pdf (accessed July 12, 2015).

Sridharan, E. (1996). *The political economy of industrial promotion: Indian, Brazilian, and Korean electronics in comparative perspective 1969–1994*. Westport, CT: Greenwood Publishing Group.

Stiglitz, J. E. (2002). Participation and development: Perspectives from the comprehensive development paradigm. *Review of Development Economics, 6*, 163–182.

Stiglitz, J. E. (2007). *Making globalization work*. New York: W. W. Norton & Company.

Stiglitz, J. E. (2008). The future of global governance. In N. Serra & J. E. Stiglitz (Eds), *The Washington Consensus reconsidered: Towards a new global governance* (pp. 309–323). Oxford: Oxford University Press.

Stoker, G. (1998). Governance as theory: Five propositions. *International Social Science Journal, 50*(155), 17–28. doi:10.1111/1468-2451.00106.

Stoll, P. T. (2008). Public goods: The governance dimension. In V. Rittberger, & M. Nettesheim (Eds), *Authority in the global political economy* (pp. 116–136). Basingstoke, Hampshire, UK and New York: Palgrave Macmillan.

Storper, J. (2015). Is benefit corporation legislation really necessary? *Conscious Company Magazine,* 128–129.

Storper, M. (2009). Roepke lecture in economic geography—Regional context and global trade. *Economic Geography, 85*(1), 1–21.

Storper, M., & Venables, A. J. (2004). Buzz: Face-to-face contact and the urban economy. *Journal of Economic Geography, 4*(4), 351–370. doi:10.1093/jnlecg/lbh027

Subramanian, C. (1992). *India and the computer: A study of planned development*. New Delhi: Oxford University Press.

Sugden, J. (2015). What IT professionals earn around the world. *Wall Street Journal*, September 21, at http://blogs.wsj.com/indiarealtime/2015/09/21/what-it-professionals-earn-around-the-world/ (accessed January 31, 2016).

Swyngedouw, E. (2005). Governance innovation and the citizen: The Janus face of governance-beyond-the-State. *Urban Studies, 42*(11), 1991–2006. doi:10.1080/00420980500279869

Teegen, H., Doh, J. P., & Vachani, S. (2004). The importance of nongovernmental organizations (NGOs) in global governance and value creation: An international business research agenda. *Journal of International Business Studies, 35*(6), 463–483.

Tellis, A. (2006). *Mahatma Gandhi's constructive program: Building a New India*. (Ph.D. Unpublished Dissertation), University of Illinois, Urbana Champaign.

The Economic Times. (2015). CSR spend may grow over 4 times to $2.5 billion. *The Economic Times*. February 15, at http://articles.

economictimes.indiatimes.com/2015-02-15/news/59166737_1_csr-activities-companies-act-top-100-companies (accessed July 12, 2015).

The Economist. (2008). Just good business. *The Economist*, January 17.

The Economist. (2015). Shareholder activism: Capitalism's unlikely heroes. *The Economist*, February 17.

The Foundation Center. (2012). *International grantmaking update: A snapshot of US foundation trends*, at http://foundationcenter.org/gainknowledge/research/pdf/intl_update_2012.pdf (accessed July 6, 2015).

The Foundation Center. (2014). *Aggregate fiscal data of foundations in the US, 2013*, at http://data.foundationcenter.org/#/foundations/all/nationwide/total/list/2013 (accessed July 6, 2015).

The World Bank. (2007). *Unleashing India's innovation: Toward sustainable and inclusive growth*. In M. A. Dutz (Ed.), Washington, DC: The World Bank.

Thomas, E. A. (Ed.) (2016). *Broken pumps and promises: Incentivizing impact in environmental health*. Heidelberg, New York, Dordrecht, London: Springer.

Tosun, C. (2000). Limits to community participation in the tourism development process in developing countries. *Tourism Management*, *21*(6), 613–633.

Tracey, P., & Jarvis, O. (2007). Toward a theory of social venture franchising. *Entrepreneurship Theory and Practice*, *31*(5), 667–685.

Tyabji, N. (1989). *The small industries policy in India*. New Delhi: Oxford University Press.

UNCTAD. (2005). *Transnational corporations and the internationalisation of R&D*. Geneva: United Nations.

United Nations. (2003). *Handbook on non-profit institutions in the system of national accounts*. Department of Economic and Social Affairs.

United Nations Development Program. (2014). *Human Development Report 2014: Sustaining human progress: Reducing vulnerabilities and building resilience*, at http://hdr.undp.org/sites/default/files/hdr14-report-en-1.pdf (accessed December 29, 2015).

Utterback, J. M., Vedin, B.-A., Alvarez, E., Ekman, S., Sanderson, S. W., Tether, B., & Verganti, R. (2006). *Design-inspired innovation*. New York: World Scientific.

Utting, P., & Marques, J. C. (2010). Introduction: The intellectual crisis of CSR. In P. Utting & J. C. Marques (Eds), *Corporate social responsibility and regulatory governance* (pp. 1–25). Houndmills, Basingstoke: Palgrave Macmillan.

Vaidyanathan, R. (2012). Can the "American Dream" be reversed in India? *BBC News*. November 5, at http://www.bbc.com/news/world-asia-india-20201666 (accessed December 14, 2014).

Vaishnav, M. (2015). *Modi's reform agenda: Change you can believe in?* Gütersloh, Germany: Bertelsmann Stiftung.

Valor, C. (2005). Corporate social responsibility and corporate citizenship: Towards corporate accountability. *Business and Society Review*, *110*(2), 191–212. doi:10.1111/j.0045-3609.2005.00011.x

Van Dyck, B., & Van den Broeck, P. (2013). Social innovation: A territorial process. In F. Moulaert, D. MacCallum, A. Mehmood, & A. Hamdouch (Eds), *The international handbook of social innovation: Collective action, social learning and transdisciplinary research.* Cheltenham, UK and Northampton, MA, USA: Edward Elgar Publishing.

Verganti, R. (2009). *Design driven innovation.* Boston: Harvard Business School Press.

Vinodrai, T. (2006). Reproducing Toronto's design ecology: Career paths, intermediaries, and local labor markets. *Economic Geography*, *82*(3), 237–263.

Vishwanath, T., Lall, S. V., Dowall, D., Lozano-Gracia, N., Sharma, S., & Wang, H. G. (2013). *Urbanization beyond municipal boundaries: Nurturing metropolitan economies and connecting peri-urban areas in India.* Washington, DC: The World Bank.

Vogel, D. (2007). *The market for virtue: The potential and limits of corporate social responsibility.* Washington, DC: Brookings Institution Press.

von Hippel, E. (1976). The dominant role of users in the scientific instrument innovation process. *Research Policy*, *5*(3), 212–239.

von Hippel, E. (1977). Transferring process equipment innovations from user-innovators to equipment manufacturing firms. *R&D Management*, *8*(1), 13–22.

von Hippel, E. (1989). New product ideas from "lead users." *Research-Technology Management*, *32*(3), 24–28.

von Hippel, E. (2001). Innovation by user communities: Learning from open-sources software. *MIT Sloan Management Review*, 82–86.

von Hippel, E. (2005). *Democratizing innovation.* Cambridge, MA: MIT Press.

Von Zedtwitz, M., & Gassmann, O. (2002). Market versus technology drive in R&D internationalization: Four different patterns of managing research and development. *Research Policy*, *31*(4), 569–588.

Waddock, S. (2000). The multiple bottom lines of corporate citizenship: Social investing, reputation, and responsibility audits. *Business and Society Review*, *105*(3), 323–345. doi:10.1111/0045-3609.00085

Waddock, S. (2004). Parallel universes: Companies, academics, and the progress of corporate citizenship. *Business and Society Review*, *109*(1), 5–42. doi:10.1111/j.0045-3609.2004.00002.x

Warhurst, A. (2005). Future roles of business in society: The expanding boundaries of corporate responsibility and a compelling case for partnership. *Futures*, *37*(2), 151–168.

Webb, J. W., Kistruck, G. M., Ireland, R. D., & Ketchen, J. D. J. (2010). The entrepreneurship process in base of the pyramid markets: The case of multinational enterprise/nongovernment organization alliances. *Entrepreneurship Theory and Practice*, *34*(3), 555–581. doi:10.1111/j.1540-6520.2009.00349.x

Weerawardena, J., & Mort, G. S. (2006). Investigating social entre-preneurship: A multidimensional model. *Journal of World Business*, *41*(1), 21–35.

Weerawardena, J., McDonald, R. E., & Mort, G. S. (2010). Sustainability of nonprofit organizations: An empirical investigation. *Journal of World Business*, *45*(4), 346–356.

Weintraub, J., & Kumar, K. (1997). *The theory and politics of the public/private distinction*. Chicago: University of Chicago Press.

Weisbrod, B. A. (1964). Collective-consumption services of individual-consumption goods. *Quarterly Journal of Economics*, *78*(3), 471–477. doi:10.2307/1879478

Weisbrod, B. A. (Ed.) (2000). *To profit or not to profit: The commercial transformation of the nonprofit sector*. Cambridge: Cambridge University Press.

Wenger, E. (1999). *Communities of practice: Learning, meaning, and identity*. Cambridge: Cambridge University Press.

Wessner, C. W., & Shivakumar, S. J. (Eds.). (2007). *India's changing innovation system: Achievements, challenges, and opportunities for cooperation. Report of a symposium*. Washington, DC: National Research Council.

White, S. C. (1996). Depoliticising development: The uses and abuses of participation. *Development in Practice*, *6*(1), 6–15.

Whitney, P., & Kelkar, A. (2004). Designing for the base of the pyramid. *Design Management Review*, *15*(4), 41–47.

Williamson, O. E. (1981). The modern corporation: Origins, evolution, attributes. *Journal of Economic Literature*, *19*(4), 1537–1568.

Williamson, O. E. (1985). *The economic institutions of capitalism. Firms, markets, relational contracting*. New York: The Free Press.

Williamson, O. E. (1993). Calculativeness, trust, and economic organ-ization. *Journal of Law and Economics*, *36*(1), 453–486.

Winston, M. (2002). NGO strategies for promoting corporate social responsibility. *Ethics & International Affairs*, *16*(01), 71–87.

Wolf, C. (1993). *Markets or governments: Choosing between imperfect alternatives*. Cambridge, MA: MIT Press.

World Bank. (1989). *Saharan Africa: from crisis to sustainable growth.* Washington, DC: The World Bank.

World Bank. (Ed.) (1994). *Governance: The World Bank's experience.* Washington, DC: The World Bank.

World Bank. (2008). *World Development Report 2009: Reshaping economic geography.* Washington, DC: World Bank.

World Bank Group. (2015a). What are public private partnerships, at http://ppp.worldbank.org/public-private-partnership/overview/what-are-public-private-partnerships (accessed February 6, 2016).

World Bank Group. (2015b). *World Development Indicators 2015.* Washington, DC: The World Bank.

Wright, M., Liu, X., Buck, T., & Filatotchev, I. (2008). Returnee entrepreneurs, science park location choice and performance: An analysis of high-technology SMEs in China. *Entrepreneurship Theory and Practice, 32*(1), 131–155.

Xu, B., & Albert, E. (2014). *Governance in India: Infrastructure.* Washington, DC: Council on Foreign Relations.

Yaziji, M., & Doh, J. (2009). *NGOs and corporations: Conflict and collaboration.* Cambridge: Cambridge University Press.

Yeung, H. (2016). *Strategic coupling: East Asian industrial transformation in the new global economy.* Ithaca: Cornell University Press.

Zaheer, S. (1995). Overcoming the liability of foreignness. *Academy of Management Journal, 38*(2), 341–363.

Zahra, S. A., Rawhouser, H. N., Bhawe, N., Neubaum, D. O., & Hayton, J. C. (2008). Globalization of social entrepreneurship opportunities. *Strategic Entrepreneurship Journal, 2*(2), 117–131. doi:10.1002/sej.43

Zelenika, I., & Pearce, J. M. (2011). Barriers to appropriate technology growth in sustainable development. *Journal of Sustainable Development, 4*(6), 12–22.

Zenger, T. R., & Hesterly, W. S. (1997). The disaggregation of corporations: Selective intervention, high-powered incentives, and molecular units. *Organization Science, 8*(3), 209–222.

Zeschky, M., Widenmayer, B., & Gassmann, O. (2011). Frugal innovation in emerging markets. *Research-Technology Management, 54*(4), 38–45.

Zhou, M. (2004). Revisiting ethnic entrepreneurship: Convergencies, controversies, and conceptual advancements. *International Migration Review, 38*(3), 1040–1074. doi:10.1111/j.1747-7379.2004.tb00228.x

Index

Aavishkaar (Venture Management)
50–51
Abraaj Capital 50–51
academic institutions, role of 13, 178,
182
accountability
financial 33, 47–8, 164
social 34, 164, 189
action
collective 1, 11, 15, 21–3, 28, 32–3,
41, 81, 191
rational 66
irrational 66
activist 42, 160
activist-entrepreneur identity 42
actors *see also* stakeholder
hierarchical 29
rational 19–20, 25
Acumen Fund 50
advocacy 12–13, 33, 39, 41, 47, 165
affordability 57, 61, 91, 94, 112, 135
affordable medical diagnostic tools 12,
115–17
Afghanistan 70, 109, 118, 123
Africa 15–16, 48, 70, 78, 106–10, 123,
179
Aga Khan Foundation 48
agency, distributed 26
agricultural practices 118–19
Agricultural Product Market
Committee (India) 120
air pollution 19, 133
altruism 20
amplification 105–6
Andhra Pradesh 98, 120–21
appropriate technology 101
Ashoka Foundation 42
Assam 121
austerity 11, 42, 53

autonomy
distributed 23
from state action 41
local 23
Azim Premji Foundation 48

Bangalore 10, 14, 100, 103–4, 106, 114,
119–21, 136, 170, 181
Bangladesh 40, 42, 109
"bank-less" banking 125–7
behavioral economics 66
benefit corporation 30, 36 *see also*
enterprise
Belgium 41
Bharti Foundation 48
Big Society Capital 50
Bihar 105, 113–14, 126, 130
Bill and Melinda Gates Foundation
47–8, 51, 114, 119, 123, 126, 137,
183
B-Corps 36–7
Bhutan 109
Big Bang Philanthropy 47 *see also*
philanthropy; venture
philanthropy
blurring of boundaries 12, 17, 29, 33,
52, 138
BOP (base/bottom-of-the-pyramid)
market 8, 12, 62–3, 65, 82–8,
90–91, 104, 135, 144–45
myth of profitability 84–7
niche segments 85
bottom-line 8, 84, 179
double 36
triple 3, 39
bottom-up 12, 28, 93–6, 106, 109, 111,
189–90 *see also* design
Boston 50, 183

223

BPO (business process outsourcing)
    centers 5, 124
BRAC (Bangladesh Rehabilitation
    Assistance Committee) 40, 85
brand 37, 83, 88, 111, 114, 141
bricolage/bricoleur 11, 26–7, 185–7
BRICS (Brazil, Russia, India, China,
    South Africa) 26, 69–71, 112–13,
    125
Brown University 44
Buffet, Warren 45–7
business model
    diverse 63
    ethical 143
    global offshore delivery 74
    innovation 57
    micro-delivery 55, 60
    micro-franchising 12, 54–5, 135–6
    Robin Hood 50, 169–73
    socially sustainable 134, 139, 142–4,
        165
    transnational access to 44

California 102
Cambridge University 44, 177
Cameroon 109
Canada 36, 45
capabilities 77, 91, 131, 143
capacity building 1, 134, 139
capitalism 31, 35, 51, 188–9
    creative 65
    global 1, 25
    inclusive 65–6
    stakeholder-driven 2
    see also philanthrocapitalism
case studies 9, 12, 68, 112, 136–7
catalyst 42–3, 100, 133–4, 171
cell phone *see* mobile phone
certification 127–8
charity 37, 39, 48, 143, 165, 171
    limits of 38, 49, 84, 143, 184
Chennai 10, 124
China 3, 59, 62, 69, 117–18, 136, 154
CICs (Community Interest Companies)
    36
civil society 3, 16, 23, 28, 31, 91, 187

civil society organization 2, 4, 8, 16, 40,
    55–6, 59, 168, 188 *see also* NGO;
    non-profit sector
closed system 31–2, 126–27
cloud (computing) 97, 99, 131, 135
club goods 19
collaboration 1, 5, 8, 13, 20, 24, 33, 35,
    52, 56–7, 59, 68, 79, 81, 98, 111,
    114, 118, 121, 130, 144–51, 153,
    170, 188–90
    among philanthropists 45
    challenges in 156–63
    cross-domain 12, 91, 137, 156,
        158–9, 171
    cross-sectoral 29–30
    multi-scalar 31
collaborative polygon 172
collective action *see* action, collective
    bargaining 34
commons
    closed 41
    creative 118
    global 20, 13
    open 41
    regional economic 20
    "tragedy of the" 66
common property resources 11, 15, 23,
    24
community *see also* user; participatory
    beneficiaries 41
    -driven innovation 120
    tribal 31, 122–3, 141
    underserved 134, 180
communities of practice 56
competition 20, 54, 95, 111, 190
complementarity 17, 51, 169
compliance 34
configural approaches 23
constraints
    bandwidth 110
    design for *see* design
    infrastructural 93, 99
    regulatory 51
    resource 57, 110
    territorial 21
construction workers 105, 127–9
consumers 35, 39, 56, 59–61, 63–5, 95,
    104, 110 *see also* user

BOP 83–4
  emerging market 89, 91, 102
  poor 8, 58
consumption 20, 32, 64, 75, 86, 90, 110
  energy 132
  non-rival 21
  of common property 23
contexts 96, 101–7, 169, 186–7
  emerging market 89, 144
  geographical 57
  institutional 55, 63, 68
contextual intelligence 8, 57, 63
conventions 24, 31
cooperatives 31, 40–41, 77, 134, 145
co-production 23
corporate citizenship 13, 34–5, 154
corporate scandals 2
corporation 2–4, 16, 20, 24, 29–30,
    33–40, 56–9, 61–3, 65, 81, 85–92,
    111–12, 118, 130, 139–42, 159,
    164, 170, 189 *see also* enterprise;
    CSR
cost arbitrage 5, 6, 12, 95, 101–2
creative capitalism *see* capitalism
creditworthiness 131, 132
crop prices 119–20
cross-cultural exchanges 26, 175–6
cross-domain 12, 30–33, 47, 91, 136–7,
    156, 159, 171 *see also*
    collaboration
CSR (corporate social responsibility) 3,
    8, 29, 33, 37–9, 56, 67, 81–2, 105,
    121, 140–43, 145, 147–9, 156,
    172, 188
  consulting 170
  limits of 138–40
  reform of 142
  strategic 141

DAC (Development Assistance
    Committee) 68
de-featuring 12, 57, 93–4, 101
Delhi 10, 44, 115, 126
Dell Foundation 51
deregulation 18
design 29, 43 54–5, 57, 59, 92–100,
    103, 105–6, 119, 131–2, 177
  bottom-up 12, 93–6, 106–7, 109, 111

engineering 8, 12, 56, 177
evidenced-based 17
for constraints 12, 93–4, 96–101, 111
institutional 3, 21, 53
pro-poor 3–4, 86
de-territorialized beneficiaries 31
development
  inclusive 70, 80–81, 91, 112
  participatory 65–6
  rural 48, 112
disaster relief 48
disruptive innovation *see* innovation
diverse economy 51–2, 17–18
division of labor 2–4, 18, 22, 31, 60,
    148–9, 156, 172, 188
domain flexibility *see* flexibility
Dominican Republic 133
"double movement" 28, 189–90
donors 48, 79, 114, 119, 170
Drucker, Peter 53

Eastern Europe 107
East Timor 109, 121
eco-innovation *see* innovation
economic crisis 2, 42
ecosystem 33, 100, 128, 130, 132, 134,
    151, 167
education 1, 19, 40, 43, 48, 55, 66–7,
    70–71, 81, 86, 91–2, 122–4, 129,
    134, 154–5, 162, 167, 172, 174
  distance 148
  online 145
  remote 141
  universal 80
  see also SSA
efficiency 16, 18, 19, 45, 54, 75, 157,
    166, 170
egalitarianism 30
e-learning 128
embeddedness 17, 43–4
emerging market, 4, 57, 63, 88–97, 102,
    105, 109, 117, 119–20, 144
employability 128–9
employment portal 129–30
empowerment 8, 11, 53, 66, 81, 145
energy 29, 43, 54, 60, 100, 103, 107–8,
    112, 139, 141, 152, 154, 171, 181

renewable 132–6, 144–5, 153, 165–6, 168, 174
-saving 95, 134–6
Engineers without Borders 179–80
enterprise *see also* corporation
  commercial 10–11, 36, 40–41, 111, 165–6, 169
  MNE (multinational) 6, 9–10, 39, 58–60, 62–3, 82–4, 87, 91, 94, 101–11, 119–21, 123, 125–6, 128–9, 131–2, 136–62, 164, 172, 187–8
  MSME (micro, small and medium-sized) 76, 77, 81
  social 2, 9–11, 13, 29–30, 36, 40–44, 47, 50–51, 64, 67, 97, 114–16, 126–8, 133–4, 136–8, 145, 153–4, 163–7, 169–74, 177–8, 183
entrepreneurship 2, 26, 44–5, 49, 75, 91, 134, 177, 189, 191
  ethnic/diaspora 43
  micro- 49, 60, 134, 139
  returnee/Argonaut 43
  serial 116
  social 4, 41–3, 48, 56–7, 140, 163–9, 179–81, 184–5
  TSE (transnational social) 8, 43–4, 104, 174–86
environmental monitoring 108
EPA (Environmental Protection Agency) 35
"etatisation of society" 38–9
ethical 65, 86
  banking 42–3
  business model *see* business model
  investment 3, 49–51
ethics 30, 34, 37, 143
Ethiopia 109, 118–19
ethnographic practice 104–5
exclusion *see* social exclusion
experimental 32, 108, 132, 145, 189–90
export-led industrialization 34
externalities 21, 188
  negative 19, 21–2, 31–2
  positive 19, 21, 31–2, 64
  social 191

face-to-face interactions 58
failure
  double 55, 189, 190
  heterarchical 25
  market 12, 18–19, 21, 25, 64, 189–90
  non-market 56
  systemic 188–9
  state 2, 4, 11, 53, 55, 57, 67, 91, 189
family planning 113–14
finance, micro- *see* micro-finance
finance, social *see* social finance
financial inclusion *see* inclusion
financial literacy 167–8
firm, theory of the 37, 39, 62 *see also* corporation; enterprise
for profit sector 39, 65, 158, 160, 162–3
flexibility
  domain 12–13, 31–3, 137–8, 188
  organizational 29–30
  scalar 13, 31, 137, 174
Ford Foundation 46, 76, 119
foundations 36, 50–51, 52, 60, 137, 153, 156, 166–7, 185, 187
  corporate 29–30, 48,
  global 10, 40, 48
  private 40, 44–7, 67, 119, 136, 170
  religious 48, 146
"fourth sector" 41, 56 *see also* enterprise; entrepreneurship
France 41
free-rider problem 23–4, 42–3

Gandhian ideals 6, 8, 70–71, 77, 80, 91
Gandhi, Indira 73
Gandhi, Rajiv 74
Gates Foundation *see* Bill and Melinda Gates Foundation
geography 8–9, 49, 57–9, 63, 191 *see also* location
Ghana 119, 152
Giving Pledge 45
"glass floor" 39, 94–5, 111
global civil society 31
Global Innovation Index 5–6, 69
global merit goods 20–22, 25, 32, 52
global public goods 11, 15–16, 20–21, 27, 44

governance 1–2, 13–18, 25–30, 56, 75
  collaborative 4, 13, 61
  corporate 11
  gap 32–4
  global 4, 22, 30, 34, 38–9, 40
  good 15–16
  hybrid 5, 31–3
  meta- 25, 32, 187
  network 1, 24–7, 187
  polycentric 1–2, 11, 15, 22–3, 25, 27, 32–3
  scales in 25
  shareholder 35
  stakeholder 22, 35
  void 28
government *see* state
government certificates 100, 155
GPPP (global public–private partnership) *see* partnership
GPS (geographic positioning system) 100–101
Grameen Bank 42
Grameen Foundation 126
Grand Challenges Canada 116, 183
grassroots innovation *see* innovation
grassroots NGOs *see* NGOs
Green Revolution 73–4
Gujarat 98, 120

Hardin, Garrett 20, 66
Harvard Business School 177–8, 181
Haryana 121
healthcare 40–41, 47, 54, 70, 80, 84, 86–7, 97, 109, 112–14, 141, 143, 149, 167–70, 176–7
heterarchical failure *see* failure
heterarchy 1–2, 11, 24–5, 27, 29–30, 32–3, 187
heterogeneity 31–2, 40, 63, 65, 188–9, 191
hierarchy 22, 24, 163, 187
HIV 70, 117, 166–7
Hivos Foundation 123, 137
HNWIs (high-net-worth individuals) 48, 50–51
Hume, David 18

hybrid domain 1–2, 4, 6, 8, 11–13, 27–34, 40, 44–5, 48, 51–2, 67–8, 136–8, 163, 172–4, 187–91
hybrid entities 2, 30, 189
hybrid governance 5, 31–3
hybrid logic 28, 190
hybrid mission 30, 56
hybrid norms *see* norms
hybrid organization *see* organization
Hyderabad 10

I3N (Intellecap Impact Investment Network) 51
ICTs (information and communication technologies) 3, 15, 23–4, 54–5, 60, 191 *see also* Internet
IIT (Indian Institute of Technology) 182
illiteracy 3, 100
IMF (International Monetary Fund) 74–5
immigrants 43, 182 *see also* migrants
immunoassays 115
impact investment 49–51, 164
impacts
  disruptive 96, 151, 191
  social 2, 55–6, 63, 67, 111, 138, 174, 189
  systemic 5, 15, 56, 188–90
import-substitution 72
incentive 76, 190
  deficient 64
  financial 47
  user 64–6, 99
inclusion
  financial 81–2, 122, 125–7
  socio-political 5, 122, 134
inclusive capitalism *see* capitalism
inclusive development *see* development
India 5–11, 69–81, 101–37
Indian Angels Network 51
indigenous
  knowledge 60
  requirement 96
  technology 72, 75
Indonesia 107, 121, 152
Industrial Policy (India) 72, 75 i
industrialization 34, 72–3, 188–9
infant mortality rate 152

informal employment 127, 129
informal retailers 131–2
informal sector 3, 77, 112, 127, 130–31
information asymmetry 29, 117–18,
    150
infrastructure 3, 6, 8, 43, 55, 57, 67,
    70–75, 80–81, 99–100, 113,
    116–17, 122, 125–7, 131, 141,
    154, 189
innovation
  business model 57
  community driven 120
  disincentives for 72–3
  disruptive 16, 151, 191
  eco- 60
  frugal 8, 57, 93–5
  grassroots 3, 6, 8
  institutional 68
  market-driven 55–6, 61–5, 68
  open 62, 68
  organizational 12, 32, 185
  pedagogical 128
  resource-constrained 57, 70, 72
  reverse 9–10, 93, 109
  social 1–6, 8–9, 53–68, 83, 89, 91–2,
    101, 103–5, 112, 136, 154,
    185–6, 189–90
  technological 3, 55, 57, 72, 107
  user-led 64
institutional bricolage 11, 26–7
institutional contexts *see* contexts
institutional design *see* design
institutional diversity 31, 52
institutional innovation *see* innovation
institutional knowledge *see* knowledge
institutional path-dependence 21–2
institutional reform *see* reform
institutional thickness 77–8, 189
interdependencies 15, 57
intergenerational responsibilities 16,
    34–5
international aid/development agency
    16, 67–8, 183
International Financial Corporation
    50
Internet 5, 59, 61–2, 64, 68, 98, 114,
    122–3 *see also* ICTs
investment

ethical *see* ethical, investment
impact *see* impact investment
PRI (program related) 50
ROI (return on) 88–9
    see also MIF
IP (intellectual property) 3, 62
Iran 121
Iraq 109
Italy 41, 49

Jan-Dhan Yojana 82
jeito 3
Jessop, Bob 24–5, 187
Jharkhand 121, 126
jugaad 3, 57, 77

Kanchipuram 116
Karnataka 105, 119–21, 124, 136, 170
know-how 9, 43–4, 155–6
know-who 155–6
knowledge
  contextual 12, 60, 96, 99
  demand-side 61
  gap 103–5, 153–4
  indigenous *see* indigenous
    knowledge
  institutional 60
  scientific 61
  spillover 59, 67
  tacit 56, 58, 120, 128
  technical 59, 181
  transfer (South–South) 106–9

L3C (Low-profit Limited Liability
    Company) 36
'last mile' problem/solution 55, 114–15
late industrializers 71–2
lead user 58, 63
leapfrog 96–7
learning 6, 96, 101, 105–6, 127, 189
  by partnering 120, 138, 144–5, 151,
    159–60
  contextual 55–6, 151
  cross-sector 33
  inter-organizational 56, 58
  through amplifying 12, 55, 105
  through collaborating 11, 59, 144–56
  through experiencing 106

through local presence 12, 102–3
legitimacy, social *see* social legitimacy
local presence 12, 102–3 *see also*
    geography; location
localization 58, 60, 96
location 5–6, 8, 43, 56–8, 63, 70, 78,
    106, 111, 114, 131 *see also*
    geography; local presence
London School of Economics 44, 181

Macarthur Foundation 123, 137
Manipur 121
market-based strategies 41–2, 45,
    47–8
market intelligence 11, 53, 61, 64, 68
market logic 53, 190
marketization of the state 2
Maslow's hierarchy of needs 109
Mastercard Foundation 40
medical device 85, 87–90, 112–13, 170
medical diagnostics 112, 115–17, 137,
    176
Meghalaya 121
merit goods 19, 28, 52, 173
Mexico 177
MGNREGA (Mahatma Gandhi
    National Rural Employment
    Guarantee Act) 80–81
micro-ATM (automatic teller machine)
    100, 132
micro-credit 54–5, 171–2, 167–8
micro-delivery 55, 60
micro-finance 95
micro-franchising 12, 54, 135–6
micro-packaging 95
micro-payment 134–5
middle class 90, 104
MIF (Multilateral Investment Fund)
    50
migrants 125–6 *see also* immigrants
millennials 30, 37–8, 179–80
missions
    dual 2, 32, 165
    hybrid 30, 56
    social 2, 27, 29, 35–6, 43, 49, 56, 135,
        141, 149, 152, 163
MIT (Massachusetts Institute of
    Technology) 44

mitigation 22, 32
MNE (Multinational Enterprise) *see*
    enterprise
mobile phone 12, 60, 63, 94, 109–10,
    114, 121–3, 135, 176–7
mobilization 1, 168
Modi, Narendra 81–2
monopoly 18–19
MOP (middle of the pyramid) market
    89–90, 144–5
moral hazards 16
Moulaert, Frank 53–4
multi-lingual 8, 97, 107
Mumbai Angels 51
Myanmar 121

National Rural Health Mission (India)
    80–82
National Skill Development
    Corporation (India) 129
national system of innovation 55, 67
needs-centered perspective 64–5
    also see Maslow's hierarchy of
    needs
Nehruvian ideals 6, 70, 72, 76, 80, 91
NGO (non-governmental organization)
    4, 8, 13, 29–30, 33, 38–41, 47, 65,
    67, 77–81, 86–7, 98, 102, 113–14,
    118–19, 121–3, 144–68, 170–73,
    178, 184, 187–9
    grassroots 8–9, 86, 118–19
    leveraged 29–30, 33, 163
    strategic 29
Niger 118–19
Nike Foundation 40
non-profit sector 32, 35, 38–9, 44–5, 56,
    138, 170–73
norms 24, 27, 29, 60, 182–3, 187–8
    hybrid 31
    shared 188
NRI (Non-resident Indian) 74, 175
nutrition 118, 141, 166

ODA (official development assistance)
    44
Omidyar Network 50
open innovation *see* innovation
open source 64, 123, 176–7

organization
　hybrid 13, 30, 32, 35–6, 138, 163–4,
　　172–3, 185
　organic 24, 26
organizational culture 158–9
organizational flexibility *see* flexibility
organizational innovation *see*
　innovation
Olson, Mancur 23
Orissa 121, 130
OSHA (Occupational Safety and Health
　Administration) 34–5
Ostrom, Elinor 11, 20, 22–4, 187

participatory development *see*
　development
partnership 16, 30–31, 33, 39, 56, 118,
　137, 140, 146, 148–9, 152–8,
　171–2, 177
　GPPP (global public–private) 44
　PDP (product development) 47
　PPP (public–private) 17–19, 24, 75
　VxDP (Vaccine Discovery) 47–8
patents 6 *see also* IP
path-dependence *see* institutional
　path-dependence
PDP (Product Development
　Partnerships) *see* partnership
philanthrocapitalism 2, 44
"philanthropreneurs" 45–7
philanthropy 20, 33, 44–5, 47–51, 84,
　143 *see also* venture philanthropy
Pitroda, Satyen 73–4
PMGSY (*Pradhan Mantri Gram Sadak
　Yojana*) 80
Polanyi, Karl 28, 189–90
populism 73–4
portable 9, 115, 133
poverty 3, 6, 43, 57, 65, 81–2, 104, 120,
　129, 135
　alleviation 21–2, 42, 65, 120
power asymmetry 8, 65
power relations 39, 60, 66, 187
PPP (public–private partnership) *see*
　partnership
pragmatic/pragmatism 12, 28, 30–31,
　65, 76
Prahalad, C. K. 12, 82–5, 91, 143

PRI (program-related investment) *see*
　investment
prisoners' dilemma 23
private interests 2, 15, 28–30, 51–2, 189
privatization 11, 53
pro-poor design *see* design
product development 64, 119, 151
productivist bias 63
profit maximization 36–7, 41
profitability 83–4, 91, 120, 142, 157,
　165
proximity 20, 57–9, 96, 101
public goods 15, 18–21, 23, 42, 60, 67,
　70, 80, 82
　global *see* global public goods
public health 21–2, 54, 80, 82
　global 20, 47
public interests 15, 17, 31, 38–9, 188
public sector reform *see* reform
Pune 10

R&D (research and development) 6–7,
　9–10, 33, 47, 58–63, 75, 82–3, 95,
　101–2, 141, 144–5, 149–50, 151,
　153, 173
　globalized 63
　hazards in 62
　market-capture 60
　public 67
Rajasthan 130
randomized control trials 66
rationality 25, 32
rational action *see* action
rational actor *see* actor
reagents 115–16
recycling 42–3
reform
　structural 34, 75
　institutional 15
　public sector 17–18
　regulatory 154
regulation 17, 18, 113
remittance 68, 82, 125–6, 172
remote diagnosis 97
remote maintenance 99
rent-seeking 18–19

reputation 30, 37–8, 65, 140, 142, 146, 159, 168 *see also* legitimacy; reputational risk
rescaling 15, 21–2, 27–9, 31
resilience 60
reterritorializing 32–3
rights-based issues 161
Rio de Janeiro 107
RIS (Radiology Information System) 97
risk
   business 88
   financial 21, 125, 159
   reputational 140–42, 146, 159
Robin-Hood *see* business model
Rockefeller Foundation 49–51
ROI (return on investment) *see* investment
RTBI (Rural Technology and Business Incubator) 125
rural development *see* development

scalar flexibility *see* flexibility
"scalar mismatch" 31, 33
scalable 5, 106–7, 116
scale
   relativization of 191
   transformative 149
   -up 107, 113, 174
Scheduled Tribes (India) 122
Schelling, Thomas 23
Schwab Foundation 163
Science and Technology Policy (India) 75
secondary marketing 12, 58, 94
self-help groups 77, 126 *see also* women
self-regulation 26, 35
self-reliance 6, 76–7, 91, 167
self-rule (*swaraj*) 76
self-sufficiency 74–5, 91, 6–8, 71–2
shanzhai 3
shared value 2, 31, 138, 140–41
shareholder
   activism 49
   primacy 36–7
Shiv Nadar Foundation 48
Silicon Valley 5, 117, 119, 180, 184
Singapore 10, 50, 169, 177

Singh, Manmohan 75
slum, 31, 84,103–5, 145, 151, 157, 161, 167, 181
SMS (short message service) 97–8, 119–20, 130, 135
social capital 43, 50, 186
social enterprise *see* enterprise; social entrepreneurship *see* entrepreneurship
social exclusion 54
social finance 33, 49–50, 60, 184–5, 187
Social Impact Bonds 50
Social Innovation Fund 183
social legitimacy 39, 164 *see also* reputation
social networks 129–30, 179, 181–3
social value 31, 39–42, 55, 189
social welfare 41, 70, 81, 190
socialism, Fabian 76
socialization of markets 2
solar PV (photovoltaic) 133, 135
South Africa 69–71, 132
South–South knowledge transfer 106–9
   see also innovation, reverse
sovereignty 22, 32, 79
Sri Lanka 133
SSA (*Sarva Shiksha Abhiyan*) 80, 124
SSBM (socially sustainable business model) *see* business model
SSN (Social Success Note) 51
stakeholder 4, 10–11, 13, 22, 27–8, 32–5, 41, 52, 56, 63, 81, 119, 131, 136–7, 145, 166, 191
   dialog 35
   hybrid 163
   self-maximizing 23–4
   see also capitalism; governance
Stanford University 44, 177
state 16, 28, 67–8, 70–81, 154–6
   bureaucratic 25
   devolution of 42
   failure 4, 11, 53, 67, 91, 189–90
   -market relations 3, 13–14, 17
   marketization of *see* marketization of the state
STPs (Software Technology Parks) 74
"strategic stickiness" 42
supply chain 103, 116–17, 119, 148

survey (questionnaire) 9–10, 144, 150,
    153
sustainability
    employment 54
    environmental 20, 54, 60, 141–2
    financial 40, 113
    livelihood 147
Swach Bharath Abhiyan (Clean India
    Mission) 81–2
"swelling of the middle" 2, 187
synergy 17–18, 140–42, 145, 148, 168
    cross-domain 17
    for-profit/non-profit 141, 168
    for-profit/CSR 140, 142
    reputational 168

talent 57, 67, 88–9, 101–2, 168, 186
Tamil Nadu 121, 124
Tanzania 118–19, 135
technology *see* indigenous technology;
    innovation; *jeito*; *jugaad*; *shanzhai*
technological transfer 59
tele-medicine 12, 97, 113–13, 169–70,
    175–6
tele-radiology 97, 169–70
thermoplastics 115–16
Thailand 107, 152
"third sector" 40–41, 56 *see also* NGOs
"Third Way" 18
TSE (transnational social
    entrepreneurship) *see*
    entrepreneurship
training 97, 105, 109, 112, 118, 124
    127–9, 170, 172
transaction cost 3, 39, 62, 135
transparency 33, 36, 47
tribal communities *see* community
triple movement 28, 189–90
trust 23–4, 135, 148
    absence of 62
    -based relationships 134
    established 113–14
    void 39

underserved 2, 56, 59, 63, 66, 122, 134,
    166, 169 *see also* BOP

United Kingdom 8, 35–7, 45, 47, 50
United States 2–4, 8, 10, 13, 30, 34–6,
    45, 47, 49, 50, 183
University of California, Berkeley 14,
    44
urban–rural gaps 6
user
    communities 64–5
    -friendly 60, 95, 161
    incentive *see* incentive
    -led innovation *see* innovation
Uttar Pradesh 113, 136

value engineering 57 *see also*
    innovation, frugal
values 29, 31, 43, 57, 143, 160, 162, 174
    also see social value
venture capital 45, 62, 183, 185–6
venture philanthropy 45–50 *see also*
    philanthropy
video-based content 118–19
Vietnam 107, 152
village council 77–8
voice 64, 97–8, 122–3, 160
voice-based applications 98
VxDP (Vaccine Discovery Partnership)
    see partnership

Washington consensus 15–16, 17–18
water 35, 70, 73, 91–3, 104, 108–9, 121,
    140, 152–3, 179
Wellcome Trust 47
wicked problems 57, 72, 93–4,
    100–101, 107
women
    poor working 167–8
    self-help group 77
    training for 147
World Bank CGAP (Consultative
    Group to Assist the Poor) 126
World Health Indicators 112

Zurich 106–7